ASCENT

ASCENT

THE CLIMBING EXPERIENCE
IN WORD AND IMAGE

Edited by

ALLEN STECK

STEVE ROPER

DAVID HARRIS

American Alpine Club Press
Golden, Colorado

The AAC Press

Published by:
The American Alpine Club
710 Tenth Street, Suite 100
Golden, Colorado 80401 USA
(303) 384-0110

The American Alpine Club was founded in 1902, and began publishing in 1907. It is a 501(c)(3) non-profit organization supported by concerned alpinists. The purposes of the American Alpine Club are: the conservation of the mountain environment; the national representation of all current interests and concerns of the American climbing community; the cultivation of mountain craft and the promotion of camaraderie among climbers; the preservation and dissemination of mountaineering art, photography, literature, and history; and the exploration and study of the high mountains and polar regions of the world.

ISBN: 0-930410-80-7

AAC Press Publications Director / Book Design and Layout: Ed Webster
Cover Design: Gordon Banks

Printed in the United States of America.

Front Cover: Approaching the summit of Chopicalqui, Cordillera Blanca, Peru. *Charlie Fowler*

Back Cover: Patrik Fransson airborne on the celebrated jump between the summit horns of the Svolvaergeita (the Svolvaer Goat), Lofoten Islands, Norway. *Ed Webster*

Frontispiece: Dick Renshaw climbing the south ridge of Kusum Kanguru, just beneath the summit, with Gongla rising behind. Sola Khumbu, Nepal. *Stephen Venables*

Right: Reflection of Shipton Spire, Karakoram Range, Pakistan. *Kennan Harvey*

THANKS TO OUR

THREE BENEFACTORS,

WHO THROUGH THEIR GENEROSITY

HELPED MAKE

THIS ISSUE OF

ASCENT

POSSIBLE

YVON CHOUINARD
FOUNDER,
PATAGONIA, INC.

DAVID SWANSON

RON ULRICH

Contents

Paul Teare alpine-style on the west ridge of Ama Dablam, Nepal. *Ed Webster*

South   217

Photographs by Gordon Wiltsie, Stephen Venables,
Gregory Crouch, and Charlie Fowler

Russel Mitrovich on *Reticent* (VI 5.9, A5). El Capitan, Yosemite Valley. *Warren Hollinger*

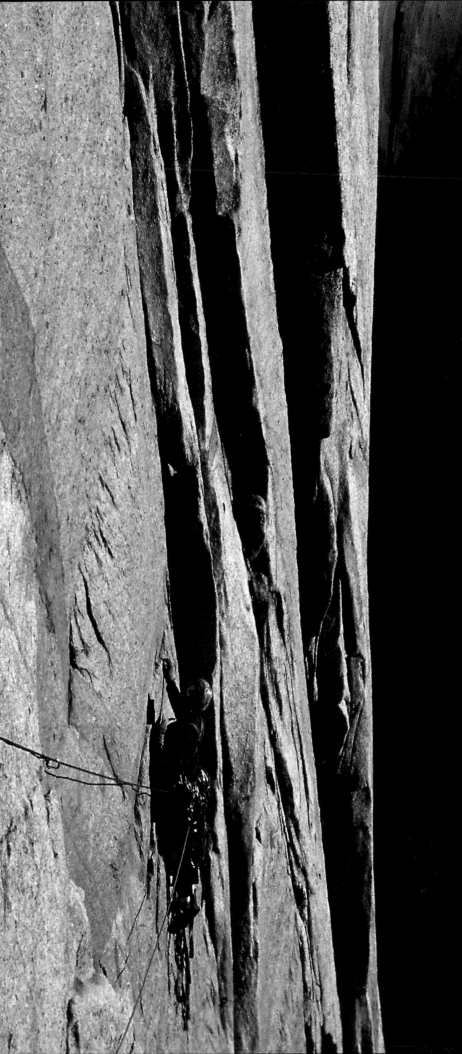

Ice dream II   Steve Wood

Introduction

Here, for the fourteenth time since 1967, is *Ascent*, its curious history to be related later. This volume is a gathering of more than thirty original selections—prose, poetry, and graphics—that we hope reflects our subtitle: the climbing experience in word and image. What you will find inside is unique, we think, especially compared to the climbing magazines. Commendable though these magazines are, they are not only jammed with confusing advertisements but tend to concentrate on ephemeral news, regional access problems, trivia, and short feature pieces dealing with cutting-edge climbing. While this last category can be a thrilling genre, these articles rarely deal with the overall "experience" of climbing as we see it. (Read the included essays by Bruce Fairley, John Hart, and David Stevenson for further insights on this subject.) *Ascent*, on the other hand, is a repository for innovative literary pieces that attempt to make sense of this imprudent activity we allot far too much time to. Our authors write exactly what they want, bound by few constraints about length, content, political correctness, or what advertisers might be ecstatic or alarmed about. We also try to edit with a light hand, preserving the idiosyncrasies of singular people. If we three editors have argued fiercely about certain pieces, this simply goes to show that climbers are a diverse group. It would be truly amazing if every reader liked every article, every poem, and every image.

Many of our pieces are essays, which we regard as a neglected climbing genre. Climbers do more than just write about their adventures: they reflect on the sport's past and worry about its future. We're delighted to have a cadre of masterful writers who examine various facets of the sport.

We do, of course, have our share of thrilling stories, several of which take place in those two familiar venues: the Himalaya and Patagonia. But the 8,000-meter peaks are barely mentioned in the Asian category, and in the second you won't find tales of daredevil first ascents. Instead, you'll read about people who persevere on "standard" routes, or get off the beaten track, or try something unusual—like the woman who leaps out of bed and solos a seemingly endless route in a remote valley in Kyrgyzstan. You'll hear also about some slightly more familiar places: Waddington, Zion, Shiprock, and the Scottish Highlands. This is truly an international volume.

Along the way you'll read about dancing on the big walls—that's right, dancing on the walls, not up them. You'll learn volumes about climbing gear, the climbing magazines, and Australian climbing of yesteryear. You'll read several pieces of fiction, including a Yosemite mystery involving Holmes and Watson.

Ascent has long been appreciated for its graphics, and in this issue's color spreads you'll travel to the ends of the earth (almost literally) and feast upon some original art. Over one hundred black and white images, scanned from slides and archival black and white photographs by the estimable Ed Webster, accompany many of the articles.

In short, every article and graphic (and our several poems) relates to the "climbing experience," a concept admittedly so nebulous that it takes our numerous authors 120,000 words to even approach dealing with the subject—one that's surely worth a million words.

Faithful readers who have followed the unconventional publication history of *Ascent* over the past three decades can either ignore this paragraph or once again endure this wondrous tale—one at least always told with slightly different language and emphasis. We began as a thin magazine, back when there were no good ones. The Dark Ages. The Sierra Club, our publisher, spared no expense and gave us every encouragement, and for this we are forever grateful. We were the world's first high-quality climbing journal, though we didn't know it at the time. We went stumbling along in this fashion for eight annual issues, each one getting bigger and more sophisticated. Then, as bi-monthly climbing magazines on both sides of the Atlantic took off, our interest waned. But soon we editors (Allen Steck and Steve Roper from the beginning, and many fine climber/editors along the way) became proud of our unpredictable publication schedule. Not for us a rigid timetable! Only five more volumes appeared during the next quarter-century, yet the magazine magically evolved into book form. Jon Beckmann was director of Sierra Club Books during these years and we, not to mention the mountaineering community, are deeply indebted to him for his courage and vision in keeping *Ascent* alive, even though it rarely produced a profit. Positive reviews in the mainstream press confirmed this fortunate decision.

By 1993, the date of the volume before this, the Sierra Club had moved out of mountaineering and into what they do best: trying to save the planet. *Ascent* didn't exactly fit into this mold, and we had an amiable divorce. Luckily, the American Alpine Club quickly stepped in as our new publisher and, shortly thereafter, Mountaineers Books, in Seattle, became the Club's new distributor. It should be a great partnership. Another recent change: climber and novelist David Harris, former editor of the *Canadian Alpine Journal*, has joined our crew, adding his expertise and sharing more than one vinous lunch at our world headquarters in Berkeley (Steck's house). It's been mostly fun working on this project, and we'd certainly appreciate feedback from readers. Shall there be yet another volume? Tell us!

We'd also like to thank Jon Waterman, past director of the American Alpine Club Press, and Ed Webster, the present director, for their expertise and encouragement in the project. As excellent climbers and writers themselves, they knew exactly what we were up to—and up against—at all times.

Linda McMillan, our rock-gym companion and a director of the AAC, took on the task of trying to raise money so that we could pay our contributors a decent pittance. After hundreds of phone calls and letters, she succeeded admirably. Thanks, Linda.

Our old friend Yvon Chouinard, ace mountaineer and founder of the Patagonia line of clothing, has long esteemed this journal, and, when asked to contribute money, he did so without blinking an eye. Two new friends, visionaries both, also contributed to the cause, and we'd like to thank David Swanson and Ron Ulrich.

We also owe a debt to a different group of visionaries, our artists and photographers. Special thanks to Jennifer Christiansen, a free-lance artist noted for her work in *Scientific American*; Colorado graphic artist, painter (and sculptor) Steven J. Wood, who has a wonderful eye for whimsy; John Svenson, the Alaskan mountaineer and artist whose work has appeared in *Ascent* several times since 1972; Gardner Heaton, renowned for his detailed topographic drawings in the *American Alpine Journal;* Freddie Snalam, former hot-dog vendor/climber turned artist/climber; photographer Gordon Wiltsie, another longtime *Ascent* contributor who has traveled the world in search of the perfect image; Canadian adventurer John Dunn, who knows the glacial landscape of Baffin Island as few do; Charlie Fowler and Gregory Crouch, Patagonian bad weather devotees both; Yosemite denizen and wall veteran Steve Schneider, and Warren Hollinger, Mark Synnott, Jared Ogden, and Kennan Harvey, four keen and youthful specialists of that rarified objective: the Karakoram big wall—plus assorted other granite precipices from Baffin Island to Kyrgyzstan.

Finally, as always, we'd like to thank everyone who sent in articles, photographs, poems, and art, some of which was accepted, some not. It was a pleasure to deal with you, and we're happy to see that a few good men and women appreciate what we are attempting to do.

THE EDITORS

KUSUM KANGURU
The Dream Pillar

Stephen Venables

For hours I had been climbing alone, in the dark, cut off from the world, and the new day caught me almost by surprise—a sudden realization of color, far below, beyond the shadowed trench of the Western Cwm, where a cluster of peaks floated in golden light. Looking down from 27,000 feet, I allowed myself a brief sightseer's smile of recognition, registering my first view of the famous peaks of the Sola Khumbu before filing the image away in my subconscious and returning to the all-consuming business of surviving Everest.

Later, at home, I recalled the image and its associations—Sola Khumbu, homeland of the Sherpas and, in particular, of Pasang Norbu, the sirdar whose gentle companionship had so enriched our 1988 Everest expedition. I decided that if I returned to the Himalaya, it would be with Pasang to one of those peaks immediately south of Everest. I say *if* because, unlike some climbers, who love their mountains unequivocally, I find myself increasingly ambivalent. There was a nagging feeling that, after catharsis on Everest, the sensible thing might be to give it all up, particularly as I was now, in 1991, the father of a baby boy.

Of course, I didn't give it up; I just compromised. By sticking to a comparatively low peak, I promised to avoid the huge risks of extreme altitude. I also gave the trip financial justification by selling the story to the *Daily Telegraph*. That meant the mortgage would be paid; it also meant that the trip had to be official, with no sneaking up illegal peaks. In Nepal the only way to be legal and keep administrative costs down is to go for one of the designated trekking peaks, where the permit fee is almost negligible. It all begins to sound depressingly like a package holiday from a catalog, until you remember that some of these so-called trekking peaks are magnificent, inspiring mountains, none more so than the one I chose, 20,889-foot Kusum Kanguru.

Most of my expeditions have been to previously unclimbed peaks—pure, virginal, unsullied. Kusum Kanguru was different. She had a past. There had been successful ascents from the east and the west and frequent suitors on the north face, because climbers tend to follow where others lead. Yet, for some inexplicable reason, no one had ever bothered with the southwest face, 4,000 feet of steep granite rising to an ethereally fluted summit and just crying out to be climbed. Not only that, but no Westerner, as far as I could tell, had even explored the valley leading to the foot of the face. Here, in the heart of the Himalaya's most popular climbing region, was a sanctuary of wilderness, with my kind of ideal climb rising out of it.

I had my dream climb, but I needed others to share the dream. I approached Dick Renshaw, who had borne my company through several trips in the early eighties. Ours had at times been rather a silent, intense partnership and he agreed happily to my suggestion of an expanded, more gregarious, team for Kusum Kanguru. Brian Davison, who was younger, stronger, and a much better climber than either of us, seemed the best choice. I also tried to persuade Paul Teare, one of my Everest companions, to join the team, but he scoffed at the idea of four people on such a small peak, so in the end we settled for three, plus Henry Day as team manager.

Henry's moment of glory had been the second ascent of Annapurna, back in 1970. He had also been to Everest in 1976 and was keen to retrace his steps along the famous trek from Jiri, this time bringing his wife, Sarah. With characteristic generosity he offered to put some money into the expedition, on the understanding that we would travel in style, with no unnecessary suffering. And so I found myself, at last, after fourteen years of Himalayan scrimping and saving, setting off on a classically pampered trek, with sahibs outnumbered by devoted staff, all under the assured direction of Pasang. We could have flown to Lukla, saving eight days and arriving weak and breathless at 11,000 feet, but our slow, measured approach was infinitely preferable.

It was October, the perfect trekking season, and I loved it. No, that is inaccurate. There were moments, particularly at one misty camp, when I felt melancholic, surprised at how much I was missing my three-month-old son. At times I found myself irritated with Brian and Dick, annoyed by the many other tourists sharing our journey along the famous Everest approach march, and doubtful about the value of our enterprise. It took a while to readapt to expedition life and lose myself in the magical moments, such as the sudden vision of Tragshindo Monastery's coppery pagoda roofs, appearing silently out of the misty rhododendron forest. It was at breakfast the next morning that we first saw our mountain, in a complete reversal of my Everest view three years earlier. Then it had been a tiny blip on the southern horizon; now it was the first great gleaming snow peak of the range, with our proposed face standing sentinel over the Dudh Kosi. Two days later, rounding a forest crest, we saw it again, this time much closer. Finally, on the eighth day of our trek we stopped immediately beneath it, at the entrance to the Kusum Khola.

Now that we were past the Lukla airstrip, we were exposed to the full reality of Sola Khumbu's burgeoning tourist industry, which made the trek from Jiri seem deserted. Our campsite at Kusum Khang felt like a highway interchange, with constant traffic shuffling past. The trekkers looked naively enthusiastic; the climbers, many returning from unsuccessful attempts on prestigious peaks, looked thin, dirty, and disappointed. As they all tramped across the wooden bridge above our tents, I wondered how many thousands—tens of thousands—had crossed that bridge and glanced up the valley above. Had they wondered about the valley and the great wall at its head? Had anyone been up there to have a look?

The wall itself appeared when the clouds lifted at breakfast. Brian scowled pessimistically. Dick got up and shut the mess-tent door. "I'm not going to let that view spoil my breakfast." Henry renewed a conversation about estate agents and other such despised parasites in Thatcherite Britain. "Usurers is the word, I think."

"Dante put them in the second circle of the inferno," added Dick. He paused for a moment, then continued. "It's very reassuring, Hell. I like the idea of somewhere for Hitler and Amin and Ceauşescu and all the rest of them to go to."

"Well," I said, "what a jolly little team we are. Shall we go and have a look at that valley?"

Two hours later, thrashing around in impenetrable jungle, it became obvious that not many people had been there. In fact, we had made a routefinding mistake, and, after retracing our steps, we found a fallen tree over the river and, beyond it, hints of an old

The southwest face
and south ridge
(on right skyline)
of Kusum Kanguru,
glimpsed from the
Kusum Khola
on day two
of the approach.

Stephen Venables

On the first attempt, Brian Davidson and Dick Renshaw inspect the Dream Pillar of Kusum Kanguru's south ridge. Renshaw and Venables' eventual route ascended the sunlit, right-facing dihedral just left of center.

Stephen Venables

trail leading to a big stack of recently cut roof shingles. The locals had obviously been at least this far, and, armed with this knowledge, we persuaded Pasang's team of porters to start up the valley the next morning.

It took us three days to travel three horizontal miles to base camp. The first day we camped near the woodpile, excavating tent sites in a mossy hollow. For the rest of our journey, right to the summit of Kusum Kanguru, we were never to find another fully flat campsite. On the second night we built projecting platforms of rotten rhododendron trunks interlaced with bamboo, while Pasang and Jeta, his brilliant cook boy, worked their magic perched on a tiny earthen ledge, in the dark, several hundred yards from the nearest water source.

We were now far beyond any traces of a trail. Already most of the porters had left, but a few stayed on to relay loads on the last day, loyal to Pasang and to my determination to see this dream through. Using *kukris* we hacked a path through dense bamboo, trying to avoid the biggest cliffs. At last we emerged onto open hillside, only to discover that the magenta shimmer we had seen from below was actually a waist-high tangle of murderously prickly barberries. Torn and bloody, we finally reached a feasible site with running water, higher than I had dared to hope, at 13,000 feet. Out came the ice axes and we set to terracing the hillside, creating a flat home where no human being had ever been. While we dug, Pasang hung the prayer flags, then lit a fire, filling the air with fragrant juniper smoke and the sweet camomile scent of the dwarf *Rhododendron anthopogon,* much favored by lamas. I always love these moments of homebuilding. Apart from the obvious, physical, practical satisfaction of creating a shelter, there is that primordial ritual of staking one's temporary claim to a particular spot on the earth's surface and calling it home—the essential dichotomy of the nomad, who deliberately seeks adventure and uncertainty in unknown lands but has to temper that adventure with moments of reassuring domesticity.

The mist swept up the valley every evening, then crept back down again at dawn. I remember one particularly fine morning, returning to base camp as the freezing fog evaporated, leaving autumnal remains of shrubs and flowers jeweled in glittering crystal. Far, far below, I could just make out the valley of the Dudh Khosi, where the daily Lukla traffic would already be starting; but up here, in our private valley, we had total tranquility. At base camp we broke the ice on the stream for a tingling wash while Pasang and Jeta cooked a huge breakfast and Tenzing whiled away the morning weaving a split-cane basket.

The doubts and the ambivalence had gone, and I was now focused properly on the climb. Basking on our sunny terrace, pen in hand, I enthused about our plans in a second dispatch to the *Telegraph.* Like all plans, these had been modified. My dream—the uncompromising direttissima straight up the center of the southwest face—had been squashed. First Dick, then Brian, had muttered the insidious words of dissent: *rockfall, avalanche funnels, no bivouac sites.* I had resisted for a while, trying to deny the problems, until

Brian had swung the telescope away from the shadowy face, over to the right, focusing on the crest of the south ridge, tempting me with the promise of a soaring granite pillar, where you could just discern the possibilities of cracks and corners. Plan B would still give us 2,000 feet of exciting mixed climbing, but up a safe spur on the right-hand side of the face. That would get us to the crest of the unclimbed south ridge and the start of the beautiful rock pillar. Above the pillar more mixed ground and a final gleaming ice ridge would lead straight to the summit.

We had done a reconnaissance, stashing food and gas several hundred feet up the initial spur. Dick had given me one of his "what did I tell you?" looks as boulders had cannonaded down my dream line on the left. I congratulated myself on choosing my team so wisely. Now, on our final rest day at base camp, I concentrated on the adventure ahead. Sarah had already left with Pasang, to visit his home in Namche Bazaar, before flying back to England. Henry would soon be following her, leaving the three of us to the serious business of climbing the mountain. We said goodbye in the morning, and by dawn the following day we were back on the lower spur, climbing to our cache of food and gas.

I think that I enjoyed the climb, but I am not sure about the other two. Earlier in the year Brian had suffered a retinal hemorrhage on Broad Peak, and since then he had been traveling the world on a shoestring. He was not at his fittest, and the altitude seemed to make him irritable. Dick, as always, was utterly dependable but seemed to be climbing very slowly, with no sense of rhythm, and he was perturbed by Brian's outbursts. We moved fitfully, delayed for a whole day by bad weather, and on the third day, despite carrying on until dusk, we did not reach the top of the spur. Our home that night was a hard-won, two-foot-wide ice ledge, and it was my turn to sleep on the outside.

It snowed the next day, but I warmed to the hard fight up dizzy, fluted slopes, with entertaining diversions over rock steps, and I particularly enjoyed the heat of battle on the final pitch, arriving just below the crest of the south ridge in driving snow to discover a huge, wind-scooped hollow beneath a perfect rock overhang. It was five-star luxury, with room for all three of us to lie down in the warm fug of our red dome tent, content with the day's work. Strong winds and snowfall prompted us to procrastinate in the morning, but after a late breakfast we got up to investigate the ridgecrest leading to the rock pillar. Dick and I fixed a rope to the foot of the pillar while Brian sat listlessly below, head leaning on the ice slope. He seemed strangely unmoved by the glitter of fresh snow, the blue autumn light, the new vista into the Hinku Valley, Chamlang, Kangchenjunga. But then, in the evening, back in the tent, he perked up. Framed in our doorway was the pillar—the dream pillar, glowing red on blue, features etched by deep shadows. Brian schemed and plotted, guessing pitch lengths,

Renshaw above the clouds.

Stephen Venables

Renshaw on
a scary rappel.

Stephen Venables

wondering about the width of that chimney, the steepness of that crack, the possibility of edging round that ledge. It was like being back on South Georgia, when his quick-thinking tactics had got us safely up and down a remote peak at the heart of the Southern Ocean. This was the positive, creative Brian I remembered, and he seemed once again fired up to complete our climb.

But it was not to be. In the morning Brian was again lethargic. Clipping on crampons, he stopped to lean over, head in hands. Dick was the first to comment. "Are you feeling okay?"

Brian tried to shrug it off, and I tried to pretend that nothing had happened, but Dick was insistent. "Can you see properly?" Nine years earlier, on the pinnacles of Everest's northeast ridge, a stroke had left Dick temporarily paralyzed and had shattered forever his dreams of the highest peaks. Before that, on K2, retinal hemorrhages had warned of possible problems. He knew how vulnerable Brian was. "Let's look at your face... it's quite puffy. You can't stay up here; it's too risky."

I thought back to the South Col, three years earlier, when Paul Teare, worried about possible edema, had given up his chance for the summit and had departed tearfully back down the Kangshung Face. Ever since then I had felt slightly uneasy about having evaded the moral dilemma by allowing Paul to descend alone while we remained to try to fulfill our summit ambitions. At least there, with tracks, marker wands, and fixed ropes on the steep terrain, a solo descent had been fairly risk free. On Kusum Kanguru, this was out of the question. There was no way of dodging the issue, although Brian nobly offered to make his way alone down the shorter far side of our ridge, into the Hinku Valley. I stared down onto the crevassed maze of the Lungsamba Glacier and blurted, "No, that would be crazy."

"Okay," he persisted, "but why don't I wait here in the tent while you two go for the top. You could bivouac in the open and I'd be fine here."

"We're almost out of food, Brian, and the gas is running out. We're at 19,000 feet and it's getting colder every day." Dick enumerated the weaknesses of our position and concluded with a firm, "We're going down." Five minutes after the conversation began, I was setting up the first of twenty abseils back down the southwest spur.

The translucent beauty of the day made retreat agonizing, particularly in the late afternoon as a silver cloud-sea washed up the valley. We left our climbing gear at advance base and continued though the dusk, following our cairns down the steep, fog-shrouded hillside, calling out through the darkness for Pasang. Late that night, over cheese omelettes, he told us how he had been away to Pheriche, taking his sick mother to hospital, carrying her on his back because there was no other way to get her there. He had damaged his knee but had still carried fresh supplies up to base camp that morning. When I asked why he had not given himself a rest, he laughed: "I am a Sherpa; I have to carry a load."

In the morning he woke us gently with the sound of chanting over the juniper fire. The sun shone and a day of luxurious rest stretched ahead. All we had to do was eat, read, and make a few preparations for the next attempt, for, already during our depressing descent the previous day, Brian had suggested magnanimously that Dick and I should have one more try at the route while he waited at base camp to be on hand for any emergency.

So, two days later, we climbed back to advance base. Going for a stroll that evening, Dick found an old battered cooking-gas cylinder, rustily camouflaged in an immense heap of red rocks. He turned this piece of archaeology over in his hands and looked up mischievously. "Are we allowed to tell?"

"Hang on a minute." I considered censorship, anxious to maintain my line on the "unexplored" valley for the benefit of a million *Telegraph* readers. My brain went into overdrive, desperate for a suitable explanation. "Why is it battered like that? If someone had just dumped it, it wouldn't have all those dents. They must have been caused by falling from a great height." We looked up at the great, untouched amphitheater above, booming with evening rockfall. "Tommy Curtiss might have chucked it off the west ridge in 1985. He and that other bloke bivouacked right up there when they topped out from the north face. That's where the cylinder came from; no one brought it up this valley." Many months later a conversation in a London pub confirmed my theory. The head of the Kusum Khola had indeed been untrodden territory until we arrived to seek my dream climb.

Dick and I settled down for a brief night's sleep at advance base. In the morning we set off before first light, repeating the well-rehearsed routine up the initial slabs and loose black walls of the spur. This time, fit, acclimated, and knowledgeable, we moved quickly and efficiently, reaching the first bivouac in time for a late breakfast. Above that, we straightened out the old line, taking the challenge of the rock head-on, rather than evading it by the snowslopes on the left. By dusk we had reached the second bivouac, where the hard-won ice ledge of the first attempt awaited us.

On the second day we raced on, again taking the prow direct, enjoying the surprise of delightful rock and mixed ground. By lunchtime we were on top of the spur, where gas and the remains of last week's food were cached. Four days work on the first attempt had now been condensed into one and a half.

A lovely alpine crest led to the steep mixed ground where Dick had fixed a rope to our high point, six days earlier. Above the rope, our pillar leaned out into the sky, split by a huge corner. The sun still shone, darkness was some way off, and there was nothing to stop us continuing. First came a short jamming crack, over a block to a ledge; then the main corner, with beautiful dark banded dikes providing reassuring toe ledges and liberal cracks for nuts and Friends. I swung up joyfully, delighting in the weird realization that this corner was formed by an immense, detached pillar a hundred feet high.

As always, there was the nagging concern about where to spend the night. The sky was darkening over Rolwaling as we reached the top of the corner and emerged into the blast of a cold November wind. The theory had been simple: find a ledge on top of the pillar. The reality was different: a sloping shelf of granite with too little snow to excavate seats. So I tried some more construction work, maneuvering huge flakes of granite, wedging them with smaller flakes, then dropping a large lump on my frozen little finger. It was now dark. I wondered if Brian, thousands of feet below, could see my flashlight. Wondered if he could hear my angry curses above the howl of the wind as I sucked the numb, bloody mess inside my glove. Immediately behind me, Dick waited patiently for the familiar Venables tantrum to subside and then, as he had done on so many other mountains in the past, he took control.

"This is ridiculous. We've got to get out of that wind, so we'll have to bivy inside the chimney." And so we did, with the tent squashed onto the sloping floor of a jammed chockstone, and another pendulous boulder winched up to a Friend to create some space above our heads. The wind howled and whistled through dark cathedral spaces, and it seemed that the whole pillar was swaying. Jammed deep in our chimney, my head rammed up against mounds of goose down and perlon, I fought waves of claustrophobia, disturbing Dick with my groans, until he shut me up with a sleeping pill.

It was a relief to emerge from our hellhole in the morning. It took an age to sort out the chaos of the bivouac, and that day, slowed by sack-hauling, we only climbed five pitches. But what perfect pitches! First steep and thuggish, then airy and light, with huge dizzy spaces beneath the toes of plastic boots, tiptoeing gratefully on firm nubbins of wrinkled granite designed expressly for our pleasure. That, surely, is the best that climbing can offer: rock pitches as fine as the most celebrated classics at home, but discovered for oneself, after much hard work, high on a Himalayan peak in a setting of glacial splendor.

Once again dusk encroached with threats of an uncomfortable night. This time we had to settle for an icy sixty-degree slope, but a bit of creative work with some large granite paving slabs improved our prospects. While Dick worked on the sleeping quarters, I back-roped myself up a final steep pitch to leave the rope fixed for the morning.

We draped the tent over the ledge and sat inside it, feet hanging over the drop. Put like that, it sounds miserable, but I was utterly content, relishing the pure, uncluttered sensation of food and warmth and security after a day of hard physical work. Sleep was delicious and all-enveloping, and I knew that waking would be hateful. But when the time came the horror of it all was soon converted to positive energy on this, our summit day.

Just before midday Brian saw the red dot, Dick, disappear over the junction of the south and west ridges. I found Dick in shadow, belayed to a deadman on the north face. It only remained for me to lead through a few feet to a little col, and then we took turns to climb up onto the white spire of Kusum Kanguru's summit. Eighteen miles to the north a vast plume blew off Everest's stark pyramid. Down here, 8,200 feet lower, it felt quite cold

Renshaw
climbing gorgeous
rock up the
Dream Pillar, with the
Lungsamba Glacier
far below.

Stephen Venables

Renshaw arriving just below the summit on a frosty November morning.

Stephen Venables

enough on November 20. Everest in May was one thing, but in winter—never! If Himalayan peaks are supposed to give pleasure, it is on the six-thousanders, in the crystal days of late fall, that I want to do my climbing.

I peered curiously down the north face, focusing on a sunlit rib of the buttress climbed by Georges Bettembourg, Doug Scott, and Mike Covington in 1979, then across at their fore-summit, separated from us by a murderously beautiful crest of extravagant baroque swirls—strictly for looking at. Doug had made some facetious comment about not wanting to mar such elegant perfection with human footprints. Now, many years later, I thought, "What a wise man!" There had always been a possibility of our descending that way but now, seeing the precarious reality of that ridge, it was a huge relief to know that we could reverse our own route easily.

Easily, but carefully. We took great pains over the belays, and when we had to resort to rappelling off snow mushrooms, they were Brobdingnagian fungi, fit for giants and backed up for the first man with deadman belays. Back on the rocks, we fussed over the anchors, taking our time and not reaching the top of the fixed rope until dusk. I was slightly dreading the battle to reestablish ourselves on the buttock-ledge bivouac when Dick happened to look round the side of a buttress and shook his head in disbelief. "Didn't you look round here when you fixed the rope last night."

"Er, no... well, it was nearly dark."

"There's a bloody great ledge here."

"What a shame we've got to go back to our little perch."

"Don't be daft." Dick, not always the quickest of thinkers himself, despaired at my stupidity. "We can bring the gear up and sleep here."

"Of course. Brilliant. I'll go down and fetch all the luggage."

Our fifth and final day on the mountain went like clockwork. We took pride in our efficiency, dispatching twenty-five rappels in just over nine hours, thrilled with our slick homeward momentum. The final loose black band was always a worry, and I remember Dick's triumphant grin as he pulled the ropes through for the last time, happy to be safely down. We pressed on down through the fog and soon after dark Brian and Jeta guided us with their flashlights through the complicated ravine to base camp, where the table was laid for a celebratory feast of soup, garlic popcorn, spring rolls, fried eggs and chips, pineapple, and the last of the whiskey.

Three days later, down in the warm, balmy air of Kusum Khang, camped once more beside the highway interchange, we were able to enjoy the breakfast view that had prompted nervous jokes four weeks earlier—able to stare up with a certain satisfaction at the symmetry of our peak, hanging blue-gray above the soft yellow and russet of the gorge we had made our own. Our failure to climb the face proper seemed irrelevant. In fact, our flanking route onto the south ridge had proved a much finer option. And it was all the more satisfying for having been so hard to reach: the winding trail through the jungle, the bamboo ledges, the little terraced garden at base camp. They were all part of the same creative experience of seeing through a dream. I felt a deep gratitude to Pasang, Jeta, Tenzing, Dawa, and Nima for making our little exploration so comfortable and enjoyable. And to Henry and Sarah and Dick, and especially Brian, who could so easily have walked off early and left us after the disappointment of missing the summit. I thought of Shelley's line, "Rarely, rarely comest thou, spirit of delight," and realized that this was one of those moments where I really felt serene, fulfilled, complete. For six weeks the journey to Kusum Kanguru had been the focus of my life. The journey had given me a wonderful variety of emotions and experience, but ultimately, in my book, mountaineering is about seeing the journey through to a successful conclusion. Perhaps that is a banal view, but I needed that sense of completeness, so that when we left on that afternoon of blue luminosity to walk up to Lukla for a final farewell party with Pasang, there were no lingering regrets to shadow the joy of returning home.

Venables safely down to earth after completing twenty-five rappels.

Dick Renshaw

12   The north face of the Eiger heavily iced after a storm. *Ascent Archives*

MY DINNER
WITH ANDERL

David Pagel

Secretly, I have always believed that lurking within me, waiting for an opportunity to manifest itself, is the ability to socialize with important people without making an ass of myself. My chosen path, largely a straight line between mountains—or bar stools—rarely affords me the opportunity to mingle with celebrities. Nevertheless, I have remained confident that if a situation should ever require it, I could muster at least some degree of grace and charm. Until now, that is; because as I pass the ornate brass mailbox proclaiming the name "Heckmair" in bold relief, I am seized with the realization that I am hopelessly out of my element. No point in kidding myself: my social skills are pretty much defined by rough manners and asinine conversation. And not a bar stool in sight.

I have traveled to this address in the picturesque Bavarian postcard-village of Oberstdorf to meet my guru—the man whose life has most influenced my own. With my girlfriend, Dina, I have come seeking a connection with the celebrated German mountain guide whose life winds like a strong thread through an extended tapestry encompassing the most famous—and infamous—of mountains and men. Anderl Heckmair is best known as the person who, in the summer of 1938, led a team of two Germans and two Austrians on the dramatic first ascent of the Eigerwand, the much-feared north face of Switzerland's Eiger. This success, so hard fought against a deadly wall, has inspired respect and sparked obsession among countless mountaineers of every subsequent generation, myself included. But for Heckmair, the Eiger climb was only the prelude to a lifetime of extreme journeys among mountains, deserts, jungles—as well as to the poles of humanity: over the course of nine decades he has crossed paths with personalities ranging from Hitler to the Dalai Lama.

And now, perhaps as a result of my own improbable success on the Eigerwand, Anderl Heckmair has agreed to meet me. But I am afraid I will barely see the man through the thick condensation clouding my glasses. And it is not the humidity causing me to steam up like a greenhouse window. This is a perspiration of nerves, and it progresses from a damp anxiety as Dina and I contemplate the Heckmairs' mailbox to a persistent fog as I finally summon the courage to ring the bell. By the time the door opens I'm almost completely blind, and I prove this by impulsively groping for Herr Heckmair's hand, only to be rewarded with a mitt-full of air. Dina is having better luck. Peering over my blinders, I perceive that the members of this household observe strict social protocol, and it is only after Dina has been shown all the proper courtesies that I am ushered inside.

I gape about in an attempt to get a fix on our hosts, and my first impression is that we have entered a time warp. It is inconceivable that the square-shouldered gentleman standing before me is more than ninety years old. His small but well-proportioned frame is neither paunchy nor stooped, and the famous profile, featuring a round face and prominent nose, is crowned with a thatch of dark hair that shows no sign of thinning or graying.

By all outward appearances Anderl Heckmair appears to have found a way to stop the clock sometime in his mid-fifties. There are signs of an inner youth here as well: he greets me with a handshake and a wink that cannot conceal a mischievous sparkle.

His wife, Trudl, is similarly tiny, trim, and goodnatured, but in her case the youthful appearance is less of a disguise; she is decades younger than her husband, and so they seem a perfectly matched couple. Frau Heckmair's most singular feature, however, is her broad smile, which beams out warmly—a defroster on my clouded spectacles.

"Welcome," she says, taking our jackets, "it is so nice you have come to visit us." As I stammer some sort of reply about what an honor it is for us to meet such a great man, the humor in Heckmair can no longer be restrained. He beats his chest importantly and utters a solemn declaration before breaking into a fit of laughter. "Yes, yes," his wife translates, "Anderl says he is very proud!"

Clearly, Anderl Heckmair is a bit of a character.

Communicating Anderl's thoughts to visitors is second nature for Frau Heckmair. Like me, Anderl speaks only his native tongue and in a thick Bavarian dialect that even Dina, whose mother grew up near Frankfurt, is hard pressed to understand. Trudl, however, knows five languages, all self-taught, and—if her English is any indication—all quite fluently. Even now she is translating effortlessly and almost simultaneously as her husband invites us "into the sitting room, where we will be more comfortable."

The Heckmairs' parlor, a dimly lit, cozy room overlooking the garden, is furnished with a sofa and three chairs arranged in close proximity around a little table. Cake has been set out, cordial bottles are nearby, and, as we settle into place, Frau Heckmair goes in search of a vase for the fresh flowers Dina has brought. I also have a gift, something I suspect will greatly surprise Heckmair. In a letter I wrote to arrange this visit I asked about the book written by Fritz Kasparek, one of Heckmair's companions on the Eigerwand's first ascent. Kasparek's autobiography, printed shortly after the war and only a few years before his fatal plunge through a Peruvian cornice, is among the rarest of published Eiger-related materials. In my letter I asked the Heckmairs if they could offer any suggestions as to where I might acquire a copy of this volume. Anderl wrote back, "It is indeed very difficult to find; I, too, have no copy." I was excited then, when only a few weeks before our trip, I received a catalog listing this title for sale. I knew I had found the perfect gift.

Now, however, I'm worried I may have mistakenly wrapped up a copy of *Mein Kampf.* Anderl is thumbing through the book, frowning and shaking his head in a decidedly negative manner. His disapproval finally extends to the point of mumbling something under his breath that even I don't need a translator to understand. Dina is giving me one of those what-have-you-done-looks, but I am shielded by my glasses, which are, once again, utterly opaque.

Thankfully, Frau Heckmair returns, and, after a short conversation with her husband, she explains: "Anderl has always climbed for his own reasons and has never been interested in doing climbs for the purpose of generating publicity. Fritz was the opposite. He was always saying to Anderl, 'We must make some important new route, or they will forget about us!' Anderl and Fritz were not close friends."

This is something of a revelation. With a personal understanding of the bond that often forms between climbing partners, I have always assumed that the four members of the successful Eiger party, united by such an epic experience, must have enjoyed a

Anderl and
Trudl Heckmair.

David Pagel

special camaraderie. It had never occurred to me that the fact that Kasparek's autobiography never made it onto Heckmair's shelf might have been intentional. And now, thanks to me, Fritz and his philosophies are back from the grave. All I can think of to say is: "I didn't know," which I suspect Dina translates to Anderl as, "He is very stupid."

It is not long, however, before the whiskey and schnapps are flowing, and Anderl is in a good humor again, happily puffing a cigar and explaining to us that the relationships between the members of the Eiger team were complicated, right from the start. The two Austrians, Kasparek and Heinrich Harrer, were initially a separate party, and had never met the Germans before encountering one another on the mountain. And the two Germans had only recently met; Heckmair originally hoped to attempt the Eiger with Hais Rebitsch, a friendly rival with whom he proposed joining forces. Rebitsch, however, had been invited to join the 1938 German expedition to Nanga Parbat, and reluctantly informed Anderl, "I leave the Eiger to you." But he also left Heckmair his partner, Ludwig Vörg, known to his friends as "Wiggerl." The previous year, Rebitsch and Vörg had retreated from the Eigerwand after climbing nearly halfway to the summit, and in doing so became the only men to return alive from a serious attempt on the face. Vörg's first-hand knowledge of the face, along with a strong recommendation from Rebitsch, made him the natural choice to accompany Heckmair.

Heckmair and
Vörg ascend the
Second Icefield
during the first
ascent of the
Eiger north wall,
1938.

Heinrich Harrer

*Photograph courtesy
of Anderl Heckmair*

"In many ways," explains Frau Heckmair, pouring us another whiskey, "Wiggerl was probably a better partner for Anderl than Rebitsch. In those days, it was common for one man to lead and the other to follow an entire climb. Both Anderl and Rebitsch were born leaders and would have competed with one another, but Vörg was ideally suited to the role of the second man; he was perfectly content to belay Anderl and remove the pitons."

The Austrians, I recalled, had a similar arrangement, with the lead falling naturally to Kasparek. I can only imagine how these dynamics must have complicated things once the two parties joined—it's no wonder he and Anderl didn't get along. The memory of this encounter gives Anderl a chuckle. His wife explains, "Anderl did not want to combine the teams. When he and Wiggerl met the others on the Second Icefield, he immediately told them, 'You must go down now, because if you continue, you will surely be killed.'"

While this must have raised Kasparek's hackles, it was a valid observation, because although the Austrians were prepared to tackle any rock pitches the Eiger might throw at them, they were poorly equipped for ice and snow. The reason the Germans caught up with them so quickly on the traverse of the Second Icefield is because without an ice axe or even adequate crampons, Kasparek was forced to chop steps for hundreds of feet using only a small hammer. Heckmair and Vörg, outfitted with the most sophisticated ice gear of the day, including twelve-point crampons, literally ran across the same ground.

"Anderl is convinced," his wife informs us, "that the reason he was successful where so many others failed is because the others prepared for the Eiger as a rock climb with just a little ice and snow. But Anderl saw that the Eiger was mainly an ice and snow climb, with only a little rock. This is what made the difference."

"Why, then," I ask, "did Herr Heckmair decide to join forces with the Austrians?" Though she has doubtlessly heard the answer a thousand times, Frau Heckmair waits patiently for her husband to finish, and then explains: "The Austrians were quite determined to continue, and Anderl was inclined to leave them to their fate. But it was Wiggerl, with his big heart, who said, 'Well, if you insist upon going on, then perhaps we should all go together.'"

Even Kasparek must have felt some relief at this proposal, since their inferior equipment meant he and Harrer could never out-pace the Germans—and if you can't beat 'em....

Anderl's glass is empty again, but his wife, ignoring his good-natured pout, has cut him off. "And one more thing," Frau Heckmair smiles warmly. "Anderl would like me to tell you that he is not 'Herr Heckmair'; he is Anderl and I am Trudl. And now he must go play cards."

Every afternoon at precisely five o'clock Heckmair plays cards with his neighbor for exactly one hour. While outsiders may view this as a curious ritual—particularly since no words are ever spoken during the game—it is, in fact, a cathartic method of relaxation for the neighbor, one that Anderl is happy to oblige. I suspect whiskey is also involved.

While he is gone, Trudl takes Dina and me

Heckmair and Vörg bivouacking on the Ramp. Eiger north face, July, 1938.

Heinrich Harrer

Photograph courtesy of Anderl Heckmair

for a walk to see the place in Oberstdorf where three major rivers merge into one—a unique geographical landmark. Dina borrows a pair of Anderl's boots for the hike; needless to say, I am proud to have a girlfriend who can fill Anderl Heckmair's shoes.

I ask Trudl if they are often pestered by climbers like us. "Oh, yes," she grins, "every now and then someone will climb the Eiger and then phone up to ask if it is possible to stop by and meet Anderl. And sometimes we are invited to visit them. Recently we went to see one young man here in Germany who went to the Eiger fifteen times before finally succeeding. His town threw him a big party with Anderl as guest of honor."

I envy this persistent and celebrated German alpinist. The Eiger took me three trips—and the only thing my town has ever given me is a parking ticket.

When we get back to the house, Anderl has returned and it is time for dinner. Dina and I insist upon taking the Heckmairs out, so we all pile into their car and Trudl drives us to a quiet little restaurant that doesn't cater to tourists (no lederhosened accordion players or dirndl-dressed barmaids). The beer, however, is classic Bavarian lager and we lift our glasses to our new friends.

Speaking of friends, I feel I must ask the Heckmairs about Heinrich Harrer. Harrer's well-publicized adventures—particularly his wartime escape from a British POW camp and subsequent journey over the Himalaya into Tibet—have made him an international celebrity. I ask Anderl and Trudl what they think about the upcoming Hollywood adaptation of Harrer's Tibetan experiences.

"Heini has just rushed off to America to help with some changes to his movie," Trudl informs us. In fact, this is a polite way of saying that he has been summoned by the film's producers to help with damage control. "He is a man who likes attention," she continues, "but now I think it has brought him serious problems." She is referring, of course, to the recent sensational disclosure that in the years surrounding the Eiger climb, Harrer was an active, card-carrying member of Hitler's SS. Although Harrer initially denied these charges, journalists, catalyzed by the publicity surrounding the film, unearthed incontrovertible proof: papers and records, some in Harrer's own handwriting, positively identifying him as an SS man.

Controversy has always surrounded the relationship between the four Eiger climbers and the Nazis. There is no doubt that after the climb the men were used to fan the flames of the nationalistic fervor that gripped Germany prior to the outbreak of World War II. Almost immediately upon their descent they were whisked away by the SS, publicly congratulated by Hitler, and held up to the nation and the world as symbols of Aryan accomplishment and pride. For this, it would be difficult to fault them, since history-making mountaineers of every time and nationality have been similarly feted by their proud governments. But it has been suggested that the motivation to climb the Eiger might have been linked to some promised compensation—or for the specific purpose of advancing a political agenda. Some have gone so far as to accuse the team of climbing under orders from the Reich. Both Heckmair and Harrer have written at length on this subject and have dismissed these theories and accusations as so much bunk. In *The White Spider,* Harrer's famous history of the Eiger, he writes, "To ascribe material motives and similar external rewards of success to our climb would be a lie and a slander. Not one of us improved his social position one whit thanks to a mountaineering feat which excited such general admiration."

Unfortunately for Harrer, history now records that it is he who lied with regard to his "social position." Membership in Nazi organizations was illegal in his native Austria until March 1938, and he had joined the SA, Hitler's paramilitary stormtroopers, many years earlier. He apparently joined the SS even before the Eiger climb. Such affiliations cannot avoid casting dark shadows across Harrer's reputation—and his character.

Despite these revelations, the Heckmairs have great respect for Heinrich Harrer—he has, after all, spent most of his life attempting to focus public attention upon the plights of oppressed peoples, particularly the Tibetans. The Heckmairs feel that his greatest blunder is in not having come clean about his youthful mistakes. As with Kasparek, however, they have clearly been uneasy with Harrer's penchant for self-promotion over the years, and they cannot hide their bemusement at his current predicament. "Now, I think he finally has more attention than he wants," Trudl says. For the Heckmairs, there is a lesson here: a person who persists in dancing close to the flame is asking to get burned.

I wonder, however, if the mutual respect between Harrer and Heckmair would have developed if the these two men hadn't survived to such ripe old ages. In fact, in the

The victorious 1938 Eiger north wall team at the Hotel "Eiger Gletscher."
From left to right: unidentified, Harrer, Kasparek, Heckmair, and Vörg.

Photograph courtesy of Anderl Heckmair

Heckmair leading on the first ascent of the north face of the Eiger, 1938.

Heinrich Harrer

Photograph courtesy of Anderl Heckmair

turbulent months following the Eiger climb, politics and personal vanities conspired to drive a wedge between them. It is clear from nearly all accounts of the Eiger's first ascent that it was Anderl who cracked this nut, always out in front finding the route, coming to terms with extreme technical difficulties, and drawing upon all his resources during the summit push to keep the team moving upward despite an intense blizzard. But soon after the Eiger ascent the four men were separated, with Harrer and Kasparek sent on tour through Austria, while Heckmair and Vörg were paraded around Germany. Considering the egos involved, it is hardly surprising that in Austria a somewhat different version of the Eiger conquest emerged, a version more generous to Kasparek and Harrer.

Tonight Anderl laughs at the memory; after all, history records a fair version of the events. Kasparek is long gone, and even Harrer, not known for minimizing his own role in anything, recently introduced Anderl to the Dalai Lama as "my life-saver."

Anderl is also determined to give credit where it is due by making the point that the Eiger ascent was a team effort, and, despite his initial misgivings, he feels the Austrians played a crucial role. "Heini and Kasparek knew the way down," he says. "They had already climbed the Mittellegi Ridge and gone down the west flank as part of their preparations for the north face." And so, when Heckmair and his exhausted companions finally crawled onto the Eiger's summit—at night and in a raging blizzard—it was the Austrians who led them to safety.

"It was a lucky thing when Wiggerl suggested they should all climb together," Trudl remarks, and Anderl chuckles his agreement.

Leading the summit icefield on the north face of the Eiger, 1938.

Photograph courtesy of Anderl Heckmair

And what of Vörg? I had read that he was a casualty of the war, killed on the Eastern Front on the very first day of fighting. But the Heckmairs reveal a chilling detail that elevates this tragedy to a new level. "He was killed by Germans," Trudl tells us, and her voice is a sad whisper. "He was posted as a sentry to watch a building until a demolition team arrived. But when the flame-throwers finally came, they didn't know he was there."

Our dinners arrive, a fabulous spread featuring curried chicken, buttered pasta, fish, and shrimp salad. The entrees that the two Eiger veterans have chosen are easily deduced from our physical appearances: Anderl is enjoying a lean portion of fish, while I wolf down the buttered pasta *and* the curried chicken. It was almost a decade ago that I climbed the Eiger, and the years have not been kind. It has been nearly six decades since Anderl climbed it and he looks like he could do it again tomorrow. This reminds me of a story.

I ask Anderl if he knows of the American climber Paul Petzoldt. As the venerable Wyoming mountain guide who pioneered the north face route on the Grand Teton—perhaps the closest American equivalent of the Eigerwand—he could be described as sort of a wild-west version of Anderl.

"Yes, Anderl has heard this name," Trudl says. Petzoldt also came close to making the first ascent of K2 the same year Anderl climbed the Eiger, and the Heckmairs remember this expedition.

I tell them of a dinner I had had with Petzoldt several years before. At some point during the meal the topic of the Eiger came up. Petzoldt had never climbed it but always wished that he had. Puffing out my chest and sucking in my gut, I seized the opportunity

On the Hinterstoisser Traverse leading to the First Icefield. Eiger north face, 1938.

Photograph courtesy of Anderl Heckmair

to mention that I had climbed the Eiger just a few years earlier. No, no, he said, he was talking about the north face. Yes, I insisted, I had climbed the north face. Petzoldt looked me up and down, slumped back into his seat, shook his head sadly, and asked, "So, does everybody climb the Eiger these days?"

Anderl and Trudl get a big kick out of this. Dina, hard-pressed to see the humor in any story that hinges upon my indolent lifestyle, rolls her eyes. I have a point, however: clearly, the Eiger is no longer a climb for just the "cream of the crop." I suggest to the Heckmairs that modern equipment is a principal reason why these days, a few curds like me are able to float to the top.

"When Anderl climbed the Eiger," Trudl tells us, "there was not even such a thing as a safety helmet. He kept a folded handkerchief under his cap to protect against falling stones."

This reminds Anderl of a story.

"Anderl once thought of adapting an Italian army helmet for climbing," his wife translates, "but first he wanted to make sure that it was strong enough. So he had his brother hit him over the head with an iron bar." To emphasize the point, Anderl grins and spreads his arms wide. Clearly, we aren't talking about some dinky little tire-iron here. "His head was okay," Trudl smiles, "but his neck was sore for weeks!" Now it is Dina and I who are cracking up, and it is Trudl's turn to roll her eyes a little.

After the meal the Heckmairs invite us back to their home again for a nightcap. Once I have been liquored up a bit, I feel I have an excuse to ask about something I'm not sure is an acceptable topic of conversation among Germans who lived through the war: Adolf Hitler. I am fascinated by the fact that Anderl actually met the man.

"Oh, yes," Trudl says—and I am relieved that I haven't offended anyone. "It is quite amazing, really. Many important Party members never met Hitler, and then there is Anderl, a simple mountaineer with no interest in politics, so poor he didn't even maintain an address, and he met Hitler on more than one occasion."

In fact, the huge public rally that Hitler used to exploit the Eiger climb as a tremendous accomplishment for the Fatherland was not the first time Anderl came face to face with *der Führer,* nor, incredibly, was it the most surreal.

Among Anderl's clients during his early years as a guide was the well-known moviemaker and actress Leni Riefenstahl. As the star of a string of popular mountain-themed motion pictures, Leni possessed both a compelling beauty and a natural athleticism that captivated German audiences. But even these extraordinary outward qualities were eclipsed by an inner measure of ambition: she courted the rich and the powerful with the intensity of a shark prowling a kiddie pool. Eventually, Leni charmed herself into the graces of Hitler himself and was selected by him to make the infamous Nazi propaganda films of the 1934 Nuremberg Rally and the 1936 Berlin Olympic Games.

After hiring Anderl for an outing in the Wolkenstein Alps and bonding with him during the epic climb and forced bivouac that followed, Leni managed to convince her resolutely apolitical guide to accompany her to a Party meeting in Nuremberg by promising him free access to the Olympic training facilities in Berlin. With the Eiger fixed firmly in his sights, it was an offer that even Anderl, despite his reservations about Nazi politics, could not refuse. While in Nuremberg, Leni was summoned to a late-afternoon tea with Party officials at a local hotel. With Anderl in tow, she was given the seat of honor at Hitler's table, and Anderl passed the time as anyone suddenly seated near his country's head of state might: trying to keep a low profile while studying the man. "I could see absolutely nothing so extraordinary about him," Anderl has said. Eventually, the conversation turned to Leni's recent mountain adventure. At this point Hitler became agitated and scolded her for risking her life so freely, especially in light of the great "mission" with which he had entrusted her. Leni answered that by hiring an experienced mountain guide—this man Heckmair—she had never been in danger. Anderl froze in mid-bite as every eye in the room suddenly drew a bead on him. Hitler insisted upon posing to Anderl the most vexing question in mountaineering: "So, why do you do it?"

The reasons that compel a person to climb mountains are such a personal mixture of sensation, emotion, and experience that attempting to communicate them satisfactorily to others is a challenge akin to proving the existence of God. And while a flip and meaningless answer like "because it's there" or "it keeps me out of real trouble" might be enough to pacify a casual friend or relative, it's not something I would want to try on a room full of Nazis. If I've never been able to explain the value of climbing to my own mother, I can't imagine having to convince Hitler.

Choosing his words carefully, Anderl did his best to explain to the *Führer* what is gained from a hard climb that cannot be found in a casual walk in the hills. Hitler was intrigued—not about climbing, but by the motivations behind it—and persisted in questioning Anderl throughout the course of the meal. Even when, at last, an aide informed the Leader that his presence was required elsewhere, Anderl was forced to tag along and continue the conversation. The two men moved out onto a balcony, where, to Anderl's astonishment, they beheld a massive throng of humanity that cheered and saluted their appearance. Hitler returned the gesture, as did the other Party leaders on the platform. And so it was that for the first time in his life, Anderl Heckmair was reluctantly obliged to raise his arm in the infamous *Heil Hitler* salute.

"But Anderl still managed to express his disapproval," Trudl tells us, "and it was a lucky thing for him that no one else noticed. He raised the wrong arm—his left one, which is something of an insult. And then he put his right hand behind his back." Anderl chuckles while

Trudl explains the significance: "In Germany, when you do this, it means you are not being truthful." In other words, standing at Hitler's elbow and before a crowd of thousands, Anderl Heckmair did the German equivalent of sticking out his tongue and crossing his fingers.

For the two hours Anderl was forced to stand on the balcony, watching the torchlit mob parade past beneath him, he yearned for the loneliness of the mountains. And the next day, at the political rally, he was gripped with a deep foreboding. Anderl has written, "I felt a kind of shudder in my soul. I understood that something was in motion that was going to sweep everything away with it, but where to I could not tell."

As Trudl finishes relating this bizarre and extraordinary tale, we all sit silently for a moment. Dina and I are so lost in thought that we barely notice when Trudl gets up to go in search of some photographs. It is Anderl who finally breaks the silence. Nudging his empty glass toward the whiskey bottle he winks, *"Schnell! Jetzt ist sie weg!"* "Quick, while she's gone!"

Anderl survived World War II by serving as a mountaineering instructor for the army troops. His skills and experience were so valuable that his commanders defied the regulations by refusing to rotate him into the fighting. After the war he made his way back to Oberstdorf and returned to the things he loved most: the mountains and guiding. With the good fortune to have had one of Germany's richest industrialists as a regular client, Anderl has explored every corner of the globe, leading climbs and treks from the Andes to the Himalaya well into his eighties. And he shows little sign of slowing down.

"At Anderl's age it is important to keep moving," Trudl remarks with a grin, "Who knows, if he stops, he may never start up again!" I tell him that I think there is little danger of this any time soon. Anderl laughs and tells another story.

"When he was young, a fortune teller told him he would die an unnatural death," Trudl explains. "To Anderl, this means he will probably die in bed." He also wants us to know that the town of Oberstdorf honored him on his ninetieth birthday by making him an Honorary Citizen. "Because of this, he gets two things," Trudl says. "First, he doesn't have to pay any city taxes. This is very nice, except his age already exempts him from these taxes."

"And the second?" I ask. Trudl smiles.

"They gave him a cemetery plot." As his laughter fills the room, I can't decide which of these honors is more useless to Anderl Heckmair.

With time growing short and the whiskey running low, I feel that the moment has come when I must say to Anderl Heckmair the thing I have come all this way to tell him. Taking a deep breath, I blurt out, "I want Anderl to understand what an important man he has been in my life."

As when we first arrived, Anderl's modesty forces him to instinctively try to get past this comment by waving me off and joking self-importantly, "Yes, I am very proud, very proud!"

But I persist. "The life Anderl has led, his climbs, and his philosophies—when a young man reads about these things and decides that these are the examples that he will follow, it can have a very profound and positive influence. It can lead a person on a very good path through life—and I really want to thank him for this."

Anderl fidgets and listens uncomfortably as Trudl translates. But when he finally responds, two things are clear: he appreciates my desire to express these feelings, and he really is proud.

The Traverse of the Gods, Eiger north wall, 1938. *Photograph courtesy of Anderl Heckmair*

Heckmair.

Anderl Heckmair collection

"Anderl says that you are making him choked-up."

Before we say goodbye, Trudl smiles and hands me the dreaded copy of Kasparek's autobiography. "In Germany, when you give someone a book, you must write something in it and sign it."

I couldn't disagree more. The unique history these men shared, from the landmark climb that brought them together, to the differing ideologies that kept them apart, seems to dictate that the pages of this particular book remain free of sentiment—especially from the likes of me.

But the Heckmairs are insistent. And so I find myself —as obscure a mountaineer as ever put pen to paper—in the awkward and unsettling position of having to compose a line of presentation to the man who first led the Eiger—in a book written by the one member of the team who probably never came to terms with this fact. Before my glasses can fog again, I manage to scribble an inscription that not only expresses my admiration at such a lifetime of unsurrendered potential, but that Fritz himself, had he lived to gain the wisdom and perspective of old age, might also have written: "To Anderl, who showed us the way."

STORM CAMP

John Hart

1

And the tent went down like an animal, fighting,
bellowing and flayed,
like a crushed man, terrible with joints
and useless openings.

And the wind upon it, stripping the steel from the cloth.

And in such hovel as remained to share
we were the tenants, leasing hour by hour.
Three days we lay in that corroding cloud
under a roof so ruinous and loud
that I have made the noise a private word
to still all other pain.

2

Three nights without sleep, and the white storm lurid,
and the spindrift probing, desiring the eyes of the brain,
on lands where it was venture to be animate:
where beauty contends with the soul, the ill-defended,
and a low grade of fear, that sets nothing in motion,
was a tax on the day and the dark.

And we each of us mounted by a private stair
to find that gap in which the stars appear
over an orchard country. Quiet there
with those cattle, and mirrors and books, and the black
    river . . .
Oh do not look down there, traveler . . .
Not yet is the night of the end, and the last effort.

3

"There is a chance," you said, "that we have come too far.
Have passed the dogs, the lines that spit at flesh,
in ignorance have crossed the saints' frontier."
And the gale belabors the paralyzed cloth,

making impossible speech:
between our frozen hoods the crystals burn:
and the air outside not air, nor a breathable substance,
but some raw ether, rigid, white, and mean.

"I have no doubt," you said, "the thing desires us.
If you could bear them, there were in that cry
	most envious voices.
The snow will imitate our stumps till spring.

"They do not rot, those alpine dead, nor bleed.
For what are they then the food, who don't climb down—
who are left behind with the skin, on the cold places?"

4

Flared once at the end of the night like a suffering stone
a sun incapable of shining on . . .
how much, then, more, of the same.

And isn't there in us a needling now
to be as lepers that endure the law—
to exit singly and obey the snow?

Go out. Why not.
Consume and be consumed.
Give up defense.
What here was worth defending?
Shred off the mortal-anyhow-undone,
this endotherm so costly to maintain . . .
It would be easier to sleep,
to lie congested in the equal storm.

> *The storm:*
> *The competent. The cured. The blast*
> *toward which all meditation must pretend.*
> *Great tree and island, resting in its wind—*
> *No enemy*
> *but some vast cogent creature, lordlier than we,*
> *possessed of a kind of speech and a kind of eye . . .*

Yet we will live to see this creature die.

No, if the monster speaks, it is not to us.
It is by accident we overhear.
It has no secret but the one we knew
(and as a clue to death it will not do):
that some of the ships of death
were beautiful.

5

There is a light on the tentcloth. The others see this, too.
    Who is it standing with a flashlight in the gale?
    I put two woolen fingers to the shine; it leaves the
    yelling fabric for the hand. It slides down toward me
    on the orange sleeve... the others see it, too.

And look, the hand that had no cause to gleam—
the hand that did not rise to meet the shine—
the dealer in sleep, with frostbite on the thumb—:

Both hands are flaming with St. Elmo's Fire.

6

In the morning I shave, and eat, and sometimes stop
to count the small elated wrist
of the surviving heart.

Say: from this day shall I number
the years of my true intention
and shall no more like a dog
go yap! and wander.

The place I stand shall always seem to be
a new town at an unaccustomed hour:
happy to have at the throat or in the foot,
infusing the narrow vessel with its heat

the beast, the beast, the beast of a small life,
the systole hard as a bean.

Aid and Free

Shipton Spire (19,700 feet)

Karakoram Range, Pakistan

Back in the summer of 1937 during his Shaksgam Expedition (later chronicled in *Blank On The Map*), renowned British mountaineer Eric Shipton first sighted the magnificent granite shark tooth that would eventually bear his name. Yet nearly sixty years passed before this striking tower above the Hainablak Glacier—an upper spur of the Trango Glacier—received its first ascent. After unsuccessful attempts by previous parties in 1992 and 1995, Greg Child, Greg Foweraker, Charles Boyd, and Greg Collum made the first ascent of Shipton Spire in July, 1996, via *The Baltese Falcon* (VII 5.11, A4). Two years later, Steph Davis, Kennan Harvey, and Seth Shaw created the nearly all-free route of *Inshallah* (VII 5.12, A1). Shipton Spire's second new route, *The Ship of Fools* (VII 5.11, A2 WI6), had earlier been achieved capsule-style by the two-man team of Jared Ogden and Mark Synnott in 1997. This photo essay celebrates the ground-breaking stylistic approaches used on the latter two routes.

The Ship of Fools

(VII 5.11, A2 WI6)

Mark Synnott and Jared Ogden July 9–August 8, 1997

Opening Pages, Left: Synnott at the Crow's Nest bivouac, top of pitch three. Great Trango Tower behind. *Jared Ogden*

Opening Pages, Right: Shipton Spire and reflection from Base Camp. *Kennan Harvey*

Left: The view down pitch nine, "the Slot from Hell" (5.9, A2), with Ogden and Fantasy Island below. *Mark Synnott*

Above Left: Synnott sorting gear at the Notch (Camp four) at 19,000 feet on *Ship of Fools*. *Jared Ogden*

Above: At Fantasy Island, Ogden prepares to lead the 5.11 crux, pitch eight. *Mark Synnott*

Above: Cleaning a tricky mixed pitch on *Ship of Fools* in stormy weather. *Mark Synnott*

Right: Synnott leading perfect 5.10 cracks on pitch sixteen. *Jared Ogden*

Above: Synnott on a hard mixed lead (pitch eighteen), fixing ropes the day before the summit. *Jared Ogden*

Right: Ogden resting and eating at the Notch after the pair's successful ascent. *Mark Synnott*

Left: Jared Ogden free climbing pitch seventeen up beautiful 5.9 cracks. *Mark Synnott*

Left:
Ogden threads
the needle on
the summit push.

Mark Synnott

Right:
Ogden leading
mixed ground
on pitch twenty,
with the summit
visible above.

Mark Synnott

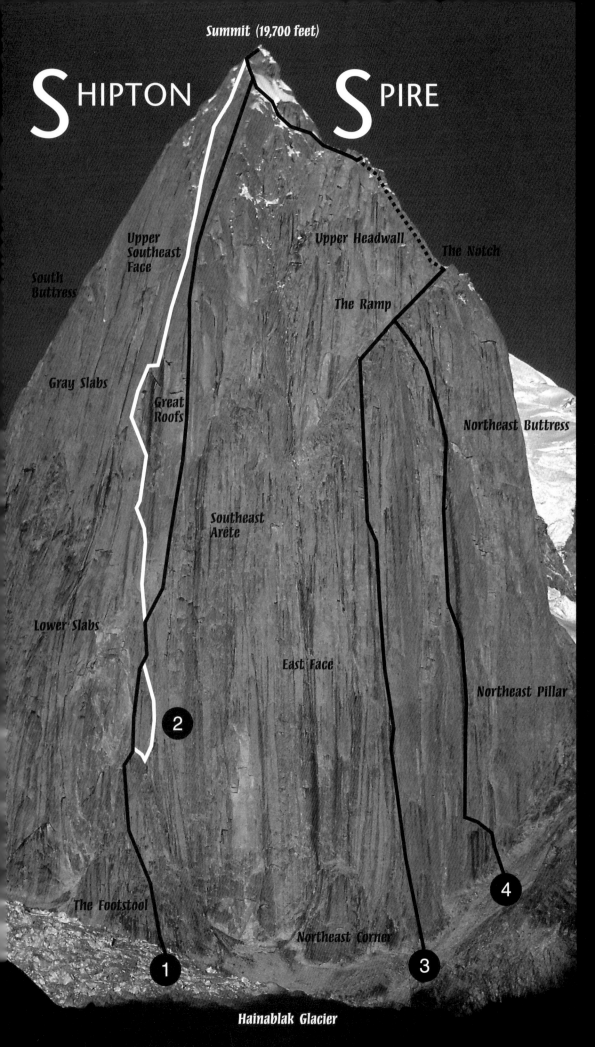

Summit (19,700 feet)

SHIPTON SPIRE

Upper Headwall

The Notch

Upper Southeast Face

South Buttress

The Ramp

Gray Slabs

Great Roofs

Northeast Buttress

Southeast Arête

Lower Slabs

East Face

Northeast Pillar

2

The Footstool

4

Northeast Corner

1

3

Hainablak Glacier

Shipton Spire's four routes:

1. *The Baltese Falcon*

   (VII 5.11, A4)

   Greg Child,
   Greg Foweraker,
   Charles Boyd,
   Greg Collum, 1996

2. *Inshallah*

   (VII 5.12, A1)

   Steph Davis,
   Kennan Harvey,
   Seth Shaw, 1998

3. *Original Route*

   (VII 5.9, A3)

   Greg Collum,
   Mark Bebie,
   Andy Selters,
   Chuck Boyd, 1992

4. *The Ship of Fools*

   (VII 5.11, A2 WI6)

   Jared Ogden,
   Mark Synnott, 1997

Jared Ogden

Right:
   Seth Shaw
   free climbing
   pitch fifteen (5.11)
   of *Inshallah*
   on Day 7.

Kennan Harvey

Above and Left: Seth Shaw leading pitch fifteen (5.11) on Day 7.

Right: Steph Davis ascends a 5.11 crack on Day 6.

Photographs: *Kennan Harvey*

Inshallah (VII 5.12, A1)

Steph Davis, Kennan Harvey, and Seth Shaw
July 13–26, 1998

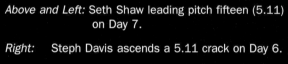

After fixing the start of the route for three days, Seth Shaw, Steph Davis, and Kennan Harvey free-climbed a total of 36 pitches up the 4,400-foot big wall. The trio very nearly made the first free ascent of Shipton Spire in a fourteen-day effort—but eventually were stymied by a single, ten-foot-high blank section.

Above: Seth Shaw, Steph Davis, and Kennan Harvey.

Left: On Day 11, Steph Davis works pitch twenty-two (5.11+), the "Suture Pitch," so named because the team used toilet paper wads to stop waterflow so that the pitch could be free climbed.

Right: Seth Shaw follows pitch twenty-two (5.11+).

Photographs: *Kennan Harvey*

TOO OLD FOR 5.12, TOO YOUNG FOR OBITUARIES

Joe Kelsey

They went, I say, partly in search of the sublime, and they found it the only way it can be found, here or there—around the edges, tucked into the corners of the days. For they were people—all of them, even the British—and despite the purity of their conceptions, they man-hauled their humanity to the Poles.

—Annie Dillard, from *An Expedition to the Pole*

The hundreds of granite formations scattered across the high desert plain that is Joshua Tree, like real mountains, simply stand. They require no climbers, no narratives, not even names. Any significance we try to impose on rock, any grails we quest for, we contrive for ourselves.

As the years trundle by and another spring finds me on rock again, hoping my feet will stick, quests and scenarios seem more distracting, as extraneous as the monogrammed silver spoons, backgammon boards, and button polish that Sir John Franklin's starved, doomed Victorians, abandoning ice-crushed ships and a search for the Northwest Passage, dragged along barren Arctic coasts. Climbing seems most profound when not burdened with such civilized impedimenta as hopes and plans, when it is simply movement on rock.

Our week-long Joshua Tree trips, requiring that life proceed haphazardly, provide a felicitous environment for scriptless climbing. During breakfast, middle-aged men of differing absences from rock, conditioning, and ambitions flock around a campground table. While stoves of diverse nationalities, vintages, and sputterings produce coffee and tea, guidebook owners alternately thumb frantically through their copies and flourish them opened to pages that suggest feasible adventure. Guidebooks are too numerous and the process too unruly for anyone's willfulness. Ambition, or even a plan, is irrelevant.

This rabble of lingerers from a few decades ago—Steve Roper, Allen Steck, Eric Beck, and I invariably, John Thackray and Walt Vennum usually, John Morton, Joe Fitschen, and Dick and Judy Erb recently, Dave Cook with wife Chloe until a few years ago, and a variable cast of other oldies—eventually decide on a crag that moments before hadn't occurred to anyone. We choose it because we happen to be pondering it when an urge to leave camp suddenly, contagiously seizes us. Horoscopes could determine our fates as serendipitously, and before the sun is high.

Then, seven or ten or fourteen rock veterans scatter through the sage like cattle thinking they're grazing, though actually being driven to a stockyard, to converge below a shapeless outcrop whose identity may be a mystery to someone who was in the outhouse when it was abruptly chosen. The coffee-nerved spill ropes below routes suitable for creaky fingers. After a leader belays atop his lead, he hands the belayee the rope's anchored

Lunchtime at Ryan
Campground.
(L-R): Eric Beck,
Lori Beck,
Allen Steck,
Steve Roper,
John Morton.

Joe Kelsey

end, tosses the free end, and zips down a rappel or trots down the crag's backside slabs and chutes. He finds ropes and belayers on nearby routes, which range from 5.6 to mid-5.10—cracks, corners, faces, whatever. A rope towed by a leader whose derring-do you missed looks about the same as a rope draped by someone who reached the anchors less gallantly, and we shamelessly top-rope what none dares lead. Someone finding no rope unoccupied may solo a handy 5.4. Before leaving for lunch, each finds his way up five or six climbs, in no order of difficulty, not catching the names of some.

Returning to camp well past the intended lunchtime, we scrutinize guidebooks trying, not always successfully, to surmise what we climbed, and sit in the shade reflecting on the morning's vicissitudes. After lunch it's off to another rockpile, though for a shorter session, and thus we wander day after day. A good day is one when enough happens that you can't think of it as unequivocally good or bad. A good week is one after which, when someone asks, "Have a good trip?" you say "Yes," knowing you're not really answering the question.

Our first spring trips, in the mid-eighties, were prologues to climbing seasons, autumn trips epilogues. But I—as did Eric and Allen and Steve and others—soon began training for JT, not training at JT. While disdaining quests, I count carabiners and retie runners so many days before a trip, wake so early on the morning of the drive down, that I must be seeking something. It isn't, as earnest writers propose, to learn why I climb—it's not the *meaning* of climbing but the *experience* of climbing. Given rock's silence, there's not much to say about the experience, other than that I'd like to hear the silence, be so at home that a cliff transfigures into Eden. Reentering Eden would make an interesting narrative, but I'm not purposeful enough to find it except by stumbling into it.

You'd think a person could attain such blessed oblivion as easily as a sunning lizard. But apparently it is human nature to concoct scenarios, follow a script leading to a resolution that would send movie-goers home whistling the theme music. We couldn't be Abstract Expressionist geniuses throwing paint at a canvas, because we couldn't resist aiming the paint to make trees and barns and cows.

A century ago, the quest was for the Poles. After men with glazed eyes reached them and there was no farther north or south to go, climbers devised absolutes: Everest, of course, the highest—the "Third Pole"—and then extremes of difficulty, length, speed, of style even. Hardest and Fastest may be temporal superlatives, challenges to someone younger and better, and Free, Pitonless, Unroped, mere way stations—as were Scoresby's Farthest North, Nansen's Farthest North—en route to the Pole of Purity, but our era offers less grandiose obsessions than so-called Golden Ages did. There is even a mania to collect the fifty states' high points, the Pole of All being an absolute you can aim your feet toward as single-mindedly as you can navigate straight north.

Greg Child didn't coin the term "pseudo-mountaineering" in a recent *Climbing* to disparage old guys happy to rope up at whatever desert lump their indecision brings them to. He had in mind folks who bypass Joshua Tree on their way to Everest. But our tribe isn't much holier than thou. As visitors from afar, camped away from other climbers, we depend on guidebooks: Vogel's and, further complicating breakfast, Bartlett's. Vogel draws routes on photos of the amorphous blobs while Bartlett sketches the blobs, adding one-liners: "Climb up and right on ledges on the southeast side of the rock." Both identify routes by inscrutable names—*Nobody Walks in L.A., Poodles Are People Too, Where Janitors Dare*—use asterisks to recommend routes, and, of course, numerically rate a route's difficulty.

With most routes less than a ropelength long, the choice may be between fifty-foot and eighty-foot climbs, a difference often not evident in guidebook illustrations. (I'm no longer surprised to walk a mile to what appears in a photo to be a Trango Tower, only to find a thirty-foot pointed block.) All that distinguishes *Rollerskating with Aliens*, say, from *Beam Me Up Scottie*, both stuck miles away out at Stirrup Tank, is one's 5.8 rating, the other's 5.10a. For pilgrims aspiring to oneness with rock, our agendas involve too much numerology: "Here's a three-star 5.8!" The numbers organize themselves into a plot: "We did nines yesterday; let's try a ten."

Eric inflicts further arithmetic by his "count," the number of routes he climbs that day. His grail is ten. He feigns nonchalance, but if we return to our Ryan campsites with a count that doesn't require all his fingers, he disappears to Cap Rock to solo a few handy 5.2s. Once, with the sun well below Mt. San Jacinto and his count teetering at nine, Eric forcibly evicted Dave from a rope so he could sprint up a worthless little top-rope before a shivering belayer could extract the rope from his belay plate. What can be said for Eric's count, though, and not for novices on Everest, is that as he tightens his sneakers below a 5.1 trough, an alter ego laughs at him as openly as his friends do.

My quest is for routes I haven't done, no matter how lichened, loose, or inaccessible. Consulting a penciled entry in my guidebook, I see that I've been up 458 Joshua Tree routes. I can only defend such stamp-collecting by pleading that with 4,000 routes in the present guidebook, even a busy week doesn't improve my insignificant fraction: aspiring pioneers are off in such JT boondocks as Oz, creating five new routes for each old route I do.

Before monomaniacs trudged straight north, Brits like Franklin put their stiff upper lips to good use looking for the Northwest Passage. I like the idea of a Northwest Passage, with its foggy labyrinth of islands and peninsulas, straits and dead-end inlets, and, given the fluctuating ice-pack, several ambiguous solutions (all useless). But seeking it still involves a story, and a story—whether convoluted or as succinct as a medieval morality play or a beer commercial—brings you no closer to rock.

Climbing, given its definition, must involve the minimal narrative of *Up*, but you can't impose much plot on granite. Flake, nubbin, crack; thin or buckets; protectable or run-out—these are not inherently heroic, tragic, or comic. On a one-pitch crag, there aren't even narrow ledges to induce epiphanies in cramped belayers.

You can impose a plot that extends beyond one climb—that spans a trip, a season, or a lifetime—but a rudderless mob tossed willy-nilly at cracks and slabs, 5.7s and 5.10s, eliminates day-to-day plot. And middle-age theoretically precludes a biographer's favorite tack: "Having mastered X, Siegfried advanced to Y." The only synopsis available to the grizzled would seem to be "Has-been" (or "never-was" in the case of some of us) "struggles ridiculously to defy decrepitude." We could be buffoons.

Buffoonery makes best drama when the buffoon is earnest and unselfconscious. A smirking tourist posing mock-heroic before the Tetons provides an insipid chuckle compared to a Grand Teton aspirant approaching his grail up the wrong canyon. Buffoonery is in the eye of the beholder, and we tend to avoid such venues as Hidden Valley Campground, where beholders are abundant.

Someone did impose buffoonery on us, but not someone who has seen Allen's annual voyage up 5.10d *Rubicon*. A book reviewer from the *Los Angeles Times*, presumably displeased with an *Ascent* article in which I celebrated our first trips, characterized this publication's creators and readership as "wilted flower children." This wasn't a curriculum vitae that had occurred to Allen, who spent the Summer of Love shoveling the Hummingbird Ridge, or Steve or Eric, who would have looked grotesque adorned with daisies, but we did name a route *Wilted Flower Children*.

We make fun of ourselves, but not really. In *Camp 4* Steve wrote that a certain fellow "climbed just well enough not to be considered a buffoon." The characterization startled me, the near-buffoon having been one of my mentors, but it could describe the ambition (and imply the fear) of everyone shouldering a rope in one of the sandy three-car turnouts where our forays begin. Plotlessness isn't frivolity: we train as seriously as our limbs and winter rain and the need to stare at computers allow—more diligently than before we realized our bodies are biodegradable. We climb near enough an edge, however idiosyncratic it may be, to remember that an edge exists. We—and I don't use *we* royally but collectively—climb at a higher level, smoother and more confident, not only than as young dervishes but than when we first ventured to the Tree and onto its four-star 5.8s.

That we now seek harder rock is a wonder to ourselves and a topic for side-canyon speculation. Training may be an explanation, but so may stickier shoes. Eric's mixed-metaphor theory is the "four-minute-mile syndrome": we're caught on a rising tide, like runners routinely surpassing that once-magic barrier. It's fun, and we may as well swim along, but climbing better because everyone is, or because shoes are stickier, isn't compelling drama. Nor is a simpler explanation—that you improve by climbing, and our communal enthusiasm gets us on the rocks, even if that enthusiasm reflects an urgency to climb while we still can. And when you've done the 5.9s along the dry wash where you've strewn quickdraws and water bottles, you tend to look at 5.10s.

To avoid being swamped by the tide, I need younger climbers to show what is possible now that wasn't then, and I'm grateful to kids who give me a taste of their generation's standards. I assume they imagine themselves eventually being old climbers, though Steve thinks me naive: "When you can't hear them, they're saying, 'Those pathetic bastards! They never found anything better to do with their lives.'"

Youth seldom witnesses our assault of Josh's spectrum of difficulties, but agelessness is often tied to the other end of the rope. It's not that Allen, a decade ahead of his ropemates, refuses to concede to time; time hasn't occurred to him. You can phone him, invite him to climb anywhere the next day, and he asks only, "What time should I be ready?" I once told him I'd just been to Red Rocks. Scowling balefully at me, he asked, "Why didn't you tell me you were going?"

"Allen," I explained, "Your daughter was getting married."

He considered that for a moment, then said quietly, "Oh, yeah."

When I began climbing, in the Shawangunks, I surreptitiously studied Hans Kraus and Fritz Wiessner. Those living legends strode placidly through the Uberfall throng and down the Carriage Road and contentedly roped up below a route, *High Exposure* say, that they'd been up countless times. I looked for an aura of former greatness reduced to pathos, but I saw instead dignity and men at home in the vertical.

Yet life can distract you not only from quests but from ignoring quests, make Eden even harder to find. When I thought I'd whittled my quest down to simple curiosity about whether I could get up the route I was standing under, along came my fiftieth birthday. Steve or I, wandering between crags, sometimes recall, no doubt imperfectly, a phrase from some educational dead-end: *In idle pursuits they whiled away the hours of their days.* As my fiftieth approached, the phrase took on an ominous inflection.

I'd decided that a belated Joshua Tree trip, a few days after my November birthday, would be the rite of passage, but on the day itself suffered quiet desperation until Allen and another friend took me to dinner. When I mentioned my dread of the shadowy side of the half-century crest, Allen looked as if he'd misunderstood. "Why fear age? I enjoyed my fortieth, my fiftieth more than that, my sixtieth even more, and I'm looking forward to my seventieth." On his sixtieth he'd reclimbed Sentinel Rock by the route he'd pioneered thirty-six years earlier, but in one day rather than the five of his youth. No short JT climb could defy time as the ascent of a long Yosemite classic could, but Allen's bold crossings of chronological cols inspired me to contemplate an insipid winter-solstice version.

Route names are a shorthand infliction of drama on rock. *Figures on a Landscape* suggests one sort of narrative, *Boogers on a Lampshade* another. However, among the

Allen Steck
brooding at
Ryan Campground.

Joe Kelsey

thousands of anonymous names we northerners scan in a guidebook, few resonate. We depend on Eric, who in San Diego hears folklore. He had breathed life into *Solid Gold*, which he'd followed, by inviting us to list the ten best pitches we'd ever done, then picturing *Solid Gold* on the list (and imagining the first of its two pitches not as the guidebook 5.9 but the word-of-mouth 5.10b). The name of its neighbor, *Figures on a Landscape*, also stands out from the mundane, but Eric's *Solid Gold* leader thought *Figures* too hard for the likes of us. *Solid Gold* sounded appropriate for showing that my fifty years on the planet hadn't been completely wasted.

Once in Ryan, though, I realized that no one at our gatherings imposes egocentric agendas and recalled that the one time I'd known Allen to script adventure he unnerved me. To prepare for Sentinel, he and I went to the Valley several days before his birthday, and he focused not on the cracks at hand but, out of character, on Sentinel's fissures. The plan was for George Lowe, Allen, me, and a fourth to march up Sentinel, but the fourth changed identity a few times, then evaporated, and I too backed out, in part because three seemed crowdlike, but also because Allen with an agenda wasn't his reassuring carpe diem self. In JT I didn't mention my recent birthday, though I did hope to steer us toward *Solid Gold* if someone mentioned it.

Beginning as always with a star-studded 5.7, we knocked off *Elusive Butterfly*, then a few neighbors, and I soon found myself twenty feet up a 5.10a, fiddling to place protection.

By the time I trusted a stopper, my hands needed recovery time. As I retreated, a youth appeared with a girlfriend and a boom box and, while the girl watched silently and the blaster didn't, soloed our route. When he reached my piece, he yanked it and tossed it down, explaining that it occupied a crucial lock. Turning fifty was picking that stopper out of the sand.

We began going to JT for paradisal spring and fall weather, but rarely have we found paradise, with the cold and wind afflicting us as often as Mojave heat. December days can be ideal, but you start late and, when the sun sets at 4:30, rappel as if stormed off the Eiger. On this trip we had Dave's bonfires, had eaten by six, then tried to postpone bedtime with the same tales of our misspent youths that had enthralled us on a dozen previous trips. But there wasn't the extensive fact-checking that prolonged earlier renditions, and the quiet soon scattered us to our tents, despite the certainty of being driven into predawn arctic air by insistent bladders.

One morning's wind discouraged us from even cranking sevens, so we hiked into the Wonderland of Rocks, taking a rope and a few nuts for easy climbs, but really to explore. Most JT climbs are on cliffs lining roads or clumps scattered around campgrounds, but the Wonderland is a labyrinth, with domes and towers hidden up ambiguously defined corridors and meandering, branching sand washes. Except for the elegant Astro Domes and the comic Freak Brothers, the amorphous outcrops—the Duckwaddle Domes and Foolproof Towers and Punk Rocks—confuse more than assist nomads trying to penetrate the Wonderland.

Our gypsy band navigated through the maze, comparing guidebook photos to reality, placemarking maps with fingers, updating our position relative to the Astro Domes when those landmarks hovered into view. Passing North Astro Dome, I saw *Solid Gold*, looking especially sunless. According to Eric, it would be north of the Arctic Circle till spring.

Needing a destination, we chose the Bighorn Mating Grotto. Its location a mile into the Wonderland, the mystery of its name, and the absence in Vogel of photos of its multi-starred routes promised the most adventure possible with gloves on. It also meant we didn't know what we were looking for. Eventually, after much head-scratching, I noted a path crashing through scrub oaks for no apparent reason and followed it to a tiny notch. Beyond was hidden a claustrophobic alcove with a surprisingly lush floor, where if I were a bighorn I'd want to mate, and overhung by dramatic cracks. Knowing we'd found the Grotto but with too little gear to be tempted upward, we could, for once, declare our day an unequivocal success—the secret of success being to aim low enough.

John Thackray and Eric Beck inspect.

Joe Kelsey

Nevertheless, en route to the cars at dusk, trying to give perspective to Eric's numerology, I asked, "What's your count?"—knowing it was two. Eric, however, told about an experiment. A group of volunteers shot basketball free throws for half an hour a day. Another group *thought* about free throws for the same half-hour. After several weeks, both groups stepped to a free-throw line. The visualizers shot as well as the practicers. "And," Eric concluded, "I've visualized climbing ten routes we saw today."

Even if you aren't as easily entertained as we are, it's hard to ignore Joshua Tree's variety: cracks, faces, steepness, smoothness. Nevertheless, Eric and I spent a day at sunny Echo Rock, where the decor is monothematic: low-angle but slippery. This isn't a genre we train for—or visualize—but in working our way up one line of bolts after another, reinforcing the mind-over-feet discipline that friction and tiny edges require, we eventually felt at home on slabs.

Two years before, I'd fallen repeatedly at *The Falcon and the Snowman*'s first bolt, eventually giving up when I ran out of combinations to fall from. Now I cruised this slick acreage—only to fail repeatedly at the third bolt, the type of slip where fingers cling to the rock, via sharp flakes, for a futile instant longer than toes. Eric relieved me and took a more sensible path, after which, grateful not proud, I followed. *Falcon* made a good-enough metaphor for Age 50: I did better than in the past, though not as well as I would have liked.

On our first trip, as we were reacquainting ourselves with old friends, Eric, apropos of nothing, turned to Steve: "I note that *Ascent* is publishing fiction." Eric's tone was accusatory, and off we went like a television talk show, equating decibels with wisdom. We resolved nothing, but I had something to ponder after leaving the smoke and babble: what a random dramatis personae we were. The sixties never foreshadowed our survival, individually or tribally, as fiction would require. Climbing fiction, in particular, can't admit chance; it is hard to imagine it being written for any purpose other than demonstrating causality.

My introduction to climbing fiction was James Ramsey Ullman's *The White Tower*. In 1944 an unclimbed Rum Doodle-height Alp attracts a downed American pilot, an Austrian *Fraülein* who romps in the edelweiss, a Swiss guide who relights his pipe before saying "*ja*," an aging Englishman who was on Everest with Mallory, a cognac-swilling Frenchman obsessed with the world's decadence, and a convalescing Nazi stormtrooper who, upon seeing the White Tower, finds his lips involuntarily forming "*Heil Hitler!*" Our Josh group may be random, but it's not improbable, as *The White Tower* melange is when they ill-advisedly tie into the same hemp rope.

The Brit, slowing the group, selflessly turns back. Pierre finds brandy in his rucksack, stays behind, and wanders into an avalanche. Too late the guide dutifully descends to check on this unfortunate debaucher. The Teuton sneaks from his tent before dawn, but the Yank catches him traversing above a strangely situated cornice. The former, after disdaining a rope and sharing thoughts on the Master Race, breaks a foothold, then the cornice, and plummets—exposing a ledge that enables our hero to conquer the Tower, then the *Fraülein*, with whom he presumably lives happily ever after.

Soon after I took up climbing, I came upon that annual compendium of mishaps called *Accidents in North American Mountaineering*. Though nonfiction, a typical accident report emphasizes causes and so foreshadows tragedy as insistently as a moral-mongering novelist. You read: "Tweedle Dum and Tweedle Dee left camp at 5 a.m. Dee hadn't eaten a warm breakfast and wasn't carrying extra socks," and are gripped with the same foreboding you are in *The White Tower*. When you read that "Tom, Dick (age 28), and Harry were ascending...." you know long before the flake comes loose who is as doomed as Ahab.

Speaking of whom, suppose that Melville, instead of going to sea, had gone to the mountains. Is it fundamentally different to cherish "a wild vindictiveness against the whale" than to not carry extra socks? Are we not merely fools for symbolism more enigmatic than inadequate footwear?

I suspect that our campfire literati, pontificating from $7.95 lawn chairs or upturned logs, would find fault with *Moby Dick*. Among scholars, Melville may get away with

Eric Beck and
Walt Vennum
about to add to
the day's count.

Joe Kelsey

drowning everyone but Ishmael—for the story to have a first-person narrator, someone
has to survive—but those of us dodging campfire sparks would note the improbability
of another ship happening by just as Ishmael is about to go under.

Ancient dramatists effected a happy ending when a narrative wasn't headed that way
by producing a deus ex machina—a benevolent god who, when things looked bleak,
arrived on a clumsy contraption. You'd think climbers would want a deus ex machina, as
cats stuck in trees presumably want fire departments—as Dave might have on *Exit Stage
Right*, when a bolt spotted from the ground turned out to be lichen. However, we're more
comfortable with a malevolent deity, the shaggy-haired Jehovah in a Far Side cartoon
labeled "God at His Computer." This Almighty hunkers over His PC; His monitor shows a
nerd shuffling down the street, oblivious to a piano being lifted to a window above. God's
finger is poised over the "Smite" key.

Accident reports imply that the fittest survive, or at least the best equipped. But while
evolution may favor those who eat warm breakfasts, much is also chance—missing the
avalanche because you forgot your ice axe and returned to camp. Someone may have
survived because of spare socks, but we wouldn't want survival to depend on socks
alone. I dread such Russian-roulette phenomena as lightning as much as the climber on
the next pinnacle, but I wouldn't want a stacked deck determining lightning's target. I
start up a route not knowing whether to expect causality or chance, and chuckling about
whichever it turns out to be. If accident-report causality were the only determinant, a different population would be embellishing Kronhofer-era stories under the Mojave moon.

Jeff Long's novel *Angels of Light* re-creates the Yosemite of the mid-1970s so realistically that you needn't correlate his ragamuffin climbers with specific nonfictional riffraff to feel you've known them. While the plot turns on a deus ex machina, Long bases his tale on a rare, real-life deus ex machina, albeit one that didn't rescue suffering climbers but financed further suffering: a plane that fell from the sky, overburdened with a marketable cash crop. So you don't question the plausibility of climbers wading through snow to a dope-laden Lodestar crashed in a Sierra lake. Then a character dies climbing, not in the shithappens way that climbers do but for a literary reason. By being a reasonable outcome of plot, the death reminds you that *Angels of Light* is fiction.

Allen Steck leading
Pinched Rib (5.10b).

Steve Roper

By killing his victim on Half Dome, though, Long avoids the temptation of fitting topography to plot. Climbing is plot resulting from topography. When I've written fiction, an alter ego has been sickened hearing me think, "They've jammed; now I'll have them chimney." Holds and cracks should exist for geologic, not narrative, reasons, and no geologic theory works on a small enough scale to predict that the next hold will be in reach or the crack take the only stopper left on your rack. Setting fiction on actual rock avoids anthropocentric geology.

Dermot Somers adroitly avoided climbing fiction's problems in "A Tale of Spendthrift Innocence." The deus ex machina is explicitly there, deciding how grim to make a bivouac, how much to make the climbers suffer, confusing typewriter with helicopter, kicking climbers off a ledge back to a bivouac at the beginning of the story. However, I have a suspicion about "Spendthrift Innocence": that it is nonfiction. I have made bad bivouacs and belays tolerable by becoming an observer hovering nearby, seeing comedy in my physical self's predicament. And who hasn't overheard a climber conversing with himself: "Damn it, asshole, your protection's perfect. Trust your foot on that freaking nubbin."

I suspect Somers of vividly recounting an actual ascent of the north face of the Dru. Climbers' names may be changed; they're irrelevant. I suspect that, with few more details, you could find your way up the Dru with "Tale" as a guidebook. The *deus* operating the *machina* is an alter ego of the climber, writing about the adventure with the separate personality we acquire away from the mountains. And it's a climb for the sake of climbing; it's not a parable.

Truth is stranger than fiction because it allows more possibilities than literary conventions do. But the most precious thing about being on rock is living in the moment—wondering if stepping on that nubbin will enable you to reach *that* crack. And, reaching the crack, deciding whether to jam or lieback. If the sequence strings together into a plot, so be it, but if you jam because you're warming up for a 5.11 or your count is three short of ten, climbing loses its essence. Fiction writers are paid to be conscious of more than one nubbin.

Climbers who script upcoming ventures, as though packaging man-days of food, miss an important essence of literature: characters don't devise plots, authors do. We write our own scenarios only by willfully roping up below one route or another. Once we step up, climbing is hoping that things work out—not that we encounter enough rockfall to validate the Eiger experience, or lightning, as a sine qua non of bivouacs.

By April, I forgot I was fifty. It was spring, when returning to rock is plot enough, time to be exhilarated by the anticipation and dread, memory and desire, that make April the cruelest month.

Steve sets a trip's "official" date: it begins on a Sunday afternoon and ends on a Saturday morning, maximizing the chance of reclaiming "our" Ryan campsites and minimizing interactions with dreaded weekend hordes. However, some of us, finding five days insufficient, began defying Steve and padding visits with unsanctioned days before or after. When I heard that Eric and San Diego friends would arrive the Friday before, I left work early on Thursday, filled water jugs, ground coffee beans, and merged into southbound freeway traffic.

Some of the supple young gurus trying to lure us into the 1990s assure us that, if we want to be 5.12 climbers, we should get in shape flailing and failing on 5.12s. Having found, though, that such masochism leads only to joint damage, Eric and I headed to Rock Garden Valley's 5.7s. But we soon saw the San Diegans' rappel ropes swaying over stiffer rock and checked the guidebook: three-star 5.9s, classics never even proposed during the morning ritual. (Had raspberry jam been sticking guidebook pages together?) Eric and I quickly revised our regimen, tagging along behind our conditioned compadres, tying to ropes tossed down *Rock Candy* and several neighbors. On Sunday afternoon, when the regulars tumbled into Ryan, we metamorphosed into 5.7 rope-guns as our group made its canonical Sunday-dusk circuit of campground crags.

The head start also proved an advantage at Monday breakfast, for I was better acclimatized for choosing a destination. Not that I had an obsession, but I'd overheard a Bay

Area boulderer reliving 5.10a *Bird on a Wire* in arm-waving detail. That eavesdropped beta was enough to give the unseen route an identity, without it suffering *Solid Gold*'s significance. For the newcomers the guidebook had starred 5.7s and 5.8s within joke-telling distance, giving our throng its necessary sociable concentration.

The boulderer had mentioned protection deficiencies, so I plugged in items at every opportunity—to arrive at the trust-your-feet crux without the cam that would make the difference between overhead protection and a bolt ten feet below. Each spring presents such an unanticipated threshold, forcing me to decide whether I'm still a climber. Passing it marks the season's start. Some spring I may back down to the bolt and lower off—perhaps even Allen will—but I jammed my fingertips as best I could, smeared my sticky rubber, and embarked on another rock year.

Not knowing what we'll be climbing, we bring El Cap racks for sixty-foot forays. With some of my venerable companions attached to artifacts that got them through the Golden Age, I bring my own packful. On Tuesday, as we lavishly packed metal for an old 5.7 favorite, *White Lightning*, Steve asked, in the disingenuous tone he uses to urge us onward, if I was bringing tiny pieces for *Poodles Are People Too*. The name didn't ring a bell, nor resound with the valor of *Solid Gold*, but a peek at the guidebook revealed a four-star 5.10b. So I clipped extra onto my rack and scrambled through the approach boulders, practicing visualization without knowing what to visualize.

Sportclimbers reduce dramatic structure to *yoyoing, hangdogging,* a *redpoint,* an *on-sight flash.* Periodicals remind us bimonthly that an on-sight flash—scaling unseen rock without trickery—is the ultimate way to "send" a climb. However, seeing *Poodles'* intermittent seams jolted my memory, made me realize that on-sight isn't the noblest style—that leading a climb after witnessing a fiasco is. A few years earlier we'd watched a bronzed Adonis botching *Poodles*. After placing enough stoppers to suture a liver transplant, he repeatedly stretched uncertainly, body tense, calves atremble, talons grasping desperately; then his body straightened as he took another dreaded three-foot plummet.

Even visualizing an abstraction, I'd psyched myself to lead near my limit, and not wanting to waste such an ephemeral state of mind, racked all my straight, curved, brass, and aluminum slivers, and set out. Too often when following a lead or repeating a route, I pay more attention to memory than rock. Didn't John step there? Couldn't I reach that flake last year? On *Poodles*, though, I was blessed with living in the present, passing what I assumed would be the crux by the simple expedient of concentrating on the rock, not my memory of witnessed failure. That was the entire story. I did pass the real crux higher, but as I belayed in the sun, the only sign that I'd climbed well was a rising-tide contagion of smoothly moving followers.

If you do six or eight or ten routes a day, euphoria is short-lived, ending abruptly and unexpectedly. That afternoon I spent too long stuffed in 5.10a *Exorcist*'s vertical crack, becoming more tired the more protection I placed and needing more protection the more tired I became. I was lowered with Steve providing Greek-chorus commentary. A chagrined failure is his cue to feign amazement and chant "What hubris!" I devoted the late afternoon to helping Eric with his count, then returned to Ryan for the evening's celebratory beer or consolatory beer, which taste about the same.

Linda McMillan following *Poodles Are People Too* (5.10b).

Joe Kelsey

For the remainder of the week, heat, rather than scenarios, determined our fates. Wednesday began with a few shaded favorites at Echo Rock; then someone proposed *Pope's Crack*, which was nearby, 5.9, and three-starred. Eric, not there to save us, later described *Pope's Crack* as a solar-paneled winter favorite. My alter ego, spectating from the shade, could see that I was leading a splendid dihedral, but my material self squirmed up the Yosemite smoothness, unexpected in the cheese-grater world of Joshua Tree. Either I or the rock—I couldn't tell where one ended, the other began—felt like melted butter. After placing belay anchors brain-fried, I had my detached-observer self double-check them.

Days of Joshua Tree rock lead less often to denouements than to abraded hands and, in heat, silliness. Our profundity fell to the following exchange, heard as we eventually reached an out-of-the-way cliff. Eric: "If we'd followed my plan, we'd be here by now." Steve: "But we *are* here." We laughed till rivulets streaked grimy cheeks. My self-conscious alter ego wondered what beginners would think, seeing what years of intimate contact with granite can do to a person.

One afternoon began at north-facing Future Games Rock, but other shade-seekers were on the reasonable routes. As the sun swung west and relentlessly narrowed the wall's shadow, each of us flattened himself against the rock, until time ran out and our wilting Valentine's Day-massacre lineup had to overcome lethargy and escape.

Nearby *Grand Canyon Donkey Trail* lured Steve, Allen, Eric, and me. It faced east, and we hadn't done it. Its one drawback was a + after its 5.9, a supposedly harmless symbol but actually a satanic mark guidebooks use to connote an evil too arcane to be expressed by numbers. Steve shouldered the rack.

Climbing directly from one bolt to the next wasn't feasible, but out left were shallow

The lustrous granite
face of *Solid Gold*.

Joe Kelsey

scoops, as if a nineteenth-century peasant-guide had hacked caverns for gentry to stand in, but spaced them erratically and botched the left-right sequence. Eric urged Steve to step far left while palming with his right hand, then move his left foot up. Each time Steve assayed a different possibility, Eric spit the seed of doubt at him. Steve's eventual lowering wasn't cheerful.

When Eric clipped to the bolt and inspected the scoops, Steve was ready: "Just step left, you miserable chickenshit; relax; bring your left foot higher." Eric looked ruefully down. "I'm better as a theoretical climber," he decided.

My turn. Unhindered by polemics, I passed the scoops but, noting that the next move might be irreversible, assessed whether a slip before the next bolt would end on planet earth. My turn to back off. Allen, more gallant—or risking less life expectancy, as Steve points out—got one move farther before contemplating the ground. Snatching a spare rope, I jogged up the descent slab. However, the dishonor of fire-department deliverance inspired Allen to ooze down until the bolt was near his feet, then slide, grabbing—as a beginner would—the bolt's carabiner. The result, as beginners learn, was a mashed finger—so our quartet top-roped *Grand Canyon Donkey Trail*. We returned to camp content to have been on rock, as always, but especially pleased to have shared misery with company amused by it.

Another hot day rousted us out of camp early, to the west side of North Astro Dome—the side facing away not only from the sun but from *Solid Gold*. I led a pleasant, bolted 5.9: *Lead Us Not into Temptation*, ideal for the day, even its name. I don't remember why we then ended up under *Solid Gold*; circling the Astro Domes involves enough thorns that you don't do it aimlessly. For all I can recall, a clumsy stage device may have transported us; at any rate, the departing noon sun found us examining *Solid Gold*.

While I felt scripted to lead—a script fermenting through two trips—I now wondered how to incorporate burn-out. Then I noted that while others indulged in ritual pointing and conjecturing—"You could use that edge"; "There's another bolt!"—Allen scanned the face silently. I've learned, particularly with Allen, that whoever isn't speculating about how a route *could* be led is the person planning to lead it.

Allen had an unassailable reason: "I'm never going to be here when I'm younger. I'll just go up to the second bolt and look."

If you were creating fiction, you'd have young climbers appear while Allen was shoeing up and comment on our antiquity, say something blunt such as "You guys look old enough to have hammered pitons!" And that's just what one lad said. Nobody proved capable of major-motion-picture repartee, but Allen, the one of us who most intrigued them, gently responded, "I guess we have hammered a few."

Dialogue dealt with, he simply led *Solid Gold* with concentration, aplomb, and disregard for his position vis-à-vis the arguably sparse bolts. An actor should *project*, but Allen betrayed less emotion than did my sweating palms, letting out rope in one-inch increments. He may have been suppressing terror, but I don't think so. He may have lost count of the bolts by the time he reached the second, but, again, I choose not to think so. Eric and I followed, tearful with gratitude for a rope from above.

Perhaps we climb to touch something inscrutable, and that's why literature misses what we experience, especially if the belayer far below is tuned in to a ground-level critique of cabernets. Then the leader is on top, out of sight, contemplating the panorama of Mojave mountains that have become familiar without our wondering at their names.

Perhaps we malign accident reports because they deny inscrutability. Maybe what sets *Moby Dick* above an accident report isn't that Ahab's rage is more profound than climbers' carelessness, but that Ahab sought inscrutability, and perhaps found it. An accident-report analysis can't reflect that "He found what he was looking for, even though he landed head first"; it can't conjecture that we climb because inscrutable shit happens.

Jim Bridwell moving over the 5.10b crux on pitch one of *Figures on a Landscape.*

Allen Steck

Endings impossibly challenge a writer trying to simulate life. A climbing life is flow; we continue climbing to avoid being frozen in time, whether in noble, ignoble, or indifferent postures. I despise time-frozen summit photos, which don't even suggest a rubble-choked descent gully. The casual photography we inflict on Joshua Tree has yet to include a summit shot.

Having a character "light out for the territory," as Huck Finn does, seems as good an ending as any, especially as readers know nothing about the territory but assume it to be uncivilized. We are free to imagine various outcomes. Our JT saga could end variously, though no ending would work as fiction. One is that within the year, I broke an ankle and Allen broke two. But we both took rehab more seriously than we'd ever taken hab and soon were climbing again, as well as we need to.

But the story hasn't yet ended. We continue to spend a week in the spring, a week in the fall, camped in Ryan. Our group fluctuates, as other relics turn from the pavement and the past onto the campground's dirt washboard. That 6,000-year-old fellow who turned up in a Tyrolean glacier a few years ago hasn't joined us yet, but some returning prodigals, who haven't stemmed a dihedral since Nixon resigned, are astonished to see ropemates of yore squeezing sockless feet into lugless magenta shoes, wrapping pelvises with paraphernalia apparently intended for sexual fetishism, and stuffing cracks with what look to be parts salvaged from a freeway when a '63 Dodge lost its engine mounts. I once kept awake driving back up I-5 by counting over twenty people who climbed or drank with us during the week. We occasionally cross sandy paths with guest rope-guns such as Charlie Fowler and Jim Bridwell, who, refusing to let us go gentle into that good night, keep the rope tight as they drag us beyond our self-imposed horizons.

Jim lured several of us up 5.10b *Figures on a Landscape*, its first pitch instantly joining the list of the ten all-time greats. *Figures* awed us too severely to make reckless old fools of us, but we now look at slightly harder routes than a few years ago. Thack arrives each spring looking a year older, climbing a year younger. Morton and the Erbs emerged from rockless exile after our first trips and caught us charter members after a few pitches, as if they'd spent their lost decades visualizing. *Poodles* has metamorphosed from a celebrated feat to someone else's turn to lead. A few of us, aided by a tailwind, turn out to have sneaked up a minimal 5.11 or two, though the routes attained this eminence only in later guidebook editions; had our internal narrator known the future rating they would have scripted failure.

I imagine I was so attuned to the granite that I could have heard silence while leading certain climbs, 5.9s typically, with routefinding dilemmas, protection problems, or corrupt rock, but I was too preoccupied with mere survival to listen. Once, on a trip's last day, I did sense I'd wandered into Eden. I'd descended from Watergate Rock, nondescript even by local standards but shady. Circling back through the yucca and creosote bushes, I paused to absorb the tapestry of friends, some plastered to interchangeable routes, others belaying above, staring at the deep sky they'd stared at all week. My modest ambitions hadn't included watching the middle-aged nonchalant their way up forgettable 5.8s, hesitating only to interrupt their belayers' mindlessness with pleas of "Up rope!" Yet I'd found whatever it is that I go to Watergate Rock and Dairy Queen Wall and the Hall of Horrors for—to be reminded that life is okay.

If I'm capable of finding paradise, I'm also capable of finding myself stranded on a ledge well above an antique bolt, irreversibly thin moves below and precarious flakes above, in an obscure cul-de-sac with only Eric. I untied and dropped our one rope and, while Eric scrambled around to the top, breathed deeply, felt as out of place as I would on television, and hoped Far Side Jehovah wasn't monitoring my *deus ex*, finger poised above the "Rattlesnake" key.

On one trip we experienced four inches of rain in two days, an amount the shallow washes don't accommodate gracefully. Campfire conviviality was once interrupted by an ominous mutter sweeping across the Mojave, then jangling pebbles and flakes on the cliff above. Before anyone could think *earthquake*, our nervous systems stampeded the dozen of us from under the cliff: a 6.2 epicentered down the road was rearranging the desert with a subtlety that in geologic terms is infinitesimal.

Once, Allen and I were enjoying perfect November weather when a "partial government shutdown" occurred. Rather than abandoning us to our cliffside fates, the shutdown government was evicting us. But while we should have been shoveling tents and coolers into the Subaru, we climbed the Headstone—because we're climbers, but also to give Newt the finger. As we drove away, though, a budget-burning Air Force *machina* shrieked by, confounding whatever plot we thought we were enacting.

One March evening I left the fire for a beer-drinker's usual reason. Looking for nothing in particular in the sky over Ryan Mountain, I noticed it—apparently larger than the stars but distinctly fuzzy, slightly blue, and suggesting, in the chilly desert air, cold beyond comprehension, its tail streaking far toward JT's outback. I could imagine a pissing Ancient being startled by a comet and attributing to it whatever upturn or downturn his fortunes then took.

Shiprock's southwest face. The main summit is on the left.

Steve Roper

THERE I WAS... ON SHIPROCK!

Alex Bertulis

Those who have climbed with Fred Beckey usually look back at the experience with mixed emotions. On the one hand, climbing with "the legend" puts one on the map, since most of his climbs are historic first ascents. Having once climbed with him, one can then contribute to bar-room banter with first-hand Beckey lore rather than listen only to the countless tall tales of others. On the other hand, climbing with Fred, even now, but especially during his prime, is like climbing with a driven madman. He has burned out hotshot climbers half his age and has gone through partners in prolific quantities. The revolving list he keeps in his "little black book," legend has it, is not just of virgin peaks and not-so-virgin women, but of potential climbing candidates from throughout North America.

I was on that list in the early spring of 1965 when Fred tried to recruit me and Eric Bjørnstad for a climb of Shiprock, a magnificent formation jutting out of the New Mexican desert. It had only one route on it, established in 1939 by a gutsy team including Raffi Bedayan and David Brower. Always a visionary, Fred saw the possibility for a second route up this gigantic and challenging peak. He had apparently found a "classic direct line" up the untouched southwest side.

The prospect of climbing such a major new route sounded attractive to me. But my boss in Seattle, neither understanding nor sharing my enthusiasm for the outdoors, bluntly informed me that I could choose between climbing and working for him. Fred, never one to take no for an answer, balked at my hesitation and told me to get my priorities straight. "You can always find another job," he argued, "but this is your chance to put your name on Shiprock!"

Eric was easier to convince, so he, his girlfriend, Christa, and Fred crammed into Fred's pink Thunderbird for the journey south. "Back in ten days," Fred shouted as he roared away.

I heard nothing for a week. Then the phone rang. My boss answered it and said, "For you. Long distance."

"Alex! This is Fred. How's work?"

"Uh, hi, Fred. Yeah, I'm pretty busy but—where are you calling from?"

"I'm in a phone booth near Shiprock. Boy, you should be here! What a stupendous peak this is and what a great route! You don't know what you're missing...." Fred went on at some length, and, had it been a local call, I would have hung up, as my boss was giving me sinister glances. Holding up the receiver in a helpless gesture, I tried to show him that I was not contributing to the conversation. Unable to convince Fred I had to go back to work, I gently hung up the phone while he was still talking.

A couple of days later, he called again. I gave my boss an apologetic smile and listened to Fred describe how great Shiprock was.

"Fred, if this climb is so great why aren't you up there on the rock?"

"Uh, well... we're here in town to get some food and extra stuff. You know, it's nice to take a break when you're this close to civilization and can have a real hamburger for a change."

As I later learned, Fred and his companions were having a miserable time. Nothing was going right. The climbing had proved much more difficult than anticipated, and the extreme cold, high winds, and sandstorms all contributed to the trio's frustration. Understandably, Christa did not relish being left alone in a tent at the base of the formation. One night, high winds caused a pole to break and the tent collapsed. The glass water bottles froze and shattered. The men fared no better. A loose boulder on the third pitch nearly killed Eric and left an ugly bruise on his arm. Frustration grew into dissension and acrimony. Rather than staying put on the climb, they made numerous forays into town to boost morale.

The phone calls to Seattle became increasingly frequent and my boss, lacking appreciation for historic first ascents, became increasingly frustrated. Fred, relentless in his recruitment, gave no hint of the abhorrent circumstances, though his tone began to take on an air of urgency. "Alex, this is such a great route. But the climbing is hard, a lot harder than we expected. We need your help. With a strong third climber we can do this thing much faster. Eric and I are getting tired. Just fly to Vegas and I'll pick you up. You'll never regret it, I promise."

Twenty days into the climb Eric and Christa mutinied. Disenchanted with the whole ordeal, they decided to return to Seattle. Fred did not accept their departure gracefully, refusing even to drive them to the nearest bus station. The two defectors collected their gear, trekked across the desert to the highway, and began hitchhiking.

Fred was furious—and alone.

When Fred called and admitted that Eric had abandoned the climb, I relented. With my boss still unwilling to give me time off, I invoked a tactic sure to improve my life one way or another: I demanded a long-overdue raise. When he refused, I quit.

Fred was delighted to see me stride off the plane at Las Vegas. And he was ready with his particular spin on the circumstances surrounding Eric and Christa's departure. "Alex, you're going to love this climb! It's a real classic. The climbing is hard, which makes it all the better, don't you think? Eric had to get back to his coffee house. I really don't blame him. After all, he can't abandon his business. I totally understand. We just had some bad luck with the weather, that's all; otherwise we would have been done with the climb by now. But, that woman, Christa, I should have never allowed Eric to bring her along. Women always cause problems on climbs. You know what I mean?"

Fred brimmed with renewed energy. He and Eric had climbed about a third of the way up the 1,500-foot route and had fixed ropes up to their high point. This section had involved much hard climbing, but Fred optimistically believed that the terrain ahead would go faster. Before leaving Seattle I had stipulated that once we started climbing we would not descend to base camp, much less go to town, until we reached the summit. We would finish the climb in a single push, I insisted. Fred readily agreed.

I had never seen Shiprock except in photographs and on a postage stamp. As we drove across the otherwise flat desert, a twin-spired outcropping appeared to float ahead of us on the distant horizon: a two-masted ghost ship sailing across a phantom sea. A well-named rock, for sure. Arriving at the base, I was definitely impressed by the monumental scale and severity of Fred's route.

That evening four young men joined us at our campfire; they planned to climb the standard route, on the other side of the peak. We drank tea together and told stories late

Fred Beckey.

Jim Stuart

into the night, and on the following morning we all awoke to placid blue skies. Perhaps this time luck and the weather would be on our side. With high hopes we wasted no time in climbing up the fixed ropes. The route Fred and Eric had completed under adverse weather conditions was admirable: two consecutive pitches, about 300 feet altogether, overhung, and the rope swung free from the wall. Hauling a week's supply of gear with us was no easy task, considering the old-fashioned prusik technique we were using.

Our first night was a sleepless one. We dangled in our slings, with base camp visible between our legs, 600 feet below. In the distance Navajos tended their sheep; it was a far cry from the lush alpine environment of the Northwest, and I relished the new experience.

The mild temperatures we had welcomed at first were gone; the days were now over 100 degrees. A heat wave! Anticipating cool weather, Fred had prescribed only one and a half quarts of water per person per day, an adequate amount in cold weather, but far too little for desert climbing in hot conditions. And yet the most vertical climbing was behind us. Ahead lay a pleasant combination of free climbing, interspersed with some aid. Fred, who normally does not shirk from leading tough pitches, relinquished most of the leading to me. After all, he had already done an impressive amount of hard climbing during the attempt with Eric, whereas I was freshly released from my desk and eager to pit myself against any and all problems. We got along fine.

After a few days the oppressively still air and the seemingly ever-present sun began to exact their toll. We were being roasted in an oven, and parched mouths and sore throats resulted from our efforts to ration the diminishing water supply. Painfully shouted belay

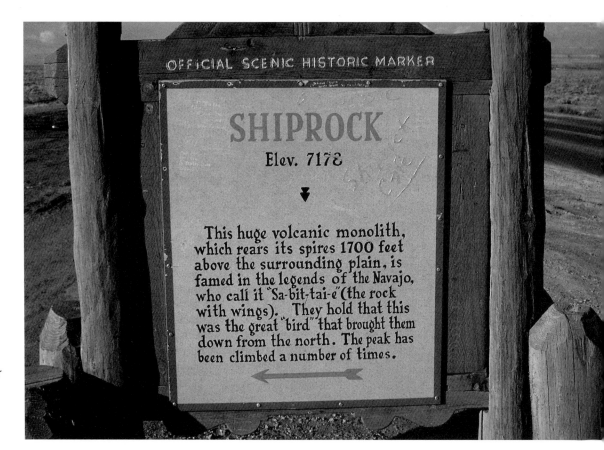

OFFICIAL SCENIC HISTORIC MARKER

SHIPROCK

Elev. 7178

▼

This huge volcanic monolith,
which rears its spires 1700 feet
above the surrounding plain, is
famed in the legends of the Navajo,
who call it "Sa-bit-tai-e"(the rock
with wings).   They hold that this
was the great "bird" that brought them
down from the north. The peak has
been climbed a number of times.

⟵

Steve Roper

instructions gave way to hand signals. Fortunately, Fred and I were used to climbing together and could anticipate each other's actions without much discussion.

The cool evenings provided desperately needed respite. The desert turned black and a canopy of stars lit up the sky; we were very much alone and utterly out of touch with the rest of the world. One night we observed a group of cars—and a patrol car with flashing lights—cluster around the base of our little mountain. We thought they had come by to check on us, but we learned later they were embarking on a less pleasant duty: retrieving the body of one of the climbers who had recently shared our campfire.

Despite the harsh conditions and demanding climbing, we made good progress. High on the peak, after rounding a buttress and traversing to the east, we encountered a flared chimney system that required strenuous stemming. Soon the south summit was within view, and I could look down into the notch between the two main summits. This meant that we were no more than 200 feet below the top! The breeze that drafted upward was most welcome. I belayed Fred up to my stance and gave him the good news. Cool and close! "Fred, look. Both summits! I'll bet it's only a couple of more leads to the top of the south one. And it may all go free."

"No way!" Fred responded with a hoarse and cracking voice. "It's going to be more than two leads. Probably hard climbing. Maybe more aid. Who knows? And look at our water bottle: that ain't enough."

I looked. We had less than half a quart left. "I agree we're low... very low. But, Fred, we're so damned close. I'll bet in a couple of hours we could be on top. And the route ahead is easier than what we just did."

"You don't know that! We can't see the whole route from here. Could be some real hard free climbing. Probably aid. We're in no position to assume anything. If we had more water I'd be willing to give it a try. I still have some strength left, but I'm not willing to risk running out of water. If we do, we're done for, way up here. Nobody would even know where to look for us. This is it. This is as far as I go!"

After a moment of silence, Fred added, "Look Alex, we've got ropes fixed all the way to the ground. We've got just enough water to make it down. Let's head back and rest a couple of days. Then we can prusik back with plenty of water. There's nothing wrong in doing that!"

I listened in disbelief. Having sacrificed a job and spent six exhausting days climbing to within a hundred feet of the summit, I was not about to turn back. Descending to camp and prusiking all the way back up at a later date held no appeal for me. Besides, we had agreed we would make the climb in one push or not at all. "Fred, if you don't want to go on, I'll go by myself."

It was a bluff and Fred did not buy it. "If you do, I'm not waiting for you. You'll die. We'll both die if we continue. I'm not hanging around to see you kill yourself."

By now both of us were arguing intensely. I've been known to be inordinately stubborn, and I used every argument I could for continuing. But Fred's stubbornness is legendary, and he was not about to give in to a young upstart like me.

But it went beyond stubbornness. Fred turned pale and his voice took on a dreadful and somber tone. He began talking about death in the mountains at great length and in detail I had never heard from him. Was he having some kind of premonition? "Alex, I've seen death many times and I'm seeing it now. I've seen it on Waddington when my guys got killed in that avalanche. I've seen it coming on Lhotse when we got trapped in bad weather. I've seen it on Mt. Baring in the North Cascades. Believe me, Alex, I know what I'm talking about. We're going to die if we stay here. I'm going down and I hope you're coming."

Fred won. I had no more resistance left, and it became apparent I couldn't persuade Fred to change his mind. "Okay, Fred, I'll go back, but remember, I'm not coming back up. You'll have to find someone else to finish it."

Fred nodded his head. No more words were spoken.

The descent proved long and uneventful, and, once the decision was made to retreat, we harbored no more ill feelings. In fact we were both greatly relieved and our sense of humor, gone for days, returned. "Alex, think there's a dance hall in town with lonely cowgirls?"

Approaching base camp, we noticed a blue pickup next to Fred's Thunderbird. As we came closer, we saw a family of twelve Navajos staring at us intensely. They had been watching us rappel, and the expressions on their faces suggested that they were curious, amazed, and perplexed. The family was lined up in a straight row, facing Shiprock. The rotund mother, attired in colorful Navajo dress, stood at one end. Next to her was her husband, a big man with a long ponytail. Next in line was an attractive daughter, about eighteen, and the only member of the family who seemed to speak English. The other children stood by silently, in order of diminishing stature.

Exuberant Fred was eager to share his recent climbing experience with anyone who would listen. First, however, we both took a few minutes to drink the water that had been stashed in our tent and to remove shoes from battle-weary feet. Then Fred planted himself in front of the family and launched into a major discourse on the trials and tribulations of our climb. How difficult it was to prusik up the overhangs! And those hanging belays, the delicate aid climbing, the hard free climbing! The wind, the cold, the heat! All the while Fred gesticulated wildly for emphasis.

The stone-faced Indians showed no reaction to Fred's oratory. After some time the father interrupted by asking his eldest daughter a brief question. She translated it for Fred

"What were you doing up there?"

"We were putting up a classic new route. Placed lots of bolts. Hard climbing. Hanging belays. Real hot up there, I'll tell you!" Fred hadn't grasped the implication of the man's question. Without waiting for a translation, the old man bent toward his daughter and asked the question another way. "Why did you go up there?"

"You see, there is only one other route on this mountain. It is very circuitous. Ours is a direct new line...." Fred continued enthusiastically, oblivious that nobody had the foggiest idea of what he was talking about. It didn't matter: Fred had an audience. He had a long story to tell—and he was bent on telling it.

The following day Fred dropped me off at the airport in Las Vegas. I wished him good luck and returned to Seattle. At my old office my boss recanted and offered me my job back—with a raise. Later I heard that Fred and Harvey Carter had completed the climb under more favorable weather conditions. Despite our fight near the top, Fred and I have remained friends and have climbed many other peaks together. Looking back at our standoff so near the summit of Shiprock, I'm glad Fred prevailed. I may have missed bagging a summit, but I'm here to talk about it (over a drink, of course).

PEREGRINE DREAMS

Amelia Rudolph

Project Bandaloop is a dance company that presses the boundaries of art, sport, and ritual by blending vertical and horizontal movement in natural and urban settings. The choreography relies on climbing movement, dance, and rigging to move aerially and at times to use a vertical rock wall as a dance floor. The company of dancers and climbers, founded in 1991 by Rudolph, has performed at sites ranging from granite cliffs in Yosemite to theaters around North America. The company has also performed on buildings such as the Space Needle in Seattle and the new public library in San Francisco.

I lay on my back in the tall grass of El Cap Meadow, the musty smell of earth filling my senses as I tried to keep the binoculars steady on a patch of headwall high on *The Shield*. The early evening light gave El Cap a mystical golden hue, a grandness, an unattainable distance that drew me like a moth. It seemed a world away. I tried to imagine what it would be like to dance on that headwall, to float and soar in arcing dives 2,500 feet above the valley floor, and I shivered with excitement and fear at the prospect. I wanted to climb the whole cliff, all the way, to earn the dance. It would be my first big wall, though I'd attempted the south face of the Washington Column, spent the night on the massively exposed third pitch of *South Seas*, and been up the east buttress to the top of the El Capitan massif. I felt ready to take care of myself up there and had a deep desire to go.

When Steve Schneider had come down from the route several months before, he gave an animated account of the incredible vertical dance floor he thought *The Shield* headwall would make. "The loft is perfect," he said, "and your ropes don't touch. I did some killer loop de loops up there; it would be perfect for a dance." Heather Baer-Schneider, who had been up the route with Steve, was a little less sure. She was so wiped out from the climbing that she thought it would be difficult to find the energy to rehearse and perform a dance once we were up there. She is strong and this made me think. An enthusiastic participant in almost every aerial dance I'd come up with, she had never before suggested that a performance might be too difficult.

I rolled over in the grass. Would my Bandaloop friends put in the time and energy to climb one of the longest routes on El Capitan in order to make a dance that would last only thirty minutes? Who could see it? Why bother? Falling into a light sleep, I began to dream of flying up there in the golden light, soaring like a bird, swooping with the downdrafts and cruising horizontally across the cliff at high speed. I could hear the cries of a falcon, the screeching of a peregrine. It woke me up. Again I heard her; the faraway sound from across the valley where I knew they nested now on Middle Cathedral Rock. How many pairs were there now in California, about 135? In 1972 they were almost extinct. I had been learning about peregrines and their near extinction from DDT and other related chemicals through my interaction with researchers in Yosemite. The more I learned

Bandaloop dancers
on the Shield
Headwall, El Capitan.

Photographs:
Steve Schneider

about them, the more I had become fascinated by their mythic symbolism in relationship to humans over time and their very real abilities as hunters and aerial geniuses. Peregrines, who catch their prey in flight, have been clocked at over 200 miles per hour. The design of some of our fastest jet fighters has been modeled on the peregrine's wing shape.

A chill ran up my spine. I knew then that we were going to make a dance on *The Shield*, up there in the sky with the falcons. This dance, "Peregrine Dreams," might do what environmental art can do at its best: remind us of our place and responsibility among other life— and reflect the beauty of that life.

That was in the fall of 1996. By early spring, with commitment from all team members— Steve Schneider, Heather Baer-Schneider, Chris Clay, Peter Mayfield, and videographer Greg Bernstein—as well as sponsorship from Sierra Designs and Boreal, we were ready to go. Karen Elliot and Suzanne Gallo, company members who weren't experienced climbers, agreed to form the ground support team, along with our set builder, Richard Kittle.

I had been communicating with Brian Walton at the Predatory Bird Research Group at the University of California at Santa Cruz, and he explained that the more the public knew about the issues facing predatory birds the better, and that he would support us in any way he could. *Life* magazine became interested in doing a feature on Project Bandaloop and decided to cover the El Cap action. I was excited about this: a dance that was isolated high on a cliff could be given a second audience through stories, film, and further theatrical performances. It would be the seed of future work.

It all came together in June 1997. We planned to spend six days on the wall, hauling all the food and gear we could possibly need. With thirty-two pounds of water per person, our haul bags were leaden—and the extras, like Greek *dolmas*, cans of beer, and video and camera gear didn't help. The beautiful wings that my mother and I had made together and our white costumes were not a problem, being as light as feathers.

Mayfield, Schneider, and Clay had fixed lines to Gray Ledges the weekend before, and we got there for our first night. Admiring the thin crack above that Scott Cosgrove and Kurt Smith had freed as part of their Muir Wall project two summers before, we wished we had time to work on it but stayed on task and kept aiding at a good speed. My lead on the roof below the headwall was a big thrill, and though rated A3, it was mostly fixed. As I was turning the roof, the wind was blowing hard, my aiders and hair flying sideways. In the ocean of air and rock around me I threw my head back and laughed, possessed by the freedom of extreme exposure.

By the time we got to the dance site we were all pretty tired, but our spirits were soaring. Our camp, two double portaledges above the Groove Pitch and one below, framed the vertical dance floor. We had gotten a little behind schedule so we had only half a day to rehearse, planning to perform that evening, June 22, solstice and full moon. *Life* had hired Galen Rowell, assisted by Schneider and Mayfield from our end, and British big-wall expert Kevin Thaw. Rowell and Thaw would rap down fixed lines for the shoot.

During rehearsal, we were all surprised by how little we felt afraid of the vast exposure. The incredible pleasure of dancing in that sublime place seemed to override the cold, the height, and the constant wind.

At 6:30 p.m. the four performers lowered into place, with the accompaniment of the wind and Steve's occasional whistles and hoots. Galen had, like the true mountain man and pro that he is, arrived right on time and dangled on the line we had fixed for him. He missed only one beat when I explained to him that the dance would last only thirty minutes and that we wouldn't pose for pictures.

It is difficult to describe what it felt like to dance on the grand, golden rock spreading for acres around us, with the falcon in our minds and hearts. Reaching out for a partner to do a lift and feeling his weight light against you, the momentum of a dancing pendulum, the synergy of the group's unison work, and the rush of fifteen feet of air between me and the rock while floating in a slow-motion back dive was like nothing I had ever experienced before. It was utterly playful after all the technical effort, and we found ourselves yelping and hooting with joy. Toward the end of the dance, when we pushed off in arcing back spins, we found ourselves turning, not single or double flips, but triples in our excitement.

As we finished the dance, we heard a faint cheer rise from the valley floor and from some parties near us on the wall. Elated, we returned to our portaledges as a peregrine swooped by silently. I believe I saw her smile.

BIG-WALL TALE OF WOE

Bob Viola

All alone I have cried
Lonely tears full of pride
In a world made of steel...
Made of stone.
                    —Kierkegaard, or was it someone else?

Trained as a man of science, I've always clung to the belief that the systematic application of logic, of learning, of the human intellect could, little by little, reveal the universe's inherent order. I naively saw the world around me as an immense clockwork, daunting in its complexity but lovely in its perfect harmony of motion. I laugh now to think what a fool I was. For now, at last, I see the universe for what is: wild and waste, chaos! It was a hard and bitter lesson I learned upon the granite altar of the Big Stone. This is my story....

Spring of this year saw me toiling in the academic vineyard of a great northern California university, but my seminal research into the social behavior of hamsters, so significant and exciting when I'd entered the Ph.D. program only eleven years ago, had bogged down. The National Science Foundation was threatening our program with draconian cuts, and my advisor had taken to barring his door and scrambling out his office window (no mean feat, given his impressive girth) whenever I appeared. Successful completion of my thesis and entry into the workplace seemed to recede ever farther into the distance. I desperately needed something to boost my flagging self-confidence and reaffirm my place in nature's order. Then and there it was decided: I would seek redemption in the cleansing granite embrace of El Capitan. And I would seek it... alone!

I had been climbing for about six months (ever since I discovered the intense concentration of lycra sport tops at the local rock gym) and had, in that short span, grown to love the sport. I read all the mags cover to cover and could spew slander with the best of them. El Cap seemed like the logical next step: a little taller than the gym and no colored tape next to the holds. Real adventure! But I needed to choose a route that would be worthy of my vision. I quickly dismissed the *Nose* and *Salathé* as mere hikes, the *Zodiac* and *Shield* as worn-out trade routes; I needed something bigger. My eye was naturally drawn to the crumbling black diorite to the left of the *NA Wall*. Here an almost constant rain of loose grit, detached flakes, and plummeting, refrigerator-sized blocks created a natural cacophony that embodied, for me, the natural world in all its savage grandeur.

Only a single route dared to cross this untamed stretch of rock. The guidebook had this to say: "*Tierra Del Fuego to the Aleutians by way of Topeka*, A5+, 5.12c/d, no second ascent." With trembling hand I traced the route's circuitous line on the topo. It had everything I was searching for: traverses, pendulums, loose rock, poor anchors, razor-sharp flakes, and copious frostings of guano on every ledge. Too perfect!

Over the next two weeks I humped loads to the base of the route. Numerous stumbles in the talus left me bruised but undaunted. Time and again climbers returning from a pleasant outing on *Moby Dick* would stare at me in amazement, shaking their heads in silent commiseration as I struggled up the trail, bent double under the crushing weight of several quarts of water and a dozen Snickers bars. Even though I was committed to a fast and light ethic, my vital supplies gradually formed a small mountain at the base of my intended route. Hardware was a different story. The topo's gear list was starkly minimalist: "two (2) pointed Leeper hooks." I gasped at the Zen purity that this rack implied and humbly accepted the challenge. To be on the safe side, however, I added a Fish hook, several more Leepers, a dozen Talons, 120 copperheads of various sizes, twenty rurps, sixty blades, seventy Lost Arrows (mostly short, thin), angles to eight inches, six chisels, carbide-tipped drills, rivets, five sets of Aliens, and a standard big-wall rack.

At last the day arrived that I had so long been dreaming of: the day I would leave the humdrum horizontal world of everyday living behind and enter, if only for a little while, a higher realm. I was soon to become absorbed in an intensely personal battle: not against the cold, uncaring stone, but against my own doubts and fears. My life would be governed by the cycles of the sun and moon, the hawks and swallows my only companions.

With a soaring heart I shouldered my rack and reached high for my first placement. Gingerly I fitted a hook into a drilled, two-inch-deep, in-cut hole with carefully chamfered edges and a slight taper designed to match that of the hook. I choked down my terror and comforted myself with the thought that *this* was what I had come for. Slowly I eased my weight onto the étrier and held my breath as the hook slid deep into the hole. I quivered for a moment, poised between heaven and earth, then lost my balance and toppled over backwards. I slammed against the unyielding ground and lay there gasping. A quick inventory told me that my injuries were not life threatening, and I redoubled my resolve to continue; yet somewhere deep in my subconscious fear took root like a bad seed.

That night I lay awake in my triple-wide A5 Wall Villa and watched as creation's starry dynamo wheeled overhead. Although exhausted, I could not sleep; I continued to replay the day's events over and over. I had managed to bypass the problematic hook placement by cleverly using my extendable cheater stick to snag a bolt twenty feet higher up. Oh, how my heart had thundered as I'd batmanned up my rope, knowing that only a slender, half-inch-diameter steel rod, driven a mere five inches into the rock, stood between me and another grounder. Above the bolt, the route really showed its teeth. Other than several more drilled hook placements, the wall was utterly blank. Never one to be afraid of thinking "outside the box," I opted for a daring and innovative tactic: I stepped out onto the limb of an adjacent ponderosa pine and fought my way through a painful tangle of branches for another fifteen feet. Here, with darkness falling, I placed an anchor, hauled (back-breaking!), and set up my first bivy.

I sat there in the darkness, warmed only slightly by the glow of my hibachi, and felt the isolation and loneliness wrap around me like a wet Persian rug. For the first time I questioned my decision to embark on this adventure solo. My heart cried out for simple human contact; the comfort of one caring, reassuring voice. I fumbled in the dark for my cell phone and dialed the Psychic Friends hotline. Hours later, emotionally drained but reassured, I sank at last into dreamless slumber.

The coming of day brought with it renewed self-confidence. I was determined, like the song says, to "screw my courage to its sticking place." I cued up my special Big Stone Party Mix tape (a thundering melange of Marilyn Manson, Ministry, and Zig Ziegler motivational speeches) and set to work. By early afternoon I had broken down the bivy and was ready to lock horns with the wall. A dicey traverse along a very creaky branch brought me abreast the rock. Again my cheater stick served me well as I reached and clipped another manky Petzl half-incher. "There's no turning back now," I thought as I swung my weight onto the bolt and committed myself, body and soul, to the wall.

By late afternoon I was at least fifty feet higher. One hour had blurred with the next as I fell into a nervewracking routine of cheater sticking between the generously spaced bolts. At one point I'd actually been forced to climb out of the bottom rungs of my étriers in order make the required reach. The incredible exposure took my breath away: each time I glanced down it got progressively more difficult to make out the insects crawling among the pine needles at the wall's base. But suddenly the routefinding became devious. Just above a bolt was a neatly painted red arrow pointing to the right. I scrutinized this traverse and noted the long hooking edge that had been carefully chiseled into the rock, punctuated by several more bolts along its length. I quickly dismissed this option as an obvious dead end and instead turned my attention to the wall above.

Just a bit higher was a tremendous block resting on a crumbling ledge. It resembled nothing so much as a great Egyptian obelisk turned upside down and balanced on its point. Separating this obelisk from the main wall was a soaring crack, widening from a few inches at its base to several feet near its top. As I recognized this crack as the key to the upper wall, my whole being was flooded with excitement! Without hesitation I ripped a four-inch bong from my rack and fitted it behind the block (a little too big but workable). With a flourish I drew my trusty, oversized wall hammer, Sister Sledge, from her holster and laid into the chrome-moly with all my might. A small crowd began to gather on the ground below, communicating their enthusiastic (though unintelligible) support through word and gesture. But the blood was up now and I needed no additional encouragement as I placed a second bong, this one significantly bigger than the first. I started to notice a deep, groaning base note above the rhythmic chant of steel on steel, almost as if the lifeless rock itself was joining me in joyous song. I had now gained enough height so that the crack's increasing width forced me to leave my aiders and go free. This happened much sooner than I expected, but crack widths are often deceiving when viewed from below. I gripped the edge of the crack and confidently swung into the classic chimney position: back pressed against the main wall, feet braced securely against the block. Every fiber of my being quivered with effort as I strained to gain height. This was my moment of truth, going free on—the Captain!

As I lie here in my hospital bed, I have all the time in the world to contemplate my incredible folly. I see again the cursed obelisk as it topples outward in exquisite slow motion; I hear the explosion of its impact on the talus below and the shrieking roar as its shrapnel splinters trees for hundreds of yards in every direction; and, worst of all, I feel the icy emptiness of a dream destroyed. Such was my shock and bewilderment that I barely felt the fall, much less the savage beating administered to me by the onlookers when they eventually emerged from their improvised shelters. All my planning, all my skill, all my courage had been for naught. The universe is a cruel and capricious taskmistress who cares nothing for these petty things. I guess it's like that guy Shakespeare said: "the fault is not with ourselves, it's with those damn stars!"

Stephen Venables braves the Jaws of Doom tyrolean traverse at 23,000 feet on Mt. Everest's Kangshung Face.

Ed Webster

COMEDY AND CLIMBING

Bruce Fairley

At a conference held as part of the 1994 Banff Festival of Mountain Films, a panel of eminent climbing writers and editors (Greg Child, David Harris, Michael Kennedy, Bart Robinson, and Joe Simpson) discussed the direction of mountaineering literature in the 1990s. The panel was chaired by Kennedy, the publisher of *Climbing,* who offered some introductory remarks about the qualities he sought in choosing material to publish. Not surprisingly, passion and integrity were virtues he discovered in the finest mountain writing. But of special interest was the last of the qualities he mentioned: humility. "We are not, after all," he observed, "working for world peace or saving the environment."

I found this last remark unexpected and gratifying and took the occasion to ask the panel why it was there were so few great works of comedy in the mountaineering genre; none at all that came to mind in continental European or American mountain writing. Only in British climbing literature is there an appreciation of the comic nature of climbing. I thought that this absence of comedy had something to do with a general lack of humility among climbers.

The panel misconstrued my question, pointing out that many climbing narratives included amusing stories and funny incidents. However, my question was not about amusing anecdotes, but about comedy. Why is it that climbing writers do not see themselves as actors in a comic (as opposed to, let us say, an epic or tragic) drama? This is not a question about whether climbers have a sense of humor, but about how they view climbing in relation to things that are of greater importance.

Almost at once I found myself thinking of the book that ushered in most completely the modern age in climbing literature, Galen Rowell's *In the Throne Room of the Mountain Gods,* a work flawed by its tone of passion without humility. Coming after the stirring exploits of Charles Houston and his comrades on K2 in 1953 (*K2: The Savage Mountain*), Rowell's account of the 1975 American K2 expedition seemed to drastically lower the tone of American mountaineering writing. One reaction to the book was that at last an expedition chronicler had demonstrated the guts to tell the *real* story—the bitchiness and competitiveness of the modern expedition game—and that it was only the delicacy of earlier writers that had kept the truth from coming out. But this interpretation had to overlook the nobility of Houston's team in the face of spirit-breaking disaster high on K2 in 1953—the "high-water mark of American mountaineering," as Royal Robbins so aptly described it. For Rowell to have written a great book would have required a comic understanding of modern Himalayan climbing endeavor, part of which is an appreciation that climbing is not important in the great scheme of things, does nothing to promote the betterment of humankind, and often leads people into absurd positions.

Consider the elements involved in that particular history. The expedition leader, the aging-but-hale executive director of REI, brings with him his younger and attractive wife and signs on numerous Washington State cronies having an unfortunate tendency to mutual congratulation, and whose résumés prominently feature multiple ascents of Mt. Rainier, sometimes numbering, as I vaguely recall, in the hundreds. The wife is an immediate flash-point for certain of the team, who (justifiably) question her climbing credentials. Rowell himself has "upstart generation" written all over him and is skeptical of more gray-haired authority; and other unlikely odd-men-in include such as the innocent Norwegian/Canadian Leif Norman Patterson (the "best of us," as Rowell fittingly calls him).

Then there is the matter of nationalistic sponsorship and all the earnestness which accompanies expeditions that take on "national" pretensions. Enormous expense and publicity are expended to achieve very little—the team barely makes it to Camp 2. A comparison might be the elephantine efforts in *Jarndyce vs. Jarndyce*, the estate wrangle that forms the subject matter of Dickens's novel *Bleak House*, in which by the time the momentous legal proceedings are ended the entire estate has been used up and the beneficiaries left destitute. The absurdity of the K2 story is capped in the end by the sudden coming-together of team spirit to counter suggestions that the team had been co-opted by the CIA to plant monitoring devices on K2's summit—a denouement that perhaps an American could take seriously, but one that generates unintended hilarity in a foreign reader.

Had Tom Patey, the great Scottish ice climber of the 1960s, whose whimsies are collected in the volume *One Man's Mountains*, been on the expedition, a very different story would have emerged than the somewhat bitter tale of *Throne Room*. Patey had a facility of being unable to completely dislike anybody. He also had a fine ability to discern the comic where others might discover uglier emotions. Consider this brief episode from the first climbing trip he made with a well-known and intense practitioner:

> We scrambled breathlessly up to the Half-way Ledge and along it as far as the Nose, where the big overhangs form a natural canopy. Bonington selected the driest and hence most overhanging crack in the vicinity. "Just keep an eye on the rope, I won't be a minute," he remarked laconically, lacing up his favorite P.A.s . True to his word he returned almost immediately, landing on the ledge in a heap. "Mild XS," he muttered. "You have a go." "I am going to try beyond the corner on your left," I replied. "At least that's the natural line." "But that's a scruffy climb!" he protested. "Personally I'd rather admit I was defeated than resort to cheating." This fairly roused my wrath. I have a proprietary interest in the Cioch dating back to our ascent of the North Wall in 1952 and our discovery of the five great buttresses in the Corrie beyond, and now this was the first time that I had heard the rock described as "scruffy." I counted it an unpardonable insult. Paradoxically it was the Lion of Llanberis [Bonington] who led the first and only dirty pitch on the climb. Here were scanty clumps of grass and heather from which he recoiled with an expression akin to revulsion, as if picking his way through a freshly manured field. "A fine orthodox line," I murmured as I passed him, "and even better things lie in store for us."

Here are present some of the elements that were present in Rowell's narrative: the suggestion of new-generation ethics versus the more orthodox, and the writer's sense that the climbing talents in the party are not equal. The comedy in the situation Patey describes is possible, however, because he is willing to expose himself to at least as much risibility as the "Lion of Llanberis," and because he realizes that really nothing is at stake here—that is to say, he shows humility. He recognizes the comic position of the discrepancy between pretension and reality. It is also important to note, in particular because of what I have to say later, that I do not think either Patey or Bonington are belittled by the anecdote, and in fact both probably grow for us somewhat as people because of the connection we are able to make with them on the level of human understanding. Haven't most climbers similar incidents to recall from their own histories, which bring a slight smile at the recollection brought on by Patey's comic presentation?

It is easy to say there is nothing funny about failure, especially when it is costly both in terms of money and human potential, as was the 1975 K2 expedition; or of human life, as was the case in 1986 and 1994 on K2, and in 1996 on Everest. Nor am I suggesting that a comic treatment should mock climbers who set out with such lofty ambitions on their way to these dangerous summits. Comedy might well mock, however, the disparity between what is hoped for and what is achieved. It is a failure of perspective not to see the comic distance between the ideal and the actual, and not to recognize one's own comic position. Failure is often the subject of comedy, and is often dignified by it. While there are many things one might call Don Quixote or Huckleberry Finn, "successful in the eyes of the world" is certainly not one of them.

To those unfamiliar with the notion of making comedy out of such material, the works of Aristophanes and Shakespeare are of special interest. Aristophanes was a playwright of Classical Greece whose plays were written during the collapse of the Athenian empire. Many of his comedies feature the prominent men of his day—politicians, philosophers, poets. Indeed, certain of the gods also appear in his plays and are portrayed in a ludicrous light. Obviously, Aristophanes' material could equally have been given tragic treatment. The disappearance of Athenian democracy and culture from the world was unmistakably tragic. However, Aristophanes chose comedy to bring home his views about the dangers of warmongering and moral decay, and he cast the important figures of his day in a ridiculous light because he knew that the issues at stake for Athens were of greater moment than the reputations of even its most outstanding citizens (Socrates and Euripides among them—two who suffer at the hands of this comic genius).

Comedy can still bring a sense of dignity to the human struggle, and, indeed, the great comic writers aim at such a thing. Who is more noble in the end than Quixote, clinging to the hope of his illusions; or Huck Finn, following his better instincts down the river with Jim even though everything he has been brought up to believe tells him that his friendship with the runaway slave is evil? Shakespeare saw no incongruity in mixing the comic and the tragic; the clown in *MacBeth* makes his most dissolute appearance immediately following the murder of Duncan; and Falstaff fences wits with Henry V, the one king whom Shakespeare unambiguously admires. Likewise Plato, considering the issue in *Symposium*, shows Socrates, having drunk all the other guests under the table, ending the banquet debating with Agathon, a tragic poet, and Aristophanes, the great comedian, that the poetic fountain of comedy and tragedy are the same—because comedy and tragedy spring from the same understanding about the nature of our human situation. We of the twentieth century have returned to this understanding of the tragic nature of comedy as the Greeks discovered it, and to an appreciation of the sinews that bind comedy and tragedy together: two aspects of the same issue.

The French thinker Henri Bergson, who wrote one of the most interesting discussions of the subject (in his book *Laughter*), thought that laughter arose from the imposition of the mechanical on the whimsical and spontaneous: "the laughable element... consists of a certain mechanical inelasticity, just where one would expect to find the wideawake adaptability and the living pliableness of a human being." Here is one explanation for the comedy in the story of those modern K2 expeditions that have been so costly in expenditure of human life—and of other expeditions or climbs where pretensions at greatness overwhelmed the participants. Climbing a mountain should be a simple thing. H. W. Tilman observed that if one wanted to go on an expedition, the procedure was straightforward: "put on your boots, and go." This is a credo that rejects rigidity in execution.

There is a kind of high comedy in the earnestness that was applied to the massive expeditions of the 1970s and into the 1980s, where the simple objective of getting to the top of something got bound up with nationalistic enterprise and a kind of *Boy's Own* enthusiasm for showing the flag for the mother country, or for the American way of life, or some other, equally murky moral objective, as opposed to just getting on with the joy of coming to grips with snow and ice. Contrasting extravaganzas like the 1963 Everest expedition with the modest affairs run by Eric Shipton and Tilman, one is struck by this thought: one never laughs at Shipton and Tilman; one laughs with them, mostly because they did not take themselves too seriously and did not subordinate the experience of getting there to the objective of reaching the top. Certainly neither ever had any pretense that they were out climbing for any other reason than personal satisfaction; it was this attitude that made Shipton so unfit in the eyes of the Mount Everest Committee to lead the 1953 British expedition, an expedition where getting to the top meant absolutely everything.

It is when climbing takes on pretensions that go beyond what the enterprise itself can sustain that the actors become comic—and mountaineering is surely susceptible to such pretensions. Comedy is the enemy of pretentiousness, and the more earnestly overstated the importance of the enterprise, the more likely the comic will appear. W. E. Bowman's farce *The Ascent of Rum Doodle* was born out of successful British expeditions, not failures. Success or failure is not ultimately important to comedy; it is understanding that counts.

The ungainly nationalistic expedition, which became an increasingly fashionable target among hard men as the 1980s wore on, has now been replaced in the 1990s by a target that presents even greater opportunities for ridicule—the guided expedition. Of course, people with enough money have always been interested in buying adventure with some built-in risk control, such as using a guide, or perhaps a helicopter. Nonetheless, there is something comic about this ethos being applied to ascents of Everest by people with little feel for the sport of mountaineering and who are climbing for reasons even more ludicrous than those held by, for example, professional mountaineers who feel they need Everest on their résumé in order to achieve respectability, not to mention a better likelihood at sponsorship. We tread on rather uneasy ground here, following the 1996 episode on Everest that has been so searingly chronicled by Jon Krakauer in his bestselling book *Into Thin Air*. But leaving the outcome in which so many died aside for a minute, had the disaster not been so terrible, a comic treatment of the 1996 guided expeditions on Everest along the lines of the pilgrimage recounted in *The Canterbury Tales* would have been more than justified.

Like Chaucer's pilgrims, all of whom had their own agendas, the clients on Fischer and Hall's teams had very disparate reasons for wanting to summit Everest, and it would not be unfair to poke fun at some of these motives, or to note the distance between the pretension and the reality. Sandy Hill Pittman, in one of her first postings to the web, noted: "It looks like I'll have as much computer and electronic equipment as I will have climbing gear....Two IBM laptops, a video camera, three 35 mm cameras, one Kodak digital camera, two tape recorders, a CDROM player, a printer, and enough (I hope) solar panels and batteries to power the whole project...." Here also, according to Krakauer, we have climbers attempting Everest who barely know how to walk in crampons; at least one "guide" who sends the clients on ahead while reclining in base camp; and a clutch of people along because they want to get their names in the record books as being early finishers in the race up the "Seven Summits." At various points during the fateful day of May 10, you have situations in which a head guide (Fischer) is ascending the mountain when all his paying clients have already summited and are going down; while another guide (Boukreev) is descending to camp when many clients are still going up! The participants on such guided trips should be thankful that Patey is no longer around to bring his comic perspective on such undertakings. It is hard to think of finer examples of the distance between pretension and reality, although that distance is so broad that the story lends itself more to parody or satire than to the whimsical comedy of Tom Patey.

Similar to Chaucer's pilgrims, Hall and Fischer's clients had somewhat the makeup of a harlequin clown's outfit; it is difficult to imagine a smooth-working team emerging from such an unlikely cast of characters with such disparate motives. One must emphasize that Chaucer really only dislikes one or two of his pilgrims, even as he pokes fun at them, and that it is not his intention to attack his characters but to let the light of clear understanding play upon their motivations and yearnings, through the medium of comedy. Or again, I repeat that Huck Finn is one of the noblest heroic figures in all of American thought, even though he is treated comically. Nobility and comedy are not mutually exclusive. The clown in *King Lear* is cracking black jokes even as the most noble characters in the play are hurtling toward tragic death. The audience is laughing while the foundations of the world collapse.

It is no longer self-evident to moderns that there is material here for comedy, and anyway, the savage ending of the unfortunate expeditions of Hall and Fischer forestalls any attempt to achieve the perspective of comedy in examining these incidents. Good taste dictates that a comic treatment of the situation will have to wait, but it will not wait forever. Pilgrims being ushered up Everest for enormous sums of money invite comic commentary on the foibles of human motivation, and are not the stuff of which we normally make tragic heroes.

I realize that there are a lot of justifications for deciding to climb Everest, even if you have limited mountaineering experience. Recently popular—and emphasized in the literature that promotes these ventures—is the "you should follow your dreams" justification. I myself don't find anything inherently noble in this idea, especially if the dreamer trashes the dreams of others en route to his or her separate conquest. Some people achieve nobility in following their dreams and some others are just stupid and wasteful. We have to admit that deciding to climb Everest is, for most people these days, a wholly selfish undertaking. Nonetheless, there was real heroism shown on Everest on May 10 and 11, 1996, and I would not want to suggest otherwise. Rob Hall sacrificed his life to remain with Doug Hanson, brushing aside suggestions that he should abandon his client and climb down alone. That was a noble decision, taken in the certain knowledge that the ultimate sacrifice would likely be the price. Andy Harris remained high on the mountain hoping to support Hall when his condition dictated that he had to descend to save himself. Ang Dorje and Lhakpa Chhiri, wasted from summiting the previous day, left the South Col in high winds and climbed to 700 feet below the South Summit in an attempt to rescue Hall. And Neal Beidleman emerges from all accounts as a clear-headed figure whose inherently good instincts as a guide brought some to safety who would otherwise have died. I am well aware that to climb high on Everest, no matter what your level of technical ability, requires exceptional determination and resolve, but none of these acts of great heroism detracts from the thesis that applying the lessons of comedy to these events can lead to an understanding of the nature of guided high-altitude climbing as it really is.

The twentieth century has not been a good age for heroes. Heroes emerge from societies in which there exists a generally accepted code of social behavior, and today social disjunction seems to prevail everywhere. Yet the great comedies reaffirm the social contract. Shakespeare's comedies inevitably end with marriage, and hence with hope and potential. So too in Aristophanes: social or political understanding is what his plays aim at. *The Frogs* was written specifically to try to bring the people of Athens to their senses. Great comedy seeks to convey a serious message. It does not follow that someone is belittled to say they are in a comic position. No one would think that Tom Patey, a master at comic self-effacement, shrunk in stature by his comic understanding of the situations he was often in. He must, on the contrary, be one of the more admired figures in mountaineering since the Second World War. As discerning a critic as David Roberts thought that his comic autobiography, *One Man's Mountains*, was the finest and most truthful account in the entire mountaineering genre.

Modern life is comfortable. It is not tragic as the ancient or classical writers understood tragedy, and the much-reported deaths of climbers on K2 in recent years, easily described as tragic in contemporary media, would not have been so considered by any age other than our own. These deaths carry more the flavor of the absurd than the tragic—to freeze to death for the glory of climbing the Abruzzi Ridge is truly to participate in an act beyond meaning. Surely, with all the noble things one might do with one's life (or with $65,000), ascending K2 or being guided up Everest must rank far down the list. Such behavior takes us into the realm of the comic, especially the comedy of the ancients that is concerned with ending and destruction. I am quite sure that these climbers were all courageous people of stamina and determination, but a proper comic understanding of the nature of climbing might have saved more than one of them from their absurd fate. As Bergson would have put it, to subordinate the mechanical idea to the reality of the situation is to make oneself a comic figure.

Even some of the greatest modern achievements in climbing seem to share the attributes of comedy to some extent. Consider, for example, the race between Reinhold Messner and Jerzy Kukuczka to be the first up the fourteen 8,000-meter peaks. Comic elements are provided by the consistent denials from the protagonists that they are in competition when they so obviously are, or that in fact the very enterprise of getting to the top of the Big Fourteen means anything to them, when it so obviously does.

Both Messner and Kukuczka are great men, and again I must emphasize that it is not necessarily the purpose of comedy to sneer at them. Quixote and Huck Finn achieve heroic stature through their awareness of the truth of things, despite the constant invitation of the reader to chuckle at their foibles. Put-upon, lied to, abused by his father and society, and forced to flee down-river with a runaway slave, Huck nonetheless possesses moral intuition superior to any other person in the world of nineteenth-century American literature. We are always smiling at Huck's apparent naiveté and innocence, but really his is the most aware and active intelligence we encounter in his world.

The comic potential that I have argued exists in the pursuit of climbing leads me to ask if there are any with Huck Finn's awareness participating at the highest levels of the game. Voytek Kurtyka seems to me one who, by having a true notion of the comedy inherent in climbing, comes into his reward by being a more complete person than many of his stature. Like Tilman, he is one whom we laugh with, not at. Interestingly, too, he is the sole survivor of the remarkable Polish triumvirate that also included Kukuczka and Wanda Rutkiewicz, both dead in the quest for the mechanical—the collecting of the 8,000-meter peaks. I believe Kurtyka has also never lost a partner. Not obsessed with the 8,000ers, as are so many of the top European alpinists, Kurtyka is known for routes of aesthetic and mental challenge. I yet remember his whimsical account of the attempt on the great wall of Trango Tower he made with three Japanese climbers, who inexplicably bailed one-third of the way up the route when everything was going smoothly. An American would likely have filled the account with invective and scorn; Kurtyka explained how his anger disappeared as he came to know these men in base camp. "Failures," he concluded, "are good things." In this story we hear the wisdom of a climber who has stepped outside the realm of physical achievements to see the comic irony inherent in the pursuit.

Among North American performers, Peter Croft also seems to me to have, through his climbing, achieved a kind of Huck-like stature; in his case this has much to do with the absence of egoism in his outlook. (Again, humility at work.) Greg Child and Jon Krakauer strike me as others who understand the comic ironies involved in risking one's neck for the sheer stubbornness of it all and whose writing shows the humility Michael Kennedy seeks. Warren Harding, with his "couldn't give a rat's ass" attitude, is the obvious satyr-like figure from the Golden Age of Yosemite, and his comic greatness continues to be misunderstood. One might even justly include Chouinard in the group—so perhaps I am wrong in asserting the relative absence of comic perspective among modern American climbers, although I think it is true that, at bottom, most lack humility.

Aristotle had no difficulty in concluding that tragedy was in every way superior to comedy. We in the twentieth century are less confident of this conclusion. This is probably because we are less likely to accept the rationality of the universe and more inclined to believe that injustice and meaninglessness confront us. This is the world that comedy speaks to: the world of surprises, absurdity, and of danger without redemption. One theory of laughter holds that the laugh arises from the sudden perception of distance between the ideal and the actual; one might say from the sudden knowledge of the absurdity of what we believe in most strongly. Of course, we laugh for many reasons—sometimes out of spite, other times from sympathy. Freud thought laughter inherently aggressive, and others have agreed. Those who believe that malice and the quest for power in individual life are the wellsprings of comedy will have no difficulty in understanding why modern climbing, with its human failures, seems infused with comic potential.

But it is still possible to adopt a more positive view of comedy. One might say that comedy brings home to us the need for honesty in human relations. The essence of comedy is to encourage humility in the face of our uncertain place in the world. In this sense, comedy is instructive and positive. Comedy is the knowledge of who we are. Comedy can give us this knowledge because almost none of us are Hamlets or Lears, and in any case we no longer inhabit the universe of the tragic and epic heroes. We are more akin to Quixote or Micawber, prone (especially climbers) to follow dreams and illusions, tending to hope that things will always turn out for the better, and hoping, like Kurtyka, to achieve stature from both the failures and the successes. The universe we inhabit is the universe of the improbable—and hence the comic. Therefore, comic understanding is ultimately the understanding of things as they truly are.

If we return to the 1975 K2 expedition, we might ask what Leif Norman Patterson, the most Huck-like of the climbers involved, would have made of the rich material had he written the account. I suspect he would have seen the irony in the situation, for it was Patterson who originally conceived the expedition, then saw it metamorphose before his eyes from a few friends getting together in the Himalaya into the great ungainly corporate enterprise it became. One might suppose that Patterson, like Huck, was swept along by the current of events, yet rescued by his awareness and refusal to become bitter about it all; the evocative photograph by Rowell, "Return to the Green," of him standing with arms spread in joy during the march out from the Baltoro breathes an appealing and simple humanity like the humanity of Huckleberry Finn. That photograph is one of the greatest legacies of the expedition, maybe its greatest.

What might the knowledge of comedy have done for the climbers on Everest or K2 who struggled there to so little moral purpose? Above all, comedy might have taught them the humility of this knowledge about who and what they were. In the words of Michael Kennedy, "we are not working for world peace." When statesmen of warring nations meet, much might hang in the balance; but when a climber faces Everest or K2 it is salutary to remember that very little hangs in the balance. Above all, comedy reminds us that it is the way of things to be unpredictable, and that it is when we start to see ourselves as tragic protagonists that we are most likely to be brought down.

There are worse failures in the world than failing to climb K2, even if you are a famous mountaineer; and it seems certain that to die in doing so is to fail most spectacularly. It also seems that those climbers at the top of the heap have lost sight of this notion that death is the greatest failure of all. Whatever comedy aims at, it is not death; comedy affirms that we can challenge our absurd position in the cosmos by the understanding of the gulf between our aspirations and our puny selves, and that in this recognition we can achieve meaning and significance in our lives. Comedy is, above all, the literature of common sense.

Indeed, it is exactly the fate of the tragic hero that such understanding is denied him; Othello pursues his theory of adultery, with mental inelasticity, to his ruin; likewise Lear's failure is the failure of a mind too rigid to contemplate his own affectation. Petheus, the doomed youth of Euripides' *The Bacchae,* is carried to his grisly end (his mother decapitates him) by a mind that is not alive to the possibilities of the Dionysian. To laugh at himself without bitterness is something that the tragic hero can rarely achieve. In reaching the knowledge that comedy brings, I believe that we impose on the irrational a meaning denied to us if we simply blunder along the path of the abstract notion (for example, the summit at all costs). Comedy is criticism of life lived according to unalterable credos and plans; it reminds us that we are human and not mechanical.

It is this absence of anything amounting to much in the way of a spirit of criticism in climbing that engendered my question to the panel in Banff. The following day I sat viewing films at the Festival, including a film documenting an impressive ascent of *The Shield* on Yosemite's El Cap. The film contained a brief discussion of the values of sport climbing, but I felt that the segment had been tossed into the film in a failed attempt to add a bit of philosophic depth—the ideas were simply too shallow. Again, the moment breathed more of comedy than of the moral seriousness the filmmaker was seeking. It is not that debates about sport climbing, or whether one should bolt on rappel, are completely unimportant, but a proper comic perspective would assign such issues their proper place in the world of climbing philosophy—somewhere near the bottom of the list of those things that matter most. Because while climbers have always shown themselves willing to furiously debate the more trivial questions, the big questions are always avoided. Where is the rapier wit who can put the ludicrous quest for the 8,000-meter peaks in perspective? Where is the comic who can do justice to the death toll on Everest or K2? (Again, to those who would protest that this is defaming the dead, all I can do is to urge you to read Aristophanes, especially *The Frogs,* written just as the light of Athens went out forever, or to consider the black comedy of Kafka, Tom Stoppard, or even Woody Allen.)

Finally, as Kurtyka discovered on Trango Tower, comedy teaches us to be tolerant of failure. As the literary critic Willie Sypher has said, "At the radiant peak of 'high comedy'... laughter is qualified by tolerance, and criticism is modulated by a sympathy that comes only from wisdom. Just a few writers of comedy have gained this unflinching but generous perspective on life, which is a victory over our absurdities, but a victory won at a cost of humility, and won in a spirit of charity and enlightenment." There is a strong lesson in these words for the writers of climbing literature in the late 1990s. Michael Kennedy's call for humility in our mountain writing is timely indeed.

MIMI DREAMING

Ken Baldwin

Gundiwinji the goanna lizard stretched out on the living Rock. He could feel the breath of the Mimi spirits deep beneath its surface releasing the sun's captured warmth, setting the blood coursing through his veins. The Rock's shadow contracted across the russet desert as the Mimi inhaled the darkness. Another dawn in the long history of the Dreaming had begun.

As Gundiwinji picked his way up the steepening, pockmarked slabs, he could feel the rush of air as the Mimi, guardians of the Rock, parted the sandstone and made their way out into the new day. The shimmering haze they left on the Rock showed that it would be hot, so Gundiwinji crept under the shade of a mallee bush. Here he could look out over the dusty panorama, safe from the piercing gaze of Werigal the wedge-tailed eagle, whose wheeling flight was the sole disturbance breaking the scorching air.

Werigal, however, had his eyes on another disturbance to the seldom-changing scene. Two figures, strangely clad and with dangling objects catching the glare of the sun, approached the Rock. As Werigal's shadow crossed over them, their faces turned upward, squinting at the burning sky. They were white in color, not like the black of the Tijantara people whose traditional lands encompassed the great red Rock. Soon the figures would reach its base, and Werigal wondered how the Mimi spirits would greet them.

The Mimi had seen people of this type before, though only very recently in the Dreaming. But the Dreaming went back a long way, to the time when the great Rainbow Serpent first crossed the desert land, carving the furrow along which waters now flowed in time of rain. These waters brought life to the desert, and with them had come the forefathers of Werigal and Gundiwinji.

To shelter from the burning midday sun, the Rainbow Serpent had buried itself deep in the sand, forming a huge mound whose outer crust had solidified in the intense heat to become the great red Rock. Grateful for the shelter that had saved its life, the Rainbow Serpent left behind the Mimi spirits to guard the Rock, then moved on to bring life to other places in the Dreaming.

Since early Dreamtime the Mimi had remained faithful to their task. They had seen the coming of the Tijantara people, who stayed in the thorny scrubland around the Rock to hunt for Gundiwinji's ancestors. These people brought fire with them and had wrought many changes to the landscape. But they had also learned from this harsh land and had taught their children—to ensure their survival—lessons from the Dreaming.

Central to these tales was the Rock itself. Aware of the sacred role the Mimi played as guardians of their past, the Tijantara proclaimed the Rock hallowed ground on which they could not tread. The caves at its base held classes for the Dreaming, and important lessons were read into the ancient rock formations imprinted on its ochre walls. Chief among these lessons was the story told about the massive cleft formed by the tail of Kurinda, the great kangaroo, who had leaped over the Rock to escape the first Tijantara warriors, whose spears, aiming too low, had left many small pockets in its weathered sandstone flanks.

Ayers Rock
at sunrise.

Ken Baldwin

It was toward this cleft that the two figures were now heading. They were unlike the first white men the Mimi had seen. Arriving in tall canoes pulled by tethered clouds, the ancestors of these people had many years ago crossed the desert on strange animals, killing Kurinda's descendants with spears of thunder. They had angered the Tijantara by climbing onto the Rock but had left it undisturbed and thus did not provoke the wrath of the Mimi, whose compassion disguised their considerable power.

It became apparent to the Mimi that these two people were also interested in the Rock. They stood in the shade near its base staring toward the cleft formed by Kurinda's tail, while the Mimi hovered invisibly above. From the skins carried on their backs they pulled out strange objects: a long, white snake resembling Namatira the blind earthworm, and shiny spearheads that rang against the desert stones. They placed these objects around them and headed for the cleft.

One of them took the snake and started to climb, his foot-coverings scratching the friable face. He had not gone far in the blazing heat when he stopped to rest. The Mimi, puzzled as to why he did not join Gundiwinji in the nearby shade, watched as he withdrew some spearheads from the skin on his back. Another object, like the war clubs of the Tijantara, followed. To the Mimi's horror, he started to club one of the spearheads into the crack! Clouds of ochre dust exploded as the white man rent asunder the sandstone walls. Kurinda's spirit shuddered, and the Mimi flew with concern into the cleft.

The man put the snake through a hole in the spearhead and, standing in a loop in the snake, moved upward. He drew another spearhead and once again wrought fearful damage to the sacred Rock. The Mimi, incensed by the object of their trust being flayed before them, blew the fiery breath of the midday air into the cleft and set the ruddy stone on fire.

The man, overcome by heat, slumped in the loop in the snake and was lowered from the Rock by the man below. With the danger passed, the Mimi ceased the wind which, spiraling into the sky, had cast the sacred dust back into the desert whence it came. The man recovered when doused with water by his friend, and the Mimi could see that all was well. But, to ensure that they did not return hurriedly, the Mimi sent the whirlwind after them, guided by Werigal's watchful eye.

Many years passed and even the Tijantara came seldom to the Rock. The far-seeing Werigal reported to the Mimi that the Tijantara now followed the ways of the white men, and no more were the classes in the caves used to pass on the lessons of the Dreaming. The Mimi did notice, however, that fire had once again returned to the landscape, tended by white men and Tijantara, side by side. Perhaps the white men were learning the lessons of the Dreaming, and perhaps now they would respect the sanctity of the Rock.

It was to the Mimi's surprise then that one day Werigal warned of two more figures in the distance, their approach heralded by jangling sounds like the ringing of the spearheads on the stones. Once again they made their way to Kurinda's cleft, and once again they uncoiled a snake taken from their skins.

But this was unlike the blanched white snake before. It was beautiful, colored with the vivid hues of the Rainbow Serpent. Mesmerized by the resurrection of their progenitor, the Mimi allowed the Rainbow Serpent to unfurl its coils across the Rock, snaking its way behind the man as he surmounted the cleft.

This time the man drew shiny laced stones from the skin and placed them in the pockets left by the Tijantara as they pursued Kurinda's desperate flight. The shiny stones fitted snugly to the Rock, leaving it untouched and reassuring the Mimi that the men could mean no harm. Up they moved under the blazing sun, their feet smearing softly on the russet surface, their palms made sweaty by exertion. The man dipped his hand into a skin filled with white dust and placed his imprint on the ochre walls, just as the Tijantara had in years gone by. The Dreaming had returned, and the Mimi were content.

Other white men came, and they too were allowed to climb the Rock. The Tijantara did not seem to mind now either. Some of them wore strange skins on their heads as they talked to the white men, showing them the sacred caves lined with the painted handprints of their forefathers. Werigal surveyed their comings and goings, and Gundiwinji shared with them the shade of the mallee tree. The Mimi watched over them all and saw to it that they and the Rock would come to no harm.

That is, until the coming of the Rainbow people.

Their first appearance was innocuous enough. They arrived dressed in skins resembling those of the Rainbow Serpent, with patterns even more complex than Gundiwinji's scaly camouflage. From one ear were suspended tiny captured sunbeams. They carried the now-familiar manyhued snake and climbed the cleft in the fashion to which the Mimi had become accustomed.

On reaching the top they threw the snake down the steepest flank of the Rock and lowered themselves slowly down the face. They stopped from time to time, inspecting the vertiginous sandstone slabs and caressing the red dust from the smallest pockets. They went up as well as down, suspended by the snake, like Nouringa the hunting spider does in its early morning dance. Then they left. The Mimi wondered at this curious ritual, but by now they had become used to the strange ways of the white men.

On their next appearance the Rainbow people made straight for the steepest flank. Out came the reincarnation of the Rainbow Serpent, and, mesmerized by its powerful magic, the Mimi followed the man's progress from inside the vertical face. His movements were truly beautiful, and even Gundiwinji found it hard to follow, so steep was the wall. On reaching a considerable height the man stopped, withdrawing what seemed to be a bulky club. And, before the Mimi could react, the man had noisily defiled the blank Rock with a thin new spear hole.

Confused by these images of the Dreaming, and concerned lest the man should fall, the Mimi watched frantically as he tied the snake to a silver-ringed spearhead placed into the hole. Up he moved, surmounting an overhanging curl in the wall, a frozen wave of rock. Resting momentarily on the shallow lip, he moved on to an even smoother and ever-steepening face.

The man was quivering now, his hands sweating and his feet smearing the granules from the Rock. In one slow movement he reached back and withdrew the bulky club again.

The Mimi, now conscious of their higher role, became agitated, swooping back and forth across the threatened face. Their breeze helped dry the man's sweat, and his quivering momentarily stopped. But the instant the club began its noisy whine, the Mimi could no longer hold their rage. The rock began to shake, imperceptibly at first, but enough to cause the grit to slide beneath the man's feet. The motion of the club ceased as he leaned tremulously against the face. Then, instantly, he parted from the Rock.

His body arced backwards and crashed against the curling ledge. Blood dripped from his head, staining the Rock as the initiation paintings of the Tijantara had done during adolescent rites. The ringed spearhead below him jangled down the snake, dislodged by the tremors of wrath. He groaned in pain and slid inexorably toward the edge.

The Mimi sensed that something was amiss. Caught between their guardianship of the Rock and their concern for those who used it, they watched the man's hands open slowly on the sloping holds. Fear gripped his face—the Mimi had to act. Diving into the Rock, they parted the living stone, into which he plunged his hand. His fist closed, his muscles flexed, and he regained the ledge.

The Rainbow people watching from below ascended the Kurinda cleft and climbed down to his aid. As they lowered him to the ground, they viewed the spear hole rent in holy stone and shook their shaven heads.

For some time the Rainbow people did not return. When they did, the Tijantara men with strange skins on their heads accompanied them and talked to them about the hole. The Mimi watched, hearing many references to the Dreaming. The Tijantara men could not tell all the stories, since to do so to the uninitiated would cause the tales to lose their magic. But the Rainbow people nodded, and the Mimi sensed they understood. White men still come from time to time to climb the Rock, though no spearheads now are seen. The Tijantara have no desire to climb it, as they wish to keep the Dreaming. The Mimi, for their part, have helped the white men keep it too. But then, that is why the Rainbow Serpent sent them in the Beginning.

Steve j. Wood

1994

two roofs – that is beautiful
looks like a pretty climb

on belay
belay on
climbing
climb on
you've got to hook in for it to work by the way
could i have a little slack
what are you going to do for your next move
and your next
you might want to think about that
these are easy moves but i am so pumped
you get here and things are going fine
then you get kicked in the face
tension TENSION
I'M SWEATING AND IT'S SLICK
AND I WON'T COMMIT
you can start your climb over at any time in your mind
TRUST YOUR FEET

Jennifer Christiansen

Steve j Wood

Freddie Snalam

Gardner Heaton

SCOTTISH PORTRAITS

Terry Gifford

We are walking across a boggy moor in northwest Scotland, heading into what is sometimes called "the Great Wilderness." We both have bulging rucksacks, but Julian is also struggling with a ski bag swinging across his chest. Since this is the end of a hot weekday in May, the sight of Julian trying it first over one shoulder, then over the other, might puzzle any other walkers, were we to meet any. Skiing in Scotland is uncertain even in winter. When we hit a path, Julian experiments with balancing the ski bag across the top of his rucksack with the band across his forehead. "Good training for Peru," he grunts. This confirms that I am the burro since I'm carrying all the camping gear and the climbing gear. Julian's rucksack slurps with turps and is weighted with tubes of oil paint. In the ski bag is a five- by six-foot rolled canvas, yard-long brushes, a collapsible alloy frame, and bulldog-clips.

From a base camp we are hoping to climb the toothy north face of Beinn Lair by its *Wisdom Buttress*, before Julian paints its portrait on the following day. This 700-foot Very Difficult (5.3) climb has the longest approach in Britain. As we settle into the fourteen-mile walk, we're hoping for two more days of dry weather. Each year at Whitsun, the end-of-May long-weekend national holiday, we've set out for a long climbing project in Scotland from which Julian hopes to produce a painting and I to write a poem to accompany it. So why don't I get to carry less? I ponder as we sweat through the humid air.

The scale and risk of this undertaking for a professional painter is typical of Julian Cooper's search for a challenge as a landscape artist. Perhaps this need to go further and attempt more comes from his being the third generation of a famous family of Lake District mountain painters. His grandfather, Alfred Heaton Cooper, moved out of industrial Lancashire to the growing tourist attraction of the mountains of the Lake District in northwest England. Julian's father, William Heaton Cooper, built the family home and gallery in Grasmere, from which Julian's brother John now runs the family business of selling paintings and prints. Like his grandfather and father, Julian is used to being able to return to his subject another day. But on these brief, annual, adrenaline-rushed trips against the Scottish weather, the outcome of both a climb and a painting can be laced with uncertainty, as the cocktails we've been forced to drink in recent years have reminded us with each remixing of ingredients.

The painting challenge Julian sets himself is not just a matter of the formidable size of the canvas, although to finish *The Cioch, Applecross* (1994) in one day was as risky a challenge as the three years' work on the monumental triptych of *The Assassination of Chico Mendes* (1992-95). The freshness of the brush strokes in *The Cioch, Applecross* that catch the roll of the heather moor, the cutting stream, and its single vivid green tree, are produced by that pressure to mediate the rhythms of the rock structure—the painting's main subject— in one day. Mediation is the key to the nature of the challenge. There was a moment that day below the Cioch when Julian felt that his body was beginning to find the rhythms of the geology, the orchestration in the great cathedral organ that rose out of the moor in front of

The Cioch, Applecross
(1994)

Julian Cooper

us. The tools are telling. Those long brushes demand an expression of the whole body in the mediation of what is being perceived. The scale of Julian Cooper's project is no less than an exploration of human nature's perception of external nature in a way that recognizes both our connections and our disconnections with the mountains. He calls it "making a third thing out of the human-mountain dialogue."

As we talked in the rare Scottish sunshine at our camp below Beinn Lair, I tried to understand why this painter needed to get his fingers into the very cracks of the mountain he was to paint. For Julian, mountains are the inner forces of our earth, exposed in formations that speak of those huge creative natural energies, while also decaying, eroding, changing before our eyes. "You're looking straight in the eye," he says, "the process that we're at the other end of. The hand that climbs the rock is at the other end of evolutionary time. The hand that paints that hand and rock is engaged in a dialogue that is a reprise." I remembered the precise positions of the hands of the climber in *Wharncliffe* (1993) to see the delicacy of evolution's achievement—and in the pylons, roads, and railway, another kind of evolutionary achievement that this painter will not avoid including in the dynamics of Sheffield's semi-industrial climbing environment.

Julian was not only talking about evolutionary time in his sense of the importance of mountains, but about a living, continuous present. The human-mountain dialogue has a number of other contemporary dimensions for him. "Mountains are primary stuff," he explains. "From them come the soil we cultivate to produce the vegetable matter we feed to animals that we eat. And paint itself is primary stuff, often made out of the earth. The earth colors are from the earth. Umber and sienna are earth and named, of course, after Umbria and Siena."

The result of this holistic approach to painting mountains, out of the experience of a climber's connectedness, is to go beyond treating mountains as objects. Painting mountains

Wharncliffe (1993)

Julian Cooper

from life, "getting out into the land that is prior to landscape," is to go beyond the photograph and sketch to perceive them as phenomena and to present them as what Julian calls "an all-over field across the whole canvas, so that the structure of the canvas is that of the mountain, a field that fills the whole vision within which you can see cause and effect at work, a field of causality, a field of stresses." In his drawing of the popular Lake District 5.7 climb *Tophet Wall* (1993), the swirl of stresses in the light and shade, the air and rock, the angles and planes, include climbers not immediately obvious in the drawing. Indeed, their rope is almost invisible. As the upper climber looks out unconcerned, his partner is crucified on the crux below. Again, the tools are telling. This airy drama, high on the Great Gable massif, was drawn with lumps of graphite scavenged from the underworld of Borrowdale, the valley's Elizabethan mine talus. This Blakean drawing is the marriage of heaven and hell that the "dialogue" of rock climbing can often become.

Notes from a Bivy Bag

Today I am lying in the heather under *Wisdom Buttress*, gloating again. Actually, I am snuggled in a bivy bag (it is summer, but this is Scotland) beside a roaring stove, doing my bit as support team for the painting project. The north face of Beinn Lair is having its portrait painted, and, somewhere over the rise further back from the crag, Julian has his huge canvas pegged to a peat bank, bulldog-clipped to his specially designed alloy frame. You can see that, for him, the climb is only another kind of preparation for the real thing, which he is working at now.

I'm not supposed to look while he's painting, so I'll tell you about *Wisdom Buttress* in between the spitting mists that drift over these craggy teeth like bad breath, slightly smudging these words in my battered notebook. Julian's working in oils, so he's not worried; a mere drizzle will do no damage.

First of all, getting here. You don't have to walk all those fourteen miles. We now have the "Letterewe Accord," negotiated for us by the British Mountaineering Council with the Letterewe Estate. "Mountain bikes are only allowed on vehicle tracks." So you can ignore the "No Cycles" sign still on the gate, lift your bike over it, and take at least two and a half miles off the walk. It's on the way out you appreciate it most as you freewheel down to the sea at Poolewe. I left my bike hidden in the heather beyond the last farm. (Julian had declined to use the bike I'd borrowed for him, after a trial ride the evening before had left him in a ditch with a scarred face and—even worse—a bruised painting arm.) Unfortunately, tire tracks in the moor on our walk in showed that some people cannot accept a reasonable compromise patiently negotiated on their behalf. I wish we'd met them.

I keep having to retreat inside this bivy bag and zip the showers out. But I've got the whole day to write, with the crag right in front of me. The climb itself is a masterpiece of routefinding up this narrow, soaring buttress of interlocking slabs and overhangs. It feels intimidating because in its 700 feet there always seems to be an overhang above you. But the incut horizontal strata of the hornblende schist gives constant encouragement against the equally constant exposure. Right from the start there's also an overhang below. That's assuming you can find the start. So you're into Scottish routefinding before you leave the ground, with a distinctly tight-lipped description from the guidebook.

I made two attempts to traverse the steep gully wall onto the undercut buttress, but I couldn't even get started. "This isn't V Diff," I kept saying, and "This can't be right!" as I moved further up the gully. I was about thirty feet above a chockstone in the gully before I found a traverse line left that was anything like V Diff. I see from a recent *Climbers' Club Journal* that Hamish Nicol approached *Wisdom Buttress* as "a VS Scottish V Diff" and just accepted that the start was an overhanging 5.8 finger traverse on rounded holds that I'd rejected.

My down-sloping footholds and series of sidepulls higher up gave entry to a huge slab of incut strata and a nut belay that was not to be missed. This route's reputation as having poor belay stances and little protection had sunk in. So did my old Moac chock. A rising gale threatened to rip us from the stance. I raced on now, anxious to make up for lost time. The cruise leftward up the slab ran out a ropelength in which only two runners were possible, but a belay ledge appeared at the right moment. Then the rain struck.

"Are we committed, now, to doing this in the rain?" asked Julian, remembering last year's epic ascent of the *Central Buttress* of Beinn Eighe, when the upper tier was awash and the outcome again uncertain. "It does say the rock gets greasy in rain," he added, anorak flapping in the wind.

"If we can find a route at V. Diff., we can do it in the rain," I said, motoring up some holds that were hidden from below because they dipped so delightfully inward.

"The rock is certainly absorbing the rain," Julian observed, as the amalgam gray of the Wisdom tooth turned black before our eyes. Julian recognized that our luck was repeating itself as, after a fortnight of dry weather, just when it broke we were committed on a big route again. This was not a place to slip on greasy rock. Although runners did, in fact, appear before every crux, people pass beneath this crag rarely and getting a rescue team here would take a day. I looked up. I'd belayed below a small overhang on the left edge of the buttress. This was the natural place to end up since the ground to the right steepened considerably. From our little platform we looked out through the rain upon miles of unpeopled emptiness. This is the fabled Last Great Wilderness of mainland Scotland. This was what we'd come all this way to climb in: the nearest thing in Britain to wilderness.

So I pushed on up, turning the overhang on its right (good nut here) and gaining entry to a smaller slab. As I pressed on, the rain stopped, rewarding the climbing spirit. I was gaining Wisdom, slowly. Another steep step right was rewarded with a final slab capped by overhangs. I followed a weakness on its left and stopped on a ledge, feeling the need to regroup. Thank goodness I'd not been tempted to lighten my load for the walk in. A crack by my knee whispered "Friend 3." It was more than friendship it wanted. It was love at first sight. Now I could relax.

Julian has just come over for a cup-a-soup lunch and the painting is going well, apparently. So, since he's gone back to the workplace, I'll tell you about this key section of the route. I was twenty feet below the roof and a traverse line out right seemed possible. I called down to Julian as he was climbing to ask if he had a big overhang to his right. I sensed that this might be the crucial place to cut right between overhangs. It was. The traverse out to the edge was sheer joy. I even got a runner in early on. Side-pulls and a toe ramp led up to the edge. A look round the arête was disheartening. More overhangs. But a delicate step across to a small platform above the void was again rewarded with a comfortingly solid block belay. I called round the arête to Julian, "You've got to be big-hearted to get up these Scottish crags. I can't believe there's a way through above here at V. Diff!"

But when it came to it, of course there was. The overhang was turned on the right once again by steep pulls on great holds on its right wall. I cut back left onto the very nose of the buttress, where exposed climbing led to a huge, unexpected sloping platform. Here I persuaded Julian to take the lead, neither of us realizing that this was the crux pitch. He barely paused to put in gear under another small overhang before swinging leftward under it and romping up the crest of the ridge to which the buttress had now narrowed.

As I came up to him, I looked past him and exclaimed, "Yet another feature! This route is amazing!" The guidebook's casual "Continue up the crest of the buttress" suggested a scramble, but here was more steep rock. The incuts kept a-coming and the position was the closest you'd get to an eagle's view, soaring over the wilderness. Heathery blocks led to the top, which could be the reason for giving this route only two stars. But that's the last memory and not typical of the route as a whole, which provides all the holds. It just keeps you guessing as to where they go. Now I'm going to sneak over and look at that painting. But before I do, let me tell you about our epic on Beinn Eighe last Whitsun and the woman we came to call "the Craggiggler."

The Craggiggler

Actually, we'd first walked in to Beinn Eighe the Whit weekend of the year before that. You know what they say about how good it is to retreat with dignity and all your limbs intact? Well, it isn't exactly true. Your head stays damaged a little, especially if you haven't even set foot on the route—and *Central Buttress* is clearly the route on the majestic Triple Buttresses of Beinn Eighe. These north-facing buttresses rise over a thousand feet above the chill mirror of the loch. You see them suddenly as you climb over the lip of the corrie. A beetling base of 300 feet of red sandstone guards access to the 700 feet of soaring quartzite crests that call out to be climbed.

When we first saw that magnificent mountain, we knew we had plenty of time to study its stark, complex beauty. We were carrying camping as well as climbing gear, and we settled in on a knoll that projected into the loch. There had been a long dry spell, as there often is in Scotland at the end of May, the sky was still clear, and there was plenty of semi-Arctic daylight left; so I persuaded Julian to leave his sketch book and answer the call of the triple goddess. Way above the loch and above some steep heather scrambling, things could actually begin. Or should have.

We found the start of *Readymix*, the recommended route up the sandstone section of *Central Buttress*. It is vertical, rounded rock and obviously has complex routefinding. Suddenly we were cream-crackered from carrying all that gear. So, thinking we might prefer to savor it the next day in less of a rush (you know how the argument goes), we passed along the ledge until the angle eased back and we could at last rope up on an easier route and make upward progress, with some delicate moves, through the sandstone tier to the grassy terrace that marks the change to quartzite and sharp, positive holds.

At the far right end of the grassy band we launched up a white slab inset into the gray quartz. For 700 feet we led through on slightly too easy, slightly too ledgy Diff (4th class) rock that suddenly leveled out onto the top of the mountain. Honor was restored for the retelling, but not really fulfilled for the frank remembering. In the last of the light I cooked a curry and Julian worked at his sketchbook. He had made the crag drawings for the 1972

Triple Buttress, Beinn Eighe.

Julian Cooper

guidebook and he now wanted to make a large oil painting from these new sketches. He was really into it. "It's not just the forms that convey the power of these buttresses," he was enthusing, " it's the violence of twisting that's gone into the making of the rock itself." We glanced back at a group of deer silhouetted on the lip of the corrie against a red sunset over the sea beyond Skye. Then, magically, the Triple Buttresses were lit by an orange after-glow that was slowly cut away by the shadow of seaward mountains creeping across the great buttresses one by one, closing them down. This is why you carry camping gear.

In the morning a single cloud drifted across the face, drizzle turned to Scottish rain, and suddenly the triple goddess had disappeared before our eyes. This is not why you carry camping gear downhill, despite limbs being intact. Rained off, we had failed even to attempt the classic route of the corrie.

Exactly one year later, after another long, dry spell in May, Julian and I were heading back to Bienn Eighe, this time without a tent. He'd got his sketches. Now we needed the route. This time the snowfields below the crag, as well as in the gullies, gave the north-facing buttresses even more drama as they reflected in the sparkling loch. We hid ruck-sacks under a boulder and racked up in the warm sunshine. Walking up the edge of the snow disoriented me, and I traversed off too early on a lower grass ledge. Julian found the right scramble, but we had yet to reach the start when suddenly a chirpy female voice came up to us: "Are you going for the classic Severe?" A woman and two men were hot on our heels. A breathless "Yes!" and we were on the correct ledge, moving along to where we knew the exact start to be. They scrambled up directly below the start and we arrived only seconds ahead of them. All we had to do was uncoil ropes, change boots, and the lead was ours. But something in the friendly banter at the start of this epic climb, and the chortles of anticipation from the young woman gearing up for the lead, made me do the unthinkable: "Do you want to go ahead of us?"

They could not believe their luck. "Oh, well, if you're sure," the Siren said. "We were going to have seconds climbing together anyway. Thanks."

"Actually, the sun comes onto the last pitches in the evening. We might catch it," I said, with a pretense of smugness. In truth, I was relieved not to have the three of them snapping at our heels.

The young woman swung off the terrace onto the steep red rock with impressive speed. At thirty feet she was stopped by an awkward corner, put gear in, and followed suggestions from below to step blindly left. It looked delicate. The rest of the pitch just flowed for her, punctuated by occasional giggles of delight: the Craggiggler. Throughout the rest of the day we knew we were on route thanks to the Craggiggler.

When the rope came tight, a young greyhound raced upward, with his friend literally on his heels, making it obvious that we would have held them back. I found this pitch intimidating. The right-leaning crack line, which the corner gives access to, has rounded jugs on a vertical to overhanging wall. Some steep bridging, and an ability to look round the corner, finally got me to an exposed belay ledge. As I was tensioning two tiny nuts against each other, the Craggiggler climbed over me with a wicked giggle—I'm not sure why.

Julian was so impressed by the first pitch that he offered me the next lead too. The quality of this next section will be hinted at by the dreaded guidebook words, "Step down from here and make an exposed traverse right." The feeling that, in fact, this was not too difficult, was just the opening of a trap to be sprung in two stages. At the end of the traverse the route goes back left across a broad ledge that is low enough to make you think you can step across to it using the pocket in front of you. I couldn't do it. The obvious holds were all in the wrong places to fit together for the move. In the end, with a deep breath, I leaned down, got two hands on the edge of the ledge and swung myself below it. Once I committed to the mantleshelf, it all fell into place. But at the far end of this shelf I was stopped again. Another long step left seemed to be required, above a gaping drop. Fine if there's something to pull across on. As I tried to escape this second trap, a voice came down again: "You're going to love this classic lieback!"

Everyone was enjoying this climb and I wanted to also, if only I could climb it. Once again a commitment to one of the options was ultimately rewarded with holds. And the lieback was indeed delightful because it was unusually positive for this subtle sandstone. A third pitch of cracks and walls led into the final few feet of a chossy chimney. *Readymix* requires a readiness for a mixture of everything.

As I was on the second stance, I had noticed a single climber scrambling up the base of the cliff. From above my head the Craggiggler shouted down, "Come for a climb, John!" While Julian was joining me on the grassy terrace at the top of the sandstone strata, the soloist climbed up beside him. When we wandered across to the start of the quartz arête he was roping up in order to partner the Craggiggler. It was John Chadwick, whom I knew as a fellow member of the Climbers' Club, joining his friends, who were apparently from the Cleveland Mountaineering Club.

As we were chatting, Julian pointed out a curtain of rain charging toward us. The forecast had been for "fair-weather cloud" all day. Well, here it came, suddenly drenching everything with Bienn Eighe's form of fair-weather cloud. John set off up rock running with water. I considered (a) waiting for the shower to pass (it did not); (b) retreat (hard snow filled the gullies at each end of this terrace); or (c) the steep, wet way upward, which was now slowing down even the fast foursome with what seemed to be technical difficulty.

"We don't think this is Severe," came from the upper pair, now in the mist.

Julian urged me upward, and once again it wasn't too bad, mainly because the rock was brilliantly flat, sharp, and more solid than it looked. But the next pitch, straight up, was definitely causing problems. So I looked round the corner (the key to Scottish routefinding) and found a slab I could romp up. Julian quickly joined me. Feeling better, if wetter by now, I launched straight up the wall above, only to be stopped again. I backed off and went walkabout along the terrace to the left. At its end there was a Friend stuck solid in a horizontal crack. This omen of desperate retreat, my sodden condition, the mist and its echoing raven, the crux still to come, together with the uncertainty of our outcome in this lengthening day, sapped my spirit. My thoughts had been wandering toward the route's possibly being capped by a cornice and then the problem of finding the descent gully in the mist. We were going to be lucky to get out of this.

Suddenly there was a horrendous rockfall in the gully to our right. It rang with that eerie presence of the forces of destruction out of control right beside you. We hoped all was well above. At this point Julian produced his secret weapon. He unclipped his Ziggy bottle and offered me a drink. It was the best whiskey I had ever tasted.

Then, miraculously, a little more looking revealed an easy line breaking back right toward where the final tower should be. Sure enough, a giggle echoed down to me, and I could just make out a figure through the mist, hunched in the bottom of a chimney like a gnome. After checking that the rockfall had not touched them, I took some advice on the line of this crux pitch at the base of the tower. From the right I climbed onto the top of a huge, detached flake. The crux is stepping off it. Hidden to the right I found a fist-jamming crack. Getting into it, with feet in the right order, was awkward, but after that everything came to my right hand, in particular, if it felt round the corner.

I'll look forward to actually doing this pitch in the evening sunshine one day, and the further 220 feet of amazing chimney climbing that follows. Out on the top Julian pointed out that, even after a year's wait, the mountain had tricked us into having to climb it in the rain anyway.

Speaking of which, the rain is setting in again, much harder now. Can't write any more. I'm going over to have a look at that painting.

I arrive to find Julian staring morosely at his canvas. Minutes earlier, in a deluge, the painting had been washed away.

The Buckler Face of Mt. Waddington in winter. *Don Serl*

SEA TO SUMMIT
The Lessons of Wadd

John Harlin

"John—"

I know what's coming. I've heard it many times over the last two years. Mark's on the other end of the line, and I've just sighed my frustrations into his ear. A resigned, depressed flatness in my voice betrays me.

"John, remember the lessons of Wadd?"

"This isn't the time. I can't think that way. Construction is way behind schedule. Really, Mark, I have to focus." Inside, I'm melting.

Adele and I are building a home, the final house in a stepping-stone series that has consumed ten years of our lives. We'll be able to move in within months, but in my heart I'm wiped out. I've lost perspective. We also have a year-old baby, conceived just after Mark's and my Waddington climb, just before Adele and I built the barn and then the house, and exactly during the collapse of our business, *Summit* magazine. We're running low on sleep. I'm not happy.

"Yeah, I know," Mark replies. "My book's been eating at me, too. I haven't been climbing either."

We pause. Finally I reach out. "These things come in seasons, Mark, like a huge expedition. We'll get there." I can say the right words, but I don't feel them. They come from my head, not my heart.

"Will we ever learn?"

1995—Waddington Dreaming

One gray Oregon office morning I check my e-mail. There's a note from Mark: "You and me. Waddington. New route. May." I stare at the message for days while the stress of my decomposing business whirlpools around me. Then Yvette takes a phone message, also from Mark. He repeats the exact same words, nothing more.

Though Mark doesn't realize it, Waddington is the Northwestern mountain I crave above all others. The highest peak in British Columbia's Coast Range, the 13,186-foot summit lies some twenty-five miles inland from the head of Knight Inlet, an eighty-five-mile saltwater fiord. These days climbers generally get there by air. I've been wanting to go by land, bushwhacking, river-fording, and glacier-navigating up to the south face to do the route established by Fritz Wiessner and Bill House in 1936. My goal is a journey wherein the summit is mostly the pretext for a grand wilderness escape. I haven't thought about going soon— Waddington will always be there, I figure. Right now I have business to take care of. But a new route? I give in and return Mark's call, knowing he's not going to let me off the hook. It turns out he has discovered that an entire face—the true south face—has never been climbed. A collection of palisades and couloirs some 3,000 feet tall and at least that wide, the face killed its only known assailant, Alec Dalgleish, who fell to his death two years before

Wiessner's arrival. Wiessner chose an elegant line that leads directly to the summit on its southwest side. His route became a classic, and Dalgleish's true south face, which lies at the head of a separate glacier, was forgotten. Mark rediscovered it in a photo. I agreed that it had to be climbed. This spring. By us.

1976—Santa Barbara

"John Harlin? Who's this John Harlin?" The voice came from the middle of the lecture hall. I was in front, perusing copies of magazines I'd never seen: *Mountain*, *Climbing*, *Summit*. It was the introductory meeting of the University of California at Santa Barbara Mountaineering Club. We'd all filled out forms. The club's officers were sorting through the documents when they'd come across the page with my name on it.

Startled, I looked up. I was twenty but new to the school. After taking a couple of semesters off, I'd transferred to UCSB from the University of Rhode Island, where my mother taught. I'd wanted to participate in more school activities, meet people. Climbing was something I'd flirted with, but in the five years I'd lived on the East Coast, I'd never met anyone who knew much about mountains, let alone climbing them. Before that I'd lived five years in Washington State, where adult friends had taken me up volcanoes.

I called back toward the paper shufflers. "That's me." Several sets of eyes turned my way. One mouth said "John Harlin died doing a new route on the Eiger."

"Yes, that was my father." I flushed with pride that my father—my name—was known by these strangers.

A couple of weeks later the club's van waited for my partner and me to descend Tahquitz Rock, where we'd just completed the *Long Climb*, 5.7. I'd never been on a rock route that long or hard. The day before, we'd climbed *Sahara Terror*, 5.6, my previous ultimate. That night on the drive home my head floated on the weekend's memories: delicate moves on steep slabs, empty space beneath my feet, carefully controlled fear, the sweet, heady rush of triumph. I felt myself a lost child suddenly returned to home's warm embrace—a home filled with wonders beyond any I remembered. Those mountaineering club officers were fast becoming my friends, their craggy world now mine, too. The next year they made me the club's president, as Dad had presided over his own Stanford Alpine Club twenty years earlier.

1995—Waddington Approach

As Mark Jenkins and I board the twin-engine prop plane on Vancouver Island, we're punching each other in boyish excitement. We've been wanting to do a trip together for seven years, ever since we'd met on the phone while I was an editor at *Backpacker* and he was a budding, bluffing freelance writer telling me he wouldn't take a penny under twice what he'd really accept. In the meantime he'd bicycled across Siberia, made the first descent of the headwaters of the Niger River, climbed in Tibet, and written a book. I'd built one house, renovated two others, and was trying to make a successful business out of *Summit*. Mark's writing had inspired me with its flair and power—but depressed me with reminders that my thirties had been crushed under the weight of timbers and spreadsheets. Now we're off on an adventure. A real mountain adventure.

When we deplane on the gravel airstrip at the head of Knight Inlet, a large guided party is waiting to board a helicopter for the flight to the south face. They offer us a lift

John Harlin (left) follows Dougal Haston on the first ascent of the *John Harlin Route* on the north face of the Eiger, 1966. Below, looking up, is Layton Kor. *Chris Bonington*

to our own camp and will drop us off wherever we want to touch down. It would save us a week of humping wilderness supplies, climbing gear, and ski equipment through thick brush, across the Franklin River, up icefalls, and across glaciers. Mark and I grin big stupid grins at each other and shake our heads no. Not hardly. We're here to begin at the beginning. Striding down the gravel logging road toward the mouth of the Franklin, we wave back toward the departing helicopter. When we reach the bay, we drop our packs and step into the salt water. Sea to summit, that's our motto. Let the adventure begin.

Autumn, 1997—Oregon

Not long after Adele and I moved *Summit* from Pennsylvania to Hood River, Oregon, I introduced myself to Mark Hudon, the owner of the local coffee-brewing company. In one of those *Mountain* magazines I'd devoured back in Santa Barbara was an article he'd written about his cross-country travels setting rock climbing's new standards. "States of the Art" was the title, and it was one of the seminal articles of the late 1970s. Mark had been my hero, and in Hood River we became friends. One evening Mark posed a question: "So, what have you done besides being born to a famous father?"

Thirty years after his death in 1966, Dad is still a household name among climbers. Out of the blue I'll get letters proclaiming the impact he'd had on people who'd only barely made his acquaintance but remembered every detail vividly. I'll meet someone who, upon hearing my name, tells me how he began climbing after reading James Ramsey Ullman's biography of my father, *Straight Up: The Life and Death of a Mountaineer*. Dad's rope broke while he was jumaring under an overhang on the new route he'd crafted on the Eiger's north face. The climb, later dubbed the *John Harlin Route*, had been a media sensation, an international race that began when a German team by coincidence launched up the wall nearly simulta-

Marilyn, John, Andréa, and John Harlin at home in Leysin, Switzerland, 1965.

Marilyn Harlin

neously. That winter a nonstop storm cycle slowed the climbers' progress. Dad expected to spend nine days on the face, but six weeks had passed when he fell on March 22.

Mom brought the news to my sister and me as we were playing in our neighbor's chalet in Leysin, Switzerland. She was eight; I would soon turn ten. I remember sitting on the bed, dazed, wordless, while tears flowed on everyone's faces. Mom didn't know details, only that Dad had been seen through the telescope falling 4,000 feet down the wall. When I could speak again, I needed facts. How was it that a rope hadn't caught his fall? I had to know that he hadn't made a mistake, that he hadn't failed.

Dad wasn't keen on mistakes, nor weaknesses. Returning from a big international ski race in Italy the year before, I told him I'd fallen twice. He'd already heard about the first one.

116

He was visibly upset about the second. Another time I'd been tackled by a bully after school. Mom was coming to pick us up, and I screamed to my sister to fetch her. Dad came instead. He was angry—that I was under the bully instead of on top of him. I felt small, ashamed of my impotence.

I hadn't had a chance to tell Dad in person that I'd done better this year in the Italian ski race. It seemed I might win in my age bracket, until faster kids followed. The race director, who had rushed over to be photographed with me, moved off to the new speedsters. But still I knew Dad would be proud.

The Harlin family outside Chalet Pollux, Leysin, 1965: Andréa, John, Marilyn, and John.

John Harlin collection

Later that year, after Dad's death, we moved to the States so Mom could go to graduate school in Seattle. Her fellow students, who knew our names from news accounts of the Eiger climb, took me climbing, backpacking, and kayaking in Washington and in Alaska's Brooks Range. Then Mom got her degree, and when I was fifteen we moved to Rhode Island where there were no mountains and, as far as I could tell at the time, no climbing.

1995—Waddington Approach

It is raining as Mark and I pitch our first camp along the Franklin River. We've covered about six miles today, mostly on a gravel logging road. For a couple of miles we might as well have taken a truck, but then alder healed the scar and we were pushing our way down a bear path. For a couple of hundred yards we even tailed its large, black-furred maker, who slipped quietly along just ahead of us until he vanished into the woods, much to our relief. Then the road became inundated by multiple beaver dams, and finally we bushwhacked to bigger gravel along the riverside. All afternoon increasingly gray clouds and ever-steepening green valley-walls tightened their grips. Here at camp it is raining lightly. On the slopes above, phantom waterfalls plunge behind gauzy veils. A few miles past the last sign of logging, there's no evidence humans have ever touched this landscape. It feels wild. Really wild. The bear helped. But why not a Bigfoot? It's a wonderful thought. We're here to explore, to respond to whatever reveals itself to us. We don't want to know what lies ahead. We want to discover it.

It's still drizzling when we strike off in the morning. We carry our skis in our hands like walking staffs on the gravel bars, and we poke and drag them through the brushy sections. When the clouds part briefly high up a hanging side valley, we glimpse cascading glaciers. The river is low, allowing us to walk on gravel for much of the distance. It's the beginning of May and the summer snowmelt hasn't yet turned this stream into the torrent it will become. In the 1930s, when Don and Phyllis Munday first forged up this valley to make the initial attempts on Waddington, the glacier came several miles further down the valley than it currently does, and getting onto it was relatively straightforward. Now, however, we've heard that the glacier's retreat has left a nearly impassable section on the north bank of the river—the side we're on—and that we'll probably need to cross the whitewater. Low as it is, we're still not seeing any place calm enough for us to consider the 100-foot ford. We put off worrying about it, confident that something will turn up.

At midday we reach a most amazing obstacle. A band of rock—diamond hard and in no mood to give way to mere liquid—blocks the river's passage. Through it is cut the narrowest of slices, in places just fifteen feet across. Through this gash surges the entirety of our river, a volume normally spread out five or more times that width. Mark and I spend hours awestruck by the power of this spectacle—and trying to find a way to cross it. Just as we'd been warned, upstream a multi-thousand-foot cliff blocks our passage. We see a ledge system about 500 feet above the river that might connect through to the Franklin Glacier beneath Waddington, but we'd much rather find a way across the river than tangle with the hideously loose wall above.

Anywhere upstream above the gash would be too dangerous to attempt our river crossing—to be swept into the maelstrom would be instant death. Could we could cut a tree that would bridge the flow somewhere in the narrows? No, we're too frightened to trust anything of a size we could manhandle into place. Hours later, after various false starts, we find a spot where we can fight our way across the hip-deep current. With our first great hurdle overcome, we gleefully make camp on the other side.

Our third morning out dawns gray and damp. Shortly after breaking camp, we're staring at the tortured tongue of the great Franklin Glacier. Skirting around its ghastly black tip, we soon are forced into a horror-filled dance across vast boulderfields where the stones are perched at the angle of repose on a substrate of black ice. Rocks, starting singly and gathering into a chaotic mob within seconds, charge angrily downslope to the glacier, now several hundred feet below our teetering bodies. Finally we find a route through the lateral moraine that we can follow onto the safety of solid glacier ice. A short way up the glacier, where soft snow mandates a switch to skis, we pitch our tent.

Day four. It's still drizzling as we weave ankle-deep on skis through a maze of snow-covered crevasses. The rain falters as we pass the first icefall and point our skis straight up the center of the glacier. Camp is up when the cloud ceiling rips apart. We gaze northeastward. Ten thousand feet above us, trailing ragged streamers of fiery snowplumes, Waddington terrorizes the landscape. As the alpenglow fades to dusk, we continue staring at the chilling spectacle. The mountain looks unimaginably cold. Horrifically high. Frighteningly harsh. Unquestionably bigger and stronger than I.

1980—Colorado

A ranger at Rocky Mountain National Park was giving me a lift. As we pulled out of Komito Boots' parking lot, he asked my name. Chuckling lightly, he retorted, "Back from the dead, I see." It was a new twist. The response I was used to went along the lines of, "Any relation to the real John Harlin?" To which I simply said—and still say—"Yes, he was my father."

Earlier that year I'd been visiting Reinhard Karl, a German climber. We were drinking beer in a pub in the Pfaltz, surrounded by sandstone towers that swarmed with climbers. My name had made it from table to table until someone stood up and called across the room, "So, John Harlin, have you come to climb the Eiger?"

Actually, I almost had. The previous year, when I knew I was returning to Europe for most of a year to be with Adele while she spent her junior year in France, my goal was to climb my father's route on the mountain he was most known for—probably after doing some of his other first ascents in the French Alps. I was in the middle of the two or three years I had given myself before entering graduate school. I wanted to tame the climbing beast within, to get it out of my system sufficiently so that I could actually concentrate on academics. Then, in the summer of 1979, the summer before Europe, I watched my climbing partner die.

We were descending beneath the Hourglass Couloir on Mt. Robson after climbing its Wishbone Arête. Above us perched a massive wall of teetering ice—a hanging glacier. I was no mountain wizard, but I knew well that hanging glaciers were things you ran away from, especially with darkness fast approaching. As Chuck Hospedales and I scrambled down snowfields punctuated by occasional short rock bands and ledges, that giant icewall kept me nervous. I forged ahead, scouting the descent route while Chuck, less experienced even than I, followed tentatively. I had climbed down a ten-foot section of vertical rock and stood waiting for my partner. It was the last bit of rock; once Chuck reached my ledge we could catwalk over to a snow couloir that would lead us safely to the glacier below. I coached him over the bulge, pointing out the moves.

"Do you have that handhold?" I yelled up.

"No!" he half screamed, half whimpered, just as gravity took control. I lunged, touched cloth but could not hold. Chuck bounced off my ledge and plunged down, his desperate cries blending in my brain with the sparks that flew duskward each time his crampons struck. By the time I reached him, 500 feet below, he was blue with death.

I ran in a blind panic through the darkness across the glacier toward the hut. I popped through the snow once, felt my legs waving in space, pulled myself up, and ran on again. Two climbers were in the hut. I'm not sure I spoke a complete sentence to them. I spent the night baring my soul into the hut's logbook and the next morning I was out before dawn.

When I called my mother, I knew that my dreams of extreme alpine climbing were over. Through Chuck, I learned the effect my own death would have on Mom. It seemed too great a price, far more upsetting than the effect of my death on me. Adele would survive, I figured. But the pain my absence would inflict on Mom seemed more than she could stand, more than I had any right to inflict.

Not that I would stop climbing altogether. I was too selfish for that. I would merely try to be safer. I would carefully control my climbing objectives, which meant above all that I would try to resist the siren call of high mountains, of the alpine routes that had been my father's passion. But I would always climb. And, inevitably, the discipline of safety would sometimes go the way of most of my disciplines, the victim of indulgence.

When the query reached me in that German pub—"Have you come to climb the Eiger?"—I wanted the mountain badly. I had to do it. Felt ashamed that I wasn't doing it. But I could not. I replied simply, "No," and drank my beer.

1995—The Great Wadd

When Mark and I peer out the tent on our fifth morning, the mountain has been reborn. Golden sunshine has replaced last evening's plumes of frozen fire. Like a Siren

route hidden

X

Mt. Waddington's Buckler Face, with *The Cowboy Way* and high camp marked.

John Harlin

perched at the source of our glacier, the summit calls out the calmness of her ice slopes, the warmth of her stony flanks. Seduced, we'll march ten miles today through icefalls and over the wide flat expanses of the Corridor Glacier, always aiming toward our virgin face, always wondering where to place our line. Our eyes attempt to undress the distant mountain through shear doggedness of focus.

Here we can finally put the mountain into perspective, something no photos we've seen have been able to do. Waddington is essentially the massive, triple-summited crest of a northwest-southeast trending ridgeline. Thus, the entire 180-degree sweep of the southwest side of the mountain became known as the "south" face. In reality, this southern flank is split into two major faces. The southwest face, which leads directly to Waddington's main summit, is where Wiessner put his route. We could reach that face by turning left up the main Franklin Glacier to its Dais Glacier tributary. Instead, we are following another tributary glacier, the Corridor, which leads to the Buckler Glacier, on the forgotten face where Dalgleish perished. This compass-true south face rises as a huge triangle pointing to the summit of the Tooth, the southeastern of the three summit towers—of which the middle is the highest. Whatever route we settle on, we see that once we've ascended the Dalgleish Face, as we're now calling it, we'll have to traverse around the northeast side of the Tooth to reach the main summit spire.

We camp where the Buckler Glacier rears upward. The next morning, after caching our skis and extra food and fuel, we point ourselves straight toward the great unclimbed wall above. Rising from our gear stash at 7,200 feet to the glacier-top platform at 9,200 feet is a moderately cascading glacier. Most of its crevasses are still full of snow this early in the season. Except where distracted by thin snowbridges and narrow fins of ice across wide crevasses, our eyes remain on the face above, probing, questing. Rock buttresses tower directly overhead. To the right we know there is a prominent cleaving couloir, the most striking line in the photo Mark had discovered. But Mark had also discovered Don Serl, a Canadian who, as luck would have it, has for years been planning to climb that very route. Indeed Don, though gracious as could be, was somewhat shaken that we might reach this face before he did. After considering the likelihood of our success, he altered his climbing plans so that he could be here with us. He and a partner should be showing up any day, arriving by helicopter. Mark and I have decided not to climb his dream line without him—unless no reasonable alternatives present themselves.

As we move up the Buckler Glacier, our eyes probe the face left of the rock buttresses. A wide icefield tapers into twin couloirs that disappear into rock walls above. We decide to try the right gully tomorrow, though its upper reaches remain inscrutable even as we climb closer and closer. By noon we reach a level platform where we can set up the tent. The afternoon passes with us sunbathing naked in a great blazing reflection oven.

At three a.m. we hardly need the alarms, we're so excited. Stars beam brightly on the snow; the taste of adventure is pungent in our mouths. There's no way that we're going to risk bad weather by waiting for Don, but at least we've chosen a line far to the left of his. In fact, his route lies hidden in a deep gully we haven't even investigated.

We rope up to cross the first crevasse and stay roped on the snow/ice slope above. Here we alternate between the steep snow/icefield and the rock from which it hangs. Occasionally, where wisdom dictates, Mark places a screw or a nut that I pull out a few minutes later on my way past. We're climbing simultaneously, moving up the slope like a wave that keeps on going, an ever-upward sweeping current. Soon we're rounding the corner where the icefield narrows. Above us, the increasingly icy slope doglegs into the still mysterious rock wall. Below, the smooth wall plunges 1,500 feet to camp, then continues more roughly for another 2,000 feet until the valley flattens.

I'm following Mark across a six-foot-wide groove in the ice directly under the mystery gully when a spindrift avalanche strikes me with its velvet glove. Powdery crystals tinkling like broken glass cover me in a gentle but completely enveloping cascade. I cling to the slope, my body lying tight against the ice, my front points and ice tools deeply embedded, holding me fast against the current. I feel embraced by the mountain, like I've been taken into her icy bosom.

When the spindrift slackens, we move upward. A few hundred feet higher Mark disappears into the snaking couloir. He's now witnessing what we couldn't see from below, and he's stopped to belay. When I reach him I look up into a couloir perhaps ten feet across with a ribbon of water ice stairstepping down its center. We're overjoyed. This will go! And quickly, too.

Two thousand feet above camp Mark and I have rendezvoused for the first time, breaking the momentum of our upward sweep. Our plan had been to swap leads whenever this time came, but I don't have the heart to take it from Mark just when the going at last gets technical. Instead, we agree that he'll lead through this gully, and that I'll take the summit pinnacle. Mark strikes off in a blaze of flashing steel. Through the rope I can feel the electric buzz of a truly happy man.

Jenkins leading in the hidden couloir on *The Cowboy Way.*

John Harlin

The ice proves casual, with vertical bulges no higher than fifteen feet each. I'm hooked into the tallest of them when a spindrift avalanche slaps me in the face. At first the flow presents no problems, but soon it swarms so thick I can't breathe. I'm beginning to get nervous when finally I figure out what to do: tilt my head into the ice and push my body out. Voilà, an air cavity opens in the space beneath my head. When the current ebbs, I dash upward to Mark.

Three ice pitches pass all too quickly, then I swing into the lead for more simul-climbing up a few hundred feet of steep snow underlain by hard ice. When I pop over Waddington's main ridgeline it is like stepping into the jet stream. Instead of stopping to belay Mark up, I simply lean into the wind and posthole in soft, fresh snow toward the summit pinnacle. It's almost flat up here, an incongruous sub-summit platform. Mark is up and also hunched into the wind when a deep roar seems to shake the mountain. It grows stronger, racing invisibly at us. Avalanche? Then a four-engine military bomber bursts directly over our shoulders and roars across the mountain, well beneath the summit.

Our composures recovered, we are back to postholing when the plane screams straight at us, flying low enough that we almost duck. Just when we think the joke has gone too far a cylinder tumbles out, trailed by a red streamer. The plane bellows by and vanishes around the mountain.

We do a clod-footed dash to where the cylinder fell into a bergschrund. I jump down into the soft snow, grab the bubble-wrapped cylinder, and Mark tensions me back out. My ice àxe slices through the tape, and I reach inside the bubblewrap to pull out a bottle of Captain Morgan rum. Mark and I stare at each other dumbfounded. Beneath the image of a grinning pirate, the label reads: "For Captain Morgan adventure was the spice of life and rum was the spirit of the adventurous." I reach into the cylinder again and pull out a copy of *Penthouse International*, a special "Girls of the World" edition. These Canadians are right friendly folks, we figure. But one last look inside the cylinder reveals a note: "To Jim and the boys, good luck." A case of mistaken identity, and now we have poor Jim's wine and women.

1963—Chamonix

Mom, Dad, and I hiked all day from the Chamonix campground where we were living that summer up to the Mer de Glace, where we roped up and weaved above deep blue crevasses on crisply crunching crampons. Then we scrambled up steel ladders and cables to reach a hut near the base of the Aiguille du Fou, where Dad had been working on a new route with Tom Frost, Gary Hemming, and Stewart Fulton. Near the hut Dad, Stewart, and I made a two-pitch climb, which I remember mostly from the photos of my gap-toothed grin beneath a helmet that overhung my head by several inches. More clearly, I recall the following night when I tossed frightened in my bunk while lightning split the sky and thunder clattered the windows. Storms didn't scare me per se; in fact, I reveled in them. But Dad was up on the cliff, and, far worse, Mom was somewhere on the glacier between the Fou and the hut. She had gone up to the base of the hidden face to see Dad off, her only mountaineering excursion since we'd moved to Europe. She was returning from her high-point with a pair of strangers when the storm rolled in. I'd find out later that her inexperienced companions pressed hard to make it all the way back to the hut. But as they struggled through the storm-wracked night on the heavily crevassed glacier, Mom forced a stop at a point where they could huddle in the safety of a small crevasse. Better to have a frightened child at the hut than to risk orphaning him with foolish, emotion-driven movement.

1995—Waddington's summit

Neither Captain Morgan nor his bevy of playmates distract us for long. Soon we're scanning, with some trepidation, the tower above. We've come 3,000 feet already and, frankly, had not expected to find the summit quite so imposing. We're standing at just over 12,000 feet, and, on any normal peak, this shoulder would be the summit ridge. Instead, bursting out of the gentle snow is a 900-foot spear of rock that skewers the sky. Actually, it's a double spear. The left point, the Tooth, rises 600 feet. A notch separates the Tooth from the true summit, which rises the extra 300 feet. Photos had given us the impression that these pinnacles would be but three pitches tall. But we'd been deluded by the massive scale of the entire mountain, which dwarfs its summit spires.

Mostly, though, we hadn't expected the rock to be so sheer. We'll find out later that while chasing the Spirits of Adventure with heads bowed against the wind, we walked right past a fourth-class ramp leading to the notch—the normal ascent route for parties who climb Waddington from the northeast. Right now we're beneath a near-vertical ice hose that plunges directly from the notch. While it's eminently climbable, ice this steep is neither Mark's nor my forte, so we look for rockier alternatives. The right wall is too steep to consider. But the left one shows a couple of weaknesses. After stashing much of our gear, I lash my crampons to my pack, holster both axes, and grab rock.

I'm aiming for a shattered concavity that seems to offer climbable features. To get to the rock, however, I have to scamper along the edge of a steep bit of snow clinging to the lowermost forty feet of the face. Delicate rock climbing takes me fifteen feet above the glacier's flat snowdeck. Then I carefully step onto the snow to my left. *Whump!* It breaks loose and together we drop to a soft glacier landing. I shake myself off and climb further across until I'm forced onto the snow again. *Whump!* Twenty-five feet this time. I consider cramponing up, then decide to try a crack to the right instead.

A hand-traverse takes me to the 5.8-ish fissure. Occasionally the rock is solid enough to hold trustworthy protection, but often the strata have separated and merely lean against the wall like a tower of cinderblocks. One hundred feet up the crack dies against a blank wall and a snow-slabbed ramp. I place a piton at the top of the crack and try climbing onto the ramp, but after several attempts I don't trust the pin enough for the delicate balance move and so I downclimb twenty feet to the last trustworthy section of the crack, where I place a backup nut. Back at the ramp I knock off loose snow to reveal a good, round foothold about thigh height, but nothing for my hands to grab. Just out of reach is a slab of soft ice. I pull out my drooped tool and hook the ice. It pops off. I wobble backwards and step down to my stance. In my other holster is a seventy-centimeter Chouinard-Frost bamboo-shaft axe, my trusty companion of nearly two decades. It nicks into thin ice two inches past the broken edge. I tug gently. The ice stays. I pull myself gingerly onto the foothold, then clear snow from the ramp above. A couple of tiny edges take me to a steep crack. At last, protection!

Later, Mark swings his arms and stomps his feet repeatedly to warm them before stepping onto the rock, glad finally to be on the move again. When he pulls above the ramp and into the steep crack above, he yells up. "John, you're a hardman!"

I know it's not true, but still a warm shock of emotion pulses in my heart. I savor the feeling, basking in its glow as Mark draws nearer. This isn't vanity, though I'm hardly immune to that weakness. No. This is a boy hearing his father's praise. Did I really do well?

On the semi-hanging belay I put on my crampons before scrambling up a face of mixed ice and rock. End of rope. Mark follows quickly. Chilled, I launch again. Soon I'm at what would be the standard fourth-class ramp except that it's filled with water ice. Near rope's end I see that my ice ramp reaches its apex at a sunlit knife-edge. I break through a small cornice and poke my head up, tumbling snowballs down the vertical gully on the other side. My eyes follow the couloir down several thousand plunging feet of evil-looking rottenness. Perched on this knife-edge, I peer rightward toward another equally steep but shorter couloir, the ice gully we'd declined three hours earlier and 400 feet below.

Despite the newfound sun (we've been climbing on the shady side of the Tooth), the wind tears away my body heat. By the time Mark pulls up, I'm chattering. Since the belay anchors here are pitiful at best, I urge Mark to quickly cross over to the base of an ice-choked chimney where he can belay. Much to my horror, when Mark reaches the chimney he begins climbing slowly upward. He doesn't feel the chill that has been growing in my bones until my body is shaking uncontrollably. By the time I catch up to Mark's belay I'm a

Jenkins exiting the hidden couloir. *John Harlin*

Jenkins on the route's penultimate pitch. The Tooth rises in the sunshine behind him.

John Harlin

changed person. I'm cold about the summit and nearly frozen toward the idea of risking a nighttime descent. I know what can happen to ropes on rappels. They get stuck. Then what, in this howling cold? Then you freeze to death. Our extra clothes and bivy sacks are in our packs guarded by Captain Morgan.

"Mark. I don't know about this. It's g-g-getting late."

Mark's gaze is quizzical. He's still in full form, ready to charge on into the great unknown. He's not used to quitting, doesn't even think about the option this close to a goal. But he doesn't question me, either. We've talked incessantly about risks and responsibilities. My threshold is obviously lower than his. I'm also much colder.

"It's nearly four o'clock now. Let's set a turn-around time."

"Five?"

At five o'clock we're two pitches higher, well above where we thought the summit would be. But when Mark reaches me at the belay, turning back isn't an option, not even for me. The summit is at last in sight, I'm sure of it, at the top of the next pitch. My front-points fly me up the ice-glazed rock until I stop to belay twenty feet shy of the apex. There is only enough room up there for one person to stand at a time.

Mark scrambles until his belly balances against the popsicle summit all frilled in rime ice. He tosses snow into the blasting sky, the low sun setting the flakes ablaze as they swirl briefly like galaxies before being whipped into space. When I take my turn I'm suddenly standing in a vast white world of emptiness curving to every horizon. Only the narrowest column of rock, it seems, forms the pedestal that suspends me at a point exactly 13,186 feet above the sea—and 2,000 feet higher than any peak in sight. At this climactic point, the massive pyramid below is as nothing. My crampons bite into one square foot of icy rock. That's all there is.

Four sloping rappels, with only one major hangup, take us back to the notch, and three vertical ones drop us to our packs at the glacier. The sky is an exploded beet this evening. Crimson clouds bleed their color into a wilderness of glaciers and craggy summits. We melt downward along the darkening ridgeline, racing against the specter of a cold and hungry night huddled in a crevasse.

No one has ever been where we're going now. Earlier in the day such thoughts quickened our blood. Now, with darkness about to envelop us far above camp, exhilaration turns to apprehension. Mostly, we're concerned with where to rappel off the ridge onto the mysterious Dalgleish Face and whether we'll find our way in the dark. Reversing our ascent route would involve endless rappelling. Instead we are descending the southeast ridge, which we can walk, then trusting that we'll find a rappel route down a relatively short cliff band back to camp. When we reach a saddle about 3,000 feet beneath the summit, there is just enough light to see a snowslope leading toward what we suspect might be a hidden couloir that could in turn lead to the Buckler Glacier, where our tent sits waiting. We rappel 150 feet to the lip of a cliff. By the time I'm done placing an anchor at the edge of the precipice, it's too dark to see into the cleavage below. We launch over the edge on the simple faith that we'll figure out each new rappel as we reach it. I slide over an overhang into a caver's blackness.

Three ropelengths later we find our hunch is right: we've touched down in a steep snow gully. Six more rappels bring us to postholing below the bergschrund. By the time we reach camp, some twenty hours after leaving it, I'm collapsing in the snow every few hundred feet. But my heart is in the constellations above. We've made it. We're home.

Voices greet us through the darkness. It's Don Serl and Jim Elzinga calling out from their tent. They had spotted our camp on the glacier and found the site just flat enough for their helicopter to drop them off. They are planning to rise in a couple of hours to try their route. We debrief them on our efforts.

Mark and I talk ourselves to sleep, as we have each night. The Lessons of Wadd, we call our philosophical ramblings. This last week we've transcended the strange, infuriating tyranny of our so-called civilized lives. Here we've found true life again, rediscovered what makes us whole. We knew it the moment we started walking. Felt it grow stronger each day. Felt the world pour into us until now we're as big as it is. This is real. This is where we belong. The workaday scene at home will have to change, will change, will never grow more important than life again. We convince ourselves this will be true.

I don't talk about my niggling doubts. My five o'clock summit deadline. My weakness. The unquiet corner of my brain that never lets me forget that I almost gave up so near the top.

1962-66—Europe

I was six when Dad took me on my first multi-pitch climb in the Calanques of southern France. We came here often because Mediterranean sun was the mirror image of storm-bound Chamonix, where Dad otherwise would have been climbing. This was also the year Dad climbed the Eiger, becoming the first English-speaker to ascend the peak's famed north face. Despite the passage of twenty-four years since the original 1938 route, there was still but one way up its great north wall, nicknamed the *Mordwand*—Murder Wall—for all its victims (twenty deaths and only twenty-seven ascents). Dad was already searching for a new route, one that would reflect the contemporary cutting edge: the pursuit of directness and purity of line. Over the next four years he returned again and again to reconnoiter, even to attempt his new route with a variety of international partners.

Finally, he could wait no longer: the time had come to pull it off. Dad resigned his teaching job at the American college and high school in Leysin, where my mother also taught. He would devote himself full time to his new climbing school, to a book he was writing about his climbs, and, above all, to making sure the Eiger Direct happened that winter. My mother would provide the family income.

Dad's Eiger partners were Layton Kor, one of America's premier rockclimbers, and Dougal Haston, a young Scottish ice climber. Dad had arranged sponsorship, including London's *Daily Telegraph*, which sent Peter Gilman to report the story, and Chris Bonington (a Briton who had been the second English-speaker to climb the Eiger's north face) as the cameraman on the sidelines. The climb was supposed to take nine days and be accomplished without fixed ropes. But fierce storms delayed the attempt, and eventually Dad dislocated his shoulder skiing beneath the face. He'd also contracted bronchitis. The team was back in Leysin waiting for better weather when they got the news that a large German team had come for the same route using full Himalayan siege tactics, ones that would allow them to climb despite the worst storm season on record. Dad's team rushed back to the face to fix their own parallel ropes. Bonington was conscripted into helping on the lower face and ended up leading a key ice passage. With a de facto international race that stretched on for six weeks, the world press had just what it needed: the climb made daily headlines.

On March 22, Dougal jumared over an overhang. Years later, after Dougal himself had been killed by an avalanche, Mom informed me that he had told her he had noticed a fray in the rope but had thought it would hold. Dad was thirty when his lifeline broke. Dougal never repeated his confession, and I don't condemn him for his mistaken judgment. As a climber, I know that judgment defines the lengths of our lives—and those of our partners. We don't always make the right call.

Had Dad lived, I may not have continued climbing. His competitiveness was as legendary as his passions and his grand dreams. Mom tells me that my skiing skills, already surpassing his, were igniting a rivalry in him. Skiing, not climbing, was my own passion back then, and, in hindsight, the idea of following Dad's handholds in the mountains once my reach could rival his would have been nearly unthinkable. But he wasn't there when I grew up. And, somehow, my adult life came to parallel his. My intended career in biology evolved by a series of inevitable mutations into mountain guiding, writing books on climbing, editing a mountain magazine. In this vertical world there was an almost seamless connection with my father. Doors opened magically, connections to prominent climbers came instantly. Sometimes I felt an impostor, that my achievements didn't live up to the standards of a name I didn't really deserve. But usually I buried such thoughts while basking in recognition gleaned from what I half-believed were my own labors.

In 1991 I was a guest at the Trento Film Festival, a prestigious event at which my father had once been a juror. I myself had judged three leading North American mountain film festivals and was relishing this brush with their classic European forebear. Afterward, a German friend and I went ski-mountaineering, and in an Alpine chalet he interviewed me for a story in a German mountain magazine. At the time I felt flush with myself. I had just relaunched the venerable *Summit* and believed I was en route to some high point, that momentum was on my side.

A few months later the story came out. Its title: "Yes, He Was My Father." I had already outlived Dad in years. I also had hoped that, at least among my friends, I might by now have emerged from his shadow.

1995—Leaving Waddington

The sun is burning through our tent as we wake. Don and Jim are still in camp. At four this morning Don's head was throbbing from the suddenness of their flight from sea level to 9,200 feet. They'll head up tomorrow instead. We're thrilled, as it gives us the day to swap lies. Turns out Mark and Jim had been on Everest together in 1986, Jim leading a disciplined Canadian team that put Sharon Wood on the summit, Mark in a dissonant gaggle of strong-willed Americans who failed. Mark and Jim haven't seen each other since.

The next morning we watch the summit-bound team posthole into the darkness, then we return to our contented slumbers. When daylight arrives it's sunless, the blue skies having been replaced by roiling clouds. Carnivorous air is tearing at the upper reaches of the buttresses above us. Mark and I know that we would never have reached the summit on a day like this; we wonder how Don and Jim are faring. Since we won't be here to greet them, we arrange in their tent a welcoming party—the worldly ladies and Captain Morgan—then pack up and head down the glacier.

By the time we're mounting Mystery Pass on our ski out to the airstrip at Scar Creek, the cloud's embrace is complete, a white darkness nearly as blinding as a moonless night. The pull of gravity tells us when we've crested the pass, but as we slide down the other side we have no perception of space. We could run straight into a crevasse or a cliff if it weren't for one thing, or rather a hundred thousand things: dead flies. They speckle the snow in lifeless droves. Evidently they've been blown toward the pass and overcome by cold. With their help we can see several feet ahead, the limit of our vision, defined by black fireflies in a white night.

Then, for a moment, the cloud lifts just enough to reveal a tent not 100 yards away. It turns out to be a party of skiers overcome by the fog. They invite us to tea and stories, which we can hardly refuse even though we'd planned to poke along for another hour or two. John Baldwin, Gordon Ferguson, and Brian Sheffield are completing the first circumski of Waddington. They can even explain the intended recipients of our airdrop—a military team training for Makalu.

The next morning we strike off on compass bearings into another windy white void. Four inches of snow fell overnight. The skiers intend to wait out the weather, but a few hours later the clouds are lifting and we see them quickly catching up. We part ways at treeline, the skiers continuing further down the ridge.

Mark and I cut down the sidehill into the Scar Creek Valley, where we know a logging road will provide brush-free passage. The adventure feels like it is drawing to a close when instead the ground grows steeper and steeper. Pretty soon we're holding onto trees. The trees thin as we approach a boxed-in drainage, and our heavy packs are tipping us off balance so badly that we decide to take them off and hold them against the slope. That way we can drop our packs if necessary while we remain clinging to the slope, or so we hope. Mark is just below me when he loses control of his pack. It tumbles 200 feet and crashes into a creek. Weightless, Mark scrabbles across a wicked dirt slope, but when I try to follow with my pack I find it's too much. So I angle down to the last trees and rappel into the creek, where Mark has found most, but not all, of his pack's contents. Another couple of hours of steep scrambling down the gully brings us to the logging road.

This time we know the adventurous part is over. We're slapping each other on the back and grinning ear to ear when 100 yards ahead of us a humped-back bear strides out of the bushes. He stops and stares at us. Grizzly, no doubt about it. Why not? We've had every other adventure we can think of. Mark and I quickly choose our respective alder trees and plan how to climb them should that become necessary. Then we wait. The bear waits. We wait. Tired of standing, the bear lies down in the middle of the road, still looking at us. Mark and I grow weary of the game; we're hoping to fly home tonight. We explain this to the bear, but he doesn't budge. So we break out our cookpot and ice axes and beat a fearsome racket as we march together sideways toward the bear, trying to make our packs look like humps more fearsome than his own. A hundred feet later our ursine sparring partner lumbers to his feet and saunters into the bushes. During the next mile, we check our backsides regularly. Sweet adrenaline tingles our spines. Hot life surges. The adventure never ends.

Winter, 1997—Oregon

The house is finished, or at least we've moved into it and signed the mortgage papers. Siena is now toddling around in the living room. She's so delightful that it's sometimes impossible to leave her and return to work.

"*Whatdis?*" she demands, pointing to whatever.

Watching Siena, I think back to the long, tent-bound conversations with Mark. A passionate father, his monologues on the joys of children helped set the baby trap for me. So did the equally smitten Jeff Bowman, with whom I'd climbed the *Salathé Wall* in another desperate escape from the office the year before. Mostly, though, my longing for a kid surfaced whenever I reflected back to the great moments of my own childhood, all of which took place outdoors. Above all, there was that magnificent summer in Chamonix, of crunching on the Mer de Glace, of boulderhopping with my sister. There was skiing on the Diableret's crevasse-free glacier, carving great sweeping backward turns at the age of eight. Some of my earliest memories: age three, waddling in a row of fellow ducklings behind our ski teacher in Grenoble, then sliding downhill through her outspread legs. Age thirteen, stepping onto the summit of Mt. Chamberlin, the highest peak in the Brooks Range, and gazing across the vast tundra landscape that I'd fallen in love with in the stories of Mowat, Chrisler, Murie, London. These and so many like them were the experiences that filled my heart, that grew my youthful brain. Each memory cried out for sharing the outdoors with a new young soul.

But babies don't conform to neatly packaged memories. And to all those who warn against building houses while cradling an infant, I confess they're right. Over and over I've lived the frightened, chattering four o'clock hour on Mt. Waddington with her summit still out of sight. I tell Mark over the phone that the quavering in my voice is a passing phase, that my circuits are but momentarily overloaded. But my heart doesn't believe the words even as they come out. Could mere reason ever subdue the unbridled fear of life's own adventure?

On Waddington we thought we'd figured it out. True life was a wilderness quest: river crossings, box canyons, bears, virgin true-south faces. We were right, of course. And wrong. There are also toddlers taking their first steps wearing nothing but an angel smile and a very crooked halo. There's fatigue from overwork and too little sleep. There are warm homes built with hard labor. There are falls in ski races, and missing fathers. You do not escape to adventure. You do not escape from it. You live it each and every day.

John and
Siena Harlin
on Mt. Adams, 1996.

Adele Hammond

Jumaring on
Trango Tower.

Warren Hollinger

132

CLIMBER AS WRITER
From the Armchair to the Tetons

David Stevenson

On my first climbing trip to the west we had maybe one day of good weather on which it would have been possible to climb. We were poised at the Lower Saddle between the Grand and Middle Teton. Our plan was to first ascend Middle by its north ridge and then do the Grand. We had a copy of Leigh Ortenburger's guide, which we felt privileged even to own—it was a yellow-covered temporary edition. Reading it was another thing. No, that wasn't the problem. We could read it all right—we just couldn't match the words on the page to the terrain we could see. We wandered up to where we thought the route on Middle should be, but never for a moment felt like we were on anything like a route. Finally, we scrambled back down, conserving our energy for the next day's attempt on the Grand. The arrival of winter that night kept us from repeating the scene on a trickier route on a larger peak. In four weeks we hadn't reached the top of a single mountain. My friend McInerney had a hundred-dollar car that was missing teeth in its flywheel, so we drove back to Michigan without turning off the ignition. It was a great trip.

I never thought that reading about climbing was anything like the act of climbing, but it is a mistake that people apparently make. Otherwise, why would litigation-conscious magazines and catalogs be compelled to print disclaimers? My favorite is the first sentence from *Rock & Ice's* disclaimer appended to their guide section: "It is impossible to perfectly describe the real changing world and what each person's experience will be in it." It's true, of course, but ironic: a magazine's goal is to work against this impossibility. This one from a recent Black Diamond catalog is more typical: "Books and catalogs like this one can help, but they are no substitute for personal instruction by a qualified person well versed in all appropriate safety techniques."

But climbing *literature* is hardly limited to guidebooks and catalog copy. More people are climbing than ever before, though not all of them would necessarily agree on what climbing is. The more participants, the more attempting to write about it, the larger the reading audience. But what of the writing? Is *more* better? Is all this writing about the mountains good writing? People agree less on this than on what climbing is.

I remember when Jeremy Bernstein's profile of Yvon Chouinard appeared in the *New Yorker*. It was the highly polished writing typical of the magazine: clear prose and impeccable style. Yet I had a friend, a climber and also a reader of the magazine, who claimed that the article was bogus. His judgment was based on Bernstein's bungled description of how jumars operate. For my friend, this invalidated the whole article; the writer, he claimed, simply didn't know what he was talking about. It was clear to me that the writer knew very well what he was talking about, but that an editor had messed up the description of jumaring in an attempt to render it in "clear prose." Climbers can be a tough audience. We're all experts, or so we think, suspicious of "outsiders" speaking for us.

I've encountered this same attitude occasionally with regard to the novel *Solo Faces*, by James Salter. I think it the best novel about climbing yet written by an American. However, among climbers there is a strange resistance to it. Why? Because, they think, who is James Salter? What routes has he done? Who has he climbed with? Did you say he's a writer, has written screenplays? Well, no wonder.

Ironically, Salter himself is tough on the book. The book is loosely based on the life of Gary Hemming, a larger-than-life climber who made his reputation in the Alps in the 1960s and later took his own life. Salter himself has always felt that the book doesn't measure up to the real-life Hemming. In other words, Salter reads his own book like a climber might! The reader who has never heard of Hemming might perhaps admire the book more. Perhaps the more one knows about the real history the less one admires the fictional re-creation.

One scene I felt was a stretch had Rand, the Hemming-based character, playing Russian roulette with his old climbing partner, now confined to a wheelchair. I remember thinking, please, spare me the Hollywood melodrama. Only recently, upon reading Pete Sinclair's *We Aspired* (which I'll discuss later), did I learn that Hemming apparently really did play Russian roulette with Barry Corbet, crippled in a helicopter crash. Double irony: the moment that rang false to me did so not because it was a fictional creation (because it isn't exactly that). Rather, the scene's shortcomings seemed aesthetically out of place: they didn't fit the art. Fiction tells us what might have been and Salter sweetly grants Hemming the reprieve Hemming never granted himself: a life after climbing. Rand survives his demons and lives on in flat desert obscurity.

In an address to the Montagna Avventura 2000 Conference, David Harris, novelist and former editor of the *Canadian Alpine Journal*, makes some interesting observations about the evolution of mountain writing. He defines climbing writing as a true "ghetto literature," written only by climbers and essentially inaccessible to anyone but climbers. Aside from the mistaken usage of "ghetto"—after all, climbers choose their lives, not so of ghetto-dwellers—there is some truth to Harris's observation. But it is a truth that goes against the grain of a writer's instinct. Wittgenstein, in his introduction to the *Tractatus*, said, "Perhaps this book will be understood only by someone who has himself already had the thoughts that are expressed in it—or at least similar thoughts." But, having said that, he devoted his life to writing as clearly as possible. As writers, we try to avoid the old excuse for the failed punch line: "I guess you had to be there." In fact, our words are supposed to stand in for being there: we know it's a poor substitute, doomed to failure, but the attempt is to create—for those who have only the authority of our words—our world for them.

Lifting my pack at the Lupine Meadows parking lot, I remind myself that this feeling isn't déjà vu. I really have done this before. A mile or so into the hike we meet Mike Friedman, just finishing a traverse that began with Teewinot, crossed over Mt. Owen, and ended with the north face of the Grand. Mike is an acquaintance from undergraduate school who works summers as an Exum guide. For a few summers I'd bump into him every year either at Jenny Lake or at Dornan's, where the view of the range from the bar window is unsurpassed, and we'd talk about our mutual friends, one of whom is Jack Lewis. It is, in fact, Jack who is just behind him on the trail, Mike informs me.

It is many years, ten or more, since I have seen Jack, but ours is the kind of friendship that time does not seem to interfere with much. In the seventies we did a thirty-five-day trip together, in and out of the St. Elias Range on skis. There were five of us and we didn't see anyone else the whole time out. We accomplished a superb climb, and the beauty and power of the experience were so fine as to be unrepeatable. So, when Jack appeared around the corner of a switchback that morning in the Tetons, it was a kind of ecstatic reunion. It was so fine to see him that I don't remember what we talked about, if anything. We just looked at each other with goofy grins on our faces, coexisting once again in that St. Elias world that the sight of each other conjured from memory.

Writers' relationships with their readers are at the far end of the spectrum from the climbers who have shared intense days in the mountains. Writers strive to share a memory with a reader who has *not* experienced the same events as they have. They must therefore cast a wider net, one that includes the climber, for whom the written word works as a public record, but extends further to the nonclimber, for whom the whole glorious vertical world must be evoked.

Climbers are a peculiar audience: sometimes easy to please, other times impossible. One of the great measures of writing's appeal to its audience, according to Aristotle, is the writer's *ethos*; that is, not his ethics, but his personal authority for speaking about his subject. Thus, for the climber/reader, a climber who is well known is, ipso facto, a good writer. This can lead to statements in recent book reviews like: "Three hundred pages of Ament and Robbins is one of the few things that could possibly upstage the Salathé Wall," or statements like, "Ament, however, is beyond critique. How can one be critical of one so supremely self-confident?" What can we learn about the book or even the reviewer's opinion by such statements? Unless we have an a priori respect for the ethos of the reviewer, all we can glean from a review of this sort is the reviewer's enthusiasm, which appears somehow misplaced. (Sometime later, I would read the book in question, Ament's *Spirit of the Age*, and found it quite compelling reading. But I couldn't help think, somewhat as the reviewer did, that it wasn't the book itself I was responding to, but rather Robbins's life itself. But wait! Isn't it the biographer's task to relate the subject's *life?* One can hardly hold it against the writer for having chosen a terrific subject.)

But ethos is a legitimate reason to be moved by a piece of writing. I doubt that many people would take up the case for Jim Bridwell being a great literary stylist. But he doesn't need to be; his written work rests on the authority of his considerable experience. So when you read "Dance of the Wu Li Master," the story of his and Mugs Stump's ascent of the Moose's Tooth, the question of how well it's written is not particularly relevant: it's written as well as it needs to be. Joe Simpson's *Touching the Void* is a better-known example. The elements of the tale are so harrowing it would be hard to mess up the telling of it: the cut rope, the abandonment, the miraculous survival, the hallucinatory crawl back to base camp. Such powerful experiences are being conveyed that the writing draws no attention to itself; it exists as a transparent window to direct experience.

Camp 4: Recollections of a Yosemite Rockclimber, Steve Roper's superb history/memoir provides a nearly perfect example of matching the ethos of the writer to the writing-task-at-hand. The undertaking was a huge one, to be sure: the chronicling of

Yosemite rock climbing from 1933 through 1970. In the first sentence of his preface Roper claims, "I avoided writing this book for many years, thirty to be exact." Our reading experience soon bears out what he doesn't tell us: that those thirty years were also spent, in effect, preparing to write this book. Roper proceeds as a good historian must, by putting events and people into context and making careful (and convincing) judgments of their significance. While it may be possible for some of those characterized to differ with Roper's conclusions, his scholarship is remarkable, and his meticulously documented sources range from published journals to personal letters, unpublished manuscripts, and conversations.

Perhaps the book's finest achievement is the fine balance struck between its mission as both a comprehensive history and a personal memoir. Roper acknowledges that "By pure happenstance... I lived in Yosemite Valley's Camp 4 during the 1960s...." Although he had done more than 260 routes in the Valley by 1963, Roper rates few of these worthy of mention. Yosemite climbing surely would have evolved without Roper, but its collective memory so accurately and beautifully evoked here might well not have.

Many years after our first attempts, McInerney and I finally climbed the Exum route. In the years between our first attempt and the last, there had been another failed attempt, a drenching night and socked-in morning at the Lower Saddle. When we finally reached the summit, we watched ourselves climb as if it were happening to someone else. The named features of the route, familiar from years of reading, appeared as abstract concepts materializing before us: the Eye of the Needle, Wall Street, the Friction Pitch. Each one was charged with history.

Pete Sinclair, like Roper, lived in a golden age of American climbing, and like Roper's book, his memoir of the climbing life in the Tetons, *We Aspired: The Last Innocent Americans*, ends around 1970. Though both books balance personal memoir with a larger history, their approaches couldn't be more different, with Sinclair far more introspective and personal, gesturing, sometimes wildly, toward deeper meanings. Taken together, the two works comprise an incredibly comprehensive portrait of climbing during the sixties in the American West.

As a twenty-three-year-old climber in 1959, Pete Sinclair was quoted in *Time*: "You can't describe climbing to people. They don't have anything to compare it with." Nonetheless, his recently published book describes climbing about as well as can be done. If I say it is well written (and I do), what do I mean? And how do I prove it? I remember a moment when I was a high-school teacher explaining to a parent his teenaged son's writing problems. The parent looked at me. "You mean *handwriting?*" he asked.

Sinclair's memoir begins with his ascent of the south face of Denali in 1959, then recounts summers of mountain rescue work in the Tetons during the sixties. But it would be an oversimplification to say that this is what the book is about. Sinclair is writing about his life during this time. As such, the book probably has more in common with a coming-of-age story like *A Portrait of an Artist as a Young Man* than with Maurice Herzog's *Annapurna* (which, incidentally, Sinclair cites as a "text of moral instruction"). But every

Tom Frost climbing the *North America Wall*, El Capitan, 1997. *Warren Hollinger*

autobiographical narrative about climbing can be said to be about the writer during a period of time. What's so special about Sinclair's version?

In most climbing books the climbing is central; what it might mean, if anything, is often tacked on, hastily. Larger meanings seem to come as after-the-fact rationalizations by the writer. Sinclair doesn't *tell* us what events mean, as in the formulaic "climbing leads to personal growth." Instead, he *shows* us how for him this leap has been accomplished. One chapter opens: "We have precious times when we glimpse the trajectory of our lives, when we are free enough from the nudge of things done and the tug of things to do to have a gravity-free movement of lucidity about what we are up to." This must also describe the space from which Sinclair's whole book arises, and also, I think, suggests the shortcomings of other works about climbing, which often feel as if their raison d'être is to "professionalize" climbing for the writer.

Sinclair's book comes twenty years after the last events it describes have taken place. Events, people, landscape, movement, and emotion percolated in his memory for years, until he could find their essences in language. In this way *We Aspired* reminds me of Norman Maclean's *A River Runs Through It:* books that were worth waiting for, until the author could set it down just right.

In the end Sinclair leaves the Tetons and, as you might guess from the subtitle, *The Last Innocent Americans*, there's a sense of melancholy to the departure, brought on by the deaths of friends (and strangers), as well as the increasing bureaucratization of the national park service. Still, when you stake a claim to being the "last innocent," you're marginalizing the experience of those who follow you. In fact, they may not be following at all—only finding their own way as young, adventurous souls must always do.

Of course, it's obvious that climbing and writing are two radically different endeavors. It should be equally obvious then that what one might *seem* to have learned by reading could be of limited value when actually climbing. Historical precedents for this view abound. In *The Sun Also Rises*, Hemingway's narrator ridicules another character for being influenced by W. H. Hudson's *The Purple Land*, "a sinister book if read too late in life."

In *Memoirs of a Mountain Guide* Lou Whittaker observes that after Roper and Allen Steck's *Fifty Classic Climbs of North America* came out in 1979, there was a noted increase in climber deaths on Liberty Ridge, a classic on the north side of Rainier. He goes on to say that they almost always found copied pages of the route description in the climber's pack. The implication is the same as Hemingway's; it's a variation on the worn maxim "a little knowledge is a dangerous thing"—"a little *book-learned* knowledge is a dangerous thing." Both writers are seemingly forgetful that they're airing this view in written language, in a book, the impact of which will be precisely the opposite of what they claim to value: the readers will be influenced by... *a book*. Whittaker, at least, tries to put it into a larger perspective: "The deaths were not caused by that book or any other, but by inexperienced climbers seeking the glory of doing a classic climb." (Later I would learn that this caveat was added after the *Classic Climbs* authors, having perused Whittaker's galleys, complained about being singled out. "How many climbers had Fred Beckey's guidebook in their pockets?" they asked.)

Whittaker is a first-rate raconteur and one of the great charms of his book, for the reader who has met him, is that his voice can be heard in the written prose. Some time after his book appeared Whittaker told the story of a midnight rescue call, and being helicoptered up to one of the high glaciers where a broken-legged climber had wrapped himself in his down sleeping bag awaiting salvation. Whittaker describes approaching the bag, uncertain whether the man is dead or alive. A face appears out of the bag and the injured climber's first words are: "I've read your book." In telling the story Whittaker laughs his great laugh, as he must have at the scene: "Well," he says, "You sure didn't read it too good!"

The last time I climbed in the Tetons was a couple of seasons ago, when I did *The Snaz* with Tom Huckin. It was the culmination of a few seasons of climbing together, a partnership that we knew would soon change when I left Salt Lake City. *The Snaz* was Tom's idea. A classic rock route first put up in the sixties, it still has a reputation, despite its now-modest grade. For us, it was not so modest, but right at the edge of our abilities.

I had been in the Wind River Range and was a bit tired physically and tired too of the weather, which couldn't seem to make up its mind as to which season it attended, summer or winter. The previous day, McInerney and I had made the long hike up to Symmetry Spire only to be chased off by lightning and a hard rain that struck so quickly we were soaked to the skin before we even donned raingear. That night I was to rendezvous with Huckin, who was newly arrived in Jackson and undeterred by my description of the weather. We found ourselves sorting gear at the Death Canyon trailhead a couple of hours before daylight.

As we approached the climb, a herd of elk thundered by us in the dark, and twice we had to skirt moose that held their ground. Despite the late season, the river roared down the canyon; I noticed a fresh fir tree, about a hundred feet long, caught haphazardly in the torrent, uprooted by some primeval force. Soon we were on the route, the long open book first written on by Chouinard and Mort Hempel. The morning's promise of good weather held all day. Though we made steady time, long blocks of hours disappeared into the effort. As on many of the best climbs, we didn't manage to take many photographs. There are a couple from the crux pitch, Tom's lead. The first shows him standing on a large detached pillar fifteen or so feet away, the sky a wedge of blue above the dihedral. The second shows him a hundred feet up, unrecognizable, the clouds in the sky completely refigured in the time it had taken him to move up. By the time we found ourselves on top, the sun had gone beyond the hanging valley to the west. And by the time we made it down to the packs, it was dark. The trail was still negotiable, but we were tired and it was late. Once again the herd of elk thundered by, and soon the lights of the valley began to appear. We drove back to Tom's sister's ranch, where we ate steak and drank a couple of beers out of longneck bottles, giddy as kids in cowboy hats. It had been perfect, the kind of day you read about.

NIGHT RAPPEL

John Hart

Though every hold was loved, we're going down.

To darkness. Crickets from the valley floor.
The mighty slope, a rack of shadow now,
receding upwards past us as we fall:
the click of all these metals
and somewhere the shepherd's pipes
from *Tristan* in the air.

By such device one does not mean to die.
But it would suit me, if I knew the year,
to do my dying on a night rappel,
or as a night rappel, so spent and clear:
the gestures accurate and left behind,
performed with precedent and heat,
the gentlest cattle of the dying mind,
action of starlight,
and the drafty masses glimmering.

What's dying but a second wind, said Yeats.
I spin suspended, hanging from the gates
so narrowly arranged, reversed, opposed,
and seeing only what a headlamp sees . . .
I do not see inimitable size:
I do not claim to run to Paradise.

But having been here once I won't cavil
at taint of deadliness on any wall.
One might as well make progress at this skill:
some hill, some dancer
will demand it all.

NORTH

Photographs by
Corina Acheson
Ed Webster
John Dunn
Mark Synnott
Warren Hollinger
and David Harris

Reine harbor on the island of Moskenesøy.

Odd-Roar Wiik
on the first ascent
of *Himmel og Helvete*
(Heaven and Hell 5.11)
on *Presten* (the Priest), Austvagøy.

Midnight sun.

Odd-Roar Wiik climbing *Solens Sønner*
(Sons of the Sun 5.10a/b) on the
Sjøsvaet (the Sea Slab)
on Austvagøy.

THE LOFOTEN ISLANDS
arctic Norway

Jan Westby climbing
the classic *Bare Blåbaer*
(Only Blueberries 5.9)
on *Pillaren* (the Pillar)
on the island of Austvagøy.

Photographs: *Ed Webster*

BAFFIN ISLAND
Canada

Mark Synnott on top
of Polar Sun Spire, beside
snow-topped Broad Peak,
with the Turrret on the left.

Warren Hollinger

Warren Hollinger
aiding pitch 17 of
The Great & Secret Show
(VII 5.11, A4 WI4)
Polar Sun Spire.

Mark Synnott

Mark Synnott
climbing Pitch 34 of
Polar Sun Spire.

Warren Hollinger

Bredablik (the sunlit rock
pillar just left of center),
Pangnirtung Pass area,
Baffin Island.

David Harris

Jeff Chapman and Warren Hollinger
on the first ascent of
The Great & Secret Show
(VII 5.11, A4 WI4), Polar Sun Spire.
Sam Ford Fjord, Baffin Island, Canada.

Mark Synnott

THE MECHANICAL ADVANTAGE
Tools for the Wild Vertical

John Middendorf

That well-known year 1492 is also the date of the first mountain expedition using mechanical tools. King Charles VIII commanded a military officer, Antoine de Ville, to climb Mont Inaccessible, a 1,000-foot rock tower south of Grenoble. With grappling hooks, ladders, and the skills gained from sieging feudal castles, de Ville and a dozen of the king's men stormed the limestone monolith. François de Bosco, a member of the expedition, reported the climb as "half a league by means of ladders, and a league by a path which is terrible to look at, and is still more terrible to descend than to ascend." (This is the first—but hardly the last—case of a climber's "emotional measurement," since "half a league" would equal nearly 8,000 feet!) De Ville called the route "the most horrible and frightful passage," and, after arriving at the summit, a large meadow, he sent a messenger scurrying over the edge with a letter for the mayor of Grenoble. It read: "I send you my hearty greetings. When I left the king he charged me to cause an attempt to be made to see whether it was possible to climb the mountain which was said to be inaccessible; which mountain I, by subtle means and engines, have found the means of climbing, thanks be to God." De Ville refused to descend until the mayor verified his ascent and so remained a week in "the most beautiful place that I have ever visited," with flowers of many colors and scents, several species of birds, and a "beautiful herd of chamois, which will never be able to get away." No longer could it be named "Inaccessible," so de Ville rechristened it with its local name, Léguille (it's known now as Mont Aiguille). This first documented mountaineering ascent took place long before mountain climbing was considered recreational exploration, and, even though the impetus for the ascent was political, it was a courageous, technical display of vertical prowess.

Ascension d'un Sérac Chamonix

Climbers ascend a serac in the French Alps, 1880.

For centuries afterward, climbing either for political reasons or for pleasure apparently didn't exist, and the ascent of Mont Blanc, in 1786, is said to mark the start of the "modern era." And tools were used again, not grappling hooks but several other innovations: a long, sturdy alpenstock for balance and for bridging gaps and tiny crevasses; ice creepers (spikes for the midsole of the boot, a form of the instep crampon present since the fifth century

B.C.); and a wood axe or modified hatchet (called, in the local dialect, a *piolette,* a term that later evolved to *piolet)*. The ropes of the day were thick and heavy, yet too fragile to catch a falling climber; instead they were used, perhaps with false security, to create human chains on glaciers and ridges. Mountaineers surmounted rock passages up to what is now called class 4 with boldness, shoulder stands, and occasionally by holding or stepping on to an iron spike hammered in with a rock. A century later, the eminent British mountaineering pioneer Edward Whymper carried a claw hook attached to a short rope for grappling an edge in order to maneuver up a short step. Such aids were used only as a supplementary handhold or foothold, as the equipment wasn't designed to support one's full weight. By the late nineteenth century, nearly every high peak in the Alps—and many in the U.S. and Canada—had been climbed by these traditional tools and methods.

As Americans were manifesting their destiny and exploring the West's more remote regions, the Scottish trailbuilder George Anderson became the first to stand atop Yosemite's Half Dome; he used sturdy eyebolt technology intended for securing trails in the Sierra Nevada wilderness. Anderson built a cabin at a spring not far from the dome and in the fall of 1875 methodically climbed the steep

150   Alpine guide Jean Charlet. *Bregeault*

MOUNTAINEERING IN THE TYROL: TURNING A CORNER.

152   On the Grépon, Chamonix, 1890. *George Abraham / Paul Teare collection*

east slab of the formation by drilling a hole and hammering in a bolt, using it as a foothold, and drilling again. Often he left the security of the anchors and free climbed up less steep or more broken sections of the gigantic slab. Since this work took many days, Anderson attached a rope to his upper bolt so that he could descend and re-ascend to his high point easily—perhaps the first-ever use of fixed ropes. John Muir, who climbed the route a short while later, thought that "the skill and courage of Anderson have not been surpassed."

Farther east, Wild West ingenuity paved the way for the first ascent of Wyoming's spectacular Devil's Tower in 1893, when ranchers Willard Ripley and William Rogers spent six weeks engineering a ladder of wood spikes, connected by rope, up a 350-foot vertical crack on the southeast side of the tower. The summit was attained during the Fourth of July celebration and the U. S. flag was proudly planted on top.

Like de Ville's ascent of Mont Aiguille four hundred years earlier, these climbs were isolated events done by rugged individualists, and, although American climbers pioneered rudimentary belay and safety techniques for the first ascent of the Grand Teton in 1898, the marriage of technology and climbing really began in Europe, where climbing techniques were more refined and specific equipment for technical climbing appeared around the turn of the century.

Mauerhaken und Karabiner und Dülfersitz

The first pitons—little more than iron spikes with rings—became available at this time. The tradition of the day, to keep purity in the passion, was to use pitons moderately, preferably only as a means to facilitate descent. But as climbers began to eye the steeper mountain faces with interest, they realized that the traditional methods would never be safe for upward passage on such vertical beasts. The imposing challenges of the unclimbed walls of the Eastern Alps required devising a new, systematic approach, broadening rules and modifying means. New and stronger manila ropes allowed for tension traverses and short lead falls, and the use of pitons for ascent became more frequent. In this time before carabiners, to supply some protection for difficult vertical climbing, a short piece of cord was tied around both the ring of the piton and the rope.

At the beginning of the twentieth century an Italian guide named Tita Piaz created intricate new techniques and climbed inspirational routes (he completed one with a Tyrolean traverse anchored by an iron ball tossed between two boulders on the summit). In 1907 he climbed the steep 1,200-foot southeast face of the Torre Est in the Dolomites, and, a year later, in the Kaisergebirge, he led a team up the 1,500-foot west face of the Totenkirchl, a challenging route even today. Piaz was willing to engineer solutions for upward passage, thus abandoning the old doctrine of not relying on gear.

In the Western Alps, where the mountains are more alpine,

Traversée du Glacier des Bossons

artificial aid was considered unsporting, but in the Eastern Alps, with its spectacular vertical limestone cliffs, a new standard arose. When the Italian expedition led by the Duke of Abruzzi returned from the Karakoram in 1909, photographer Vittorio Sella's lithographs of the stupendous rock walls of the Baltoro must have sparked many a climber's imagination and provided additional rationale for scaling the steep cliffs at home. Climbing then was still largely a gentleman's—and gentlewoman's—sport, and guided excursions were the norm, but some of these outings were anything but leisurely. In 1910 the Italian guides Angelo Dibona and Luigi Rizzi, plus German clients Guido and Max Mayer (who were as expert and experienced as their guides) climbed the north face of the Cima Una in the Dolomites, a 2,600-foot wall with continuous steepness and exposure. The team had developed customized pitons (*Mauerhaken*) and ascended with the help of new rudimentary aid techniques and rope maneuvers.

Better climbing through technology is not just about improved ropes and specialized hardware. Equipment for surviving the elements contributed equally to rising standards. Before his disappearance in 1895 while reconnoitering Nanga Parbat, Albert Mummery had developed lightweight silk bivouac tents and insulating gear sufficient for living in extreme conditions. Prior to World War I, warm, lightweight garments were evolving, and, with this all-weather equipment, climbers could spend multiple days and nights in harsh conditions.

Tom Frost

Beginning around 1910, a trio of inventive German climbers took advantage of modern metallurgical materials. Otto Herzog, having seen a pear-shaped *karabiner* on members of a fire brigade, developed the first steel carabiner for climbing. Hans Fiechtl, a master of roped climbing maneuvers, invented and manufactured a piton with an eye to supplement the ones with rings. Hans Dülfer developed a new set of methods, including a belay device using two carabiners; frictionless tension traverses; sturdier belay anchors; and the *Dülfersitz*, the body rappel that would be used for the next half century by climbers worldwide.

154

These three innovators of new tools and techniques were great friends and together and separately they pioneered the most visionary big walls of the day, some requiring several days of difficult free and aid climbing. The new protection devices allowed a bolder style of climbing that combined traditional "free" methods with technical "aid" methods, allowing the climber and the belayer to remain firmly affixed to the rock on routes whose sheer steepness and frequent overhangs had previously been unthinkable. In 1912 Dülfer climbed the imposing east face of the Fleischbank, and a year later he did the west face of the Cima Grande, the centerpiece of the Tre Cime di Lavaredo group. His death at twenty-three, on the Western Front in 1915, cut short what surely would have been an incredible climbing career.

The Sporting Way

The era of mechanically assisted rock climbs of the Eastern Alps was not without competition. Incredibly bold vertical routes were climbed without any mechanical protection at all—what we would call "free-solo" today. Georg Winkler, a pioneer in such climbing, made a number of impressive climbs, including the first ascent in 1887 of the eastern Vajolet Tower, a year before his death at age eighteen during a solo attempt of the Weisshorn. Many climbers in later years were to emulate Winkler and reject the use of ropes and aid, even though he himself used a grappling hook on occasion. Footwear evolved from heavy nail-spiked boots to lighter felt-soled shoes developed by the Simond firm, opening a new era of free climbing with leaders who morally opposed reliance on gear.

Paul Preuss, a vocal and influential Austrian, vigorously denounced the use of pitons and rope maneuvers as a lower standard. He wrote six climbing rules:

> First, one should not only be equal to any climb that one undertakes, but be more than equal to it. Second, the standard of difficulty which a climber can conquer with safety when descending, and for which he can consider himself competent, with an easy conscience, should represent the limit of what he should attempt on his ascent. Third, hence the use of artificial aids only becomes justifiable in case of sudden threatening danger. Fourth, the piton is an emergency aid and not the basis of a system of mountaineering. Fifth, the rope may be used to facilitate matters, but never as a sole means to make a climb possible. Finally, the principle of safety is one of the highest principles. Not the spasmodic correction of ones own want of safety, obtained by the use of artificial aids, but that true primary safety which should result, with every climber, from a just estimate of what he is able, and what he desires, to do.

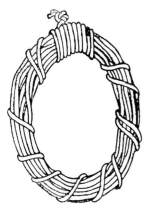

Among Preuss's 1,200 ascents, his routes with Paul Relly up the 3,000-foot northeast face of the Crozzon di Brenta and the 800-foot vertical northeast face of the Cima Piccolissima, plus his solo of the east face of the Campanile Basso, were incredibly bold for 1911, with some pitches still rated 5.9. In 1913 Preuss died at age twenty-seven while attempting to solo the north face of the Manndlkogen. It was an era when not many of the top climbers made it to thirty. Perhaps the new safety methods had some merit after all.

The year 1919 saw the publication of Guido Rey's book *Alpinisme Acrobatique*, a treatise on the "artificial" techniques utilizing the latest, easily available pitons and carabiners. And, after World War I, international climbing organizations exchanged information about remote expeditionary climbing in the Andes, Caucasus, Himalaya, Canadian Rockies, and Alaska, increasing the collective knowledge regarding extended human survival in cold con-

ditions. One of the outstanding alpinists of the era, Willo Welzenbach, was the innovator of both ten-point crampons that fit the entire sole of the boot and shorter ice tools. He also created a standard rating system (Grades I to VI) based on his experience with hundreds of routes in both the Western and Eastern Alps. The post-war era also brought higher-quality woven ropes and stronger carbon steel for carabiners.

Big walls were coming of age, and pre-war pioneers—those who were still alive after the war—continued to push standards in the 1920s. Gustav Haber and Otto Herzog climbed the 1,000-foot *Ha-He Dihedral* on the Dreizenkenspitze in 1923, a technical big-wall route requiring two bivouacs; it was not repeated, despite many attempts, until the 1950s. Hans Fiechtl's *Ypsilon Riss* (5.9, A1) on the 1,200-foot north face of the Seekarlspitze was perhaps the most difficult of the era.

Prior to his 1928 immigration to the United States, Dresden native Fritz Wiessner teamed up with aid master Roland Rossi and adventurer Emil Solleder for some of the wildest long rock adventures in the Alps, including the southeast face of the Fleischbank (V+), and the north wall of the Furchetta (VI). Trusting the security of the newer pitons, climbers became willing to risk lead falls and free climbing standards rose. In 1925 Solleder and Gustl Letten-bauer climbed the northwest face of the Civetta in a day, a 3,700-foot 5.9 route in the Dolomites, carrying only fifteen pitons for protection and belays.

Fritz Wiessner on the first ascent of Mt. Waddington, Canada, 1936. Note his rope-soled shoes.

William P. House

A year later, in the Julian Alps (now part of Slovenia), Stane Tominsek and Mira Marko Debelakova spent two days climbing the technical 3,000-foot north face of the Spik, their reliance on the new gear making it possible. Tools for safe upward passage were improving, and in 1929 Luigi Micheluzzi and team climbed the Marmolata, the highest peak in the Dolomites, by its steepest route, the 1,800-foot south pillar. Pitons were used for protecting the lead climber and for occasional aid on these historic big walls, but in deference to the strict anti-piton standard of the Western Alps, they were used sparingly.

New Ideas Come to America

It took some time for European tools and techniques to filter into North America. In 1916 Conrad Kain climbed two imposing Canadian peaks, South Howser Tower and Bugaboo Spire, without the use of any hardware. These were the most difficult rock routes yet done in the Western Hemisphere (rated 5.6 today), and Kain considered them harder than his alpine route on Mt. Robson, today considered a far more serious proposition due to its length and objective hazards. In the Adirondacks, John Case, an early president of the Appalachian Mountain Club (AMC), applied skills and belay techniques learned in Europe, using a rope to belay, but without protection. Albert Ellingwood, a Colorado College political science professor (who had also learned climbing techniques during visits to Europe) introduced rudimentary belay techniques to the Rockies and pioneered technical climbing in Colorado when he scaled Lizard Head in 1920, using three iron spikes similar to telephone-pole steps. Today it is a loose and scary 5.7+ route and still the most difficult Colorado summit to attain. Ellingwood became the finest rockclimber in the land, and his improbable 1925 route on the 2,000-foot northeast buttress of Crestone Needle (5.7) with Eleanor Davis, Stephen Hart, and Marion Warner, using only a rope and an unanchored belayer for safety, was the most inspiring and the highest (to a 14,197-foot summit) rock climb in America at the time.

A wooden wedge.

Ascent Archives

In 1927 protection specifically designed for rock climbing was introduced to North America. Brothers Joe and Paul Stettner emigrated from Germany after getting their first vertical experiences in the Kaisergebirge, inspired by Hans Dülfer and his steep routes and techniques. After a few years of working in Chicago, they found themselves missing the mountain life they had been born into. They ordered ring-angle pitons and carabiners from Munich and headed out on their motorcycles to Colorado. There they procured a rope at a hardware store and pioneered their historic 5.7 route on the east face of Longs Peak, using "running belays" and the European pitons for protection. This ascent of *Stettners' Ledges* marks the dawn of mechanically protected climbing in the U. S.

In France that same year a seed was germinating that would change the nature of climbing profoundly. This was the development of a portable set of tools for anchoring in rock anywhere: the drill and expansion bolt. The inventor/manufacturer, Laurent Grivel, used these new tools on the first ascent of the spectacular Pére Eternal, a 200-foot sliver on the north ridge of the Aiguille de la Brenva. Bolts were used sporadically in the following years, including on the south ridge of the Aiguille Noire de Peuterey, but little concerning this technique is described in the literature. The official inauguration of bolts to the climbing world was not to come for a while.

Bill House and Bob Bates on the first ascent of the *Henderson Route* (5.5), Cannon Cliff, New Hampshire, 1940. (Note the ball-peen hammer and sneakers.)

Kenneth A. Henderson

On the eastern edge of North America, members of the AMC who had visited Chamonix and the Dolomites returned with new ropes, hardware, and safer belay methods. Robert Underhill, brother and sister Lincoln and Miriam O'Brien (later Underhill), Fritz Wiessner, Bill House, Elizabeth Knowlton, Ken Henderson, and cousins Bradley Gilman and Hassler Whitney all made belayed ascents of the steep rock faces of Cannon Cliff and Cathedral and Whitehorse Ledges in the White Mountains of New Hampshire. Underhill exported the knowledge west when, as chairman of the AMC's Committee on Rock Climbing, he wrote an article for the 1931 annual *Sierra Club Bulletin* describing the latest rope-management techniques. This vital information enabled California pioneers to open a whole new range of routes in the Sierra, laying the groundwork for the technical big-wall routes to come.

"Impossible" Walls

Back in Europe, at the same time, a bold new era for big-wall climbing began when the first of the famous "last great problems of the Alps," the north face of the Matterhorn, fell to the brothers Toni and Franz Schmid. Pitons began to appear more widely in both the Western and Eastern Alps, and climbers began to recognize that the use of protection systems was facilitating superb achievements on extremely difficult vertical terrain. As the popularity of the sport increased, the climbing population evolved from consisting of exclusively aristocrats and guides to a broader set of athletes, doctors, lawyers, engineers, and a new breed of working-class heroes, one of whom became legendary.

Emilio Comici was an Italian longshoreman when he began caving on weekends. After a particularly difficult cave exploration—setting the world's depth record near Trieste—he ran to the nearest summit and made a pact to forever spend his free time in the open air of the mountains instead of underground. He became an expert in the techniques pioneered by Dülfer, Herzog, and Fiechtl, and revolutionized climbing by perfecting a new style well suited for the extreme cliffs of the Dolomites, and ultimately, the big walls of the world. Comici was the inventor of modern aid techniques, such as using multi-step aid ladders, solid belays, complex rope maneuvers, hanging bivouacs, and climbing with a trail rope as a means to stay connected to the belayer for hauling up extra equipment. Realizing that he had a choice either to reject the use of mechanical aids or to accept them wholeheartedly, he chose the latter and made heavy use of the new tools.

In 1931 he put the new systems to the test on the 3,600-foot northwest face of the Civetta, and the result was the steepest and perhaps the most difficult climb in the world (to this day it is still a challenging twenty-six pitch vertical adventure). Not satisfied, he wrote, "I wish some day to make a route and from the summit let fall a drop of water and this is where my route will have gone." He realized his dream of such a route—a direttissima, as it became known—with his direct line up the incredibly steep 1,500-foot north wall of the Cima Grande in 1933. True, his line wavers slightly but no more than if the wind had buffeted the mythical drop of water back and forth. On the lower half of the wall Comici, Giuseppe Dimai, and Angelo Dimai used just seventy-five pitons—one every ten feet, on average—hardly excessive considering that the wall overhangs continuously and is composed of less-than-solid rock.

Comici freely shared his expertise, inspiring many with his dream of the ultimate aesthetic route. He died climbing, at age thirty-nine, never knowing that his dreams and philosophies were to create passionate splits in climbing attitudes as new technologies developed.

The 1930s were an age of innovation in Europe. The leader of a talented new group of climbers from Fontainebleau, Pierre Allain, developed lightweight goose-down clothing and bivouac equipment suitable for surviving on the steep, icy faces of the Western Alps. In 1935 he made the first ascent of the frigid north face of the Petit Dru, near Chamonix, with Raymond Leininger. This was a pioneering, two-day free and aid route that combined the challenges of an alpine route with the technical aspects of the Dolomite and Kaisergebirge vertical walls.

Around the same time, the Simond firm, near Chamonix, began to manufacture high-quality pitons, equipping a new breed of extreme climbers. Gino Soldà, Raffaele Carlesso, Domenico Rudatis, Ettore Castiglioni, Raimund Schinko, Alfred Couttet, and Giusto Gervasutti all made incredible technical climbs during this period, but the climber who stands out most prominently, both for the quality of his routes and the breadth of his vision, was Riccardo Cassin. This sturdy Italian mastered aid techniques and took them to new extremes on the major routes of the period, including the *Walker Spur* of the Grandes Jorasses (with Gino Esposito and Ugo Tizzoni), the northeast face of the Piz Badile (with Esposito and Vittorio Ratti), and the north face of the Cima Ovest (with Ratti). Cassin's routes continually pushed standards of difficulty and commitment.

Illustration courtesy of Anderl Heckmair

Perhaps the best description of the marriage of technology and human boldness during the interwar period came from Heinrich Harrer, in his account of the first ascent of the north face of the Eiger in 1938. Harrer had elected not to take a pair of crampons for the ascent, while his partner Fritz Kasparek had a pair of traditional ten-point crampons with sharp points evenly spaced around the sole of the boot. As they finished a long session of step-cutting across the Second Icefield, they were surprised to see below them Anderl Heckmair and Ludwig Vörg rapidly approaching, using the "fashionable" twelve-point crampons invented by Laurent Grivel, a guide and blacksmith of Courmayeur, in 1931. The addition of two front-facing prongs allowed a climber to ascend on his toes, facing forward rather than using the traditional French method of keeping the foot flat on the ice, as if frictioning up a slab. "I looked back, down our endless ladder of steps," Harrer wrote later. "Up [the Second Icefield] I saw the New Era coming at express speed; there were two men running—and I mean running, not climbing—up it." The two teams joined forces for the historic first ascent of the Eigerwand. This climb should have marked the opening of a whole new era, but the outbreak of another tragic European conflict soon put an end to the risky vertical games.

In the less frenetic U.S., technical climbing developed slowly. Transatlantic travel was still expensive and slow, and information about the new European techniques was hard to come by. The only available English literature came from Britain, where traditional mountain guide/client excursions up the 4,000-meter Alpine peaks were still the norm. But that is not to say there was no progress. Dwight Lavender designed and produced the first pitons made in the U.S. at the engineering workshop of Stanford University. In 1932 the *American Alpine Journal* published a note explaining the world's climbing systems, including the use of "safety snaps" (carabiners), then a rare item in America. The article begins, "Not withstanding feeble protests by a few climbers, mostly of the past generation, hammers, pitons, and safety snaps have definitely entered into modern climbing technique." With the new tools and safety methods becoming more widely known, climbers began to eye the challenges unpeeling in the Tetons, Yosemite, and the Southwest.

Big-Wall Epicenter

Dick Leonard, a San Francisco Bay Area law student, formed the Cragmont Climbing Club in 1932 and, with a few others, began practicing the new techniques on the local rocks in Berkeley. He ordered carabiners and pitons from Sporthaus Schuster in Munich and in 1933

Larry Coates climbing the *Original Route* up Shiprock, New Mexico.

Ed Webster

began putting them to use on the spectacular granite cliffs of Yosemite, marking the first use of climbing hardware in the Sierra Nevada. The European pitons were made from mild steel, and, though well suited for the limestone of the Alps where their softness allowed them to conform securely to undulating cracks in the brittle rock, they were usually difficult to remove once placed, and far from ideal in California granite. Leonard made sure he had an adequate supply of of them (fifty-five, all told) and in 1934 teamed up with Jules Eichorn and Bestor Robinson for the first ascent of Higher Cathedral Spire, the most technical aid climb in North America at the time, and the first of a long lineage of its kind in Yosemite.

Leonard, a student of rope dynamics, developed the body, or hip, belay, with the rope surrounding the waist (Europeans often used a shoulder belay, which presented torque problems unless one's feet were perfectly braced). This Leonard combined with a refinement in which the belayer absorbed the shock of a fall by letting the rope hum around his waist for a few feet before stopping the fall with a gloved "brake" hand. This "dynamic" belay resulted in a lower load on the anchors and the rope; the falling climber and the belayer also experienced a less severe jolt. Using this new system, Leonard and others felt more confident risking longer falls on their bold forays.

Further east, the 1,700-foot volcanic plug of Shiprock, rising from the New Mexico desert, stood as one of the last prominent mountaineering challenges in the continental U.S. In 1937 Bob Ormes and Bill House attempted a direct route to the summit via what is now known as Ormes Rib, where they encountered difficulties placing gear. With marginal protection and with no way of using aid in the shattered rock, the team's efforts culminated in a twenty-foot fall by Ormes. He retrieved the deformed piton that had stopped him and later wrote an article entitled "A Piece of Bent Iron" in the *Saturday Evening Post*, offering a warning to those who would push their luck on such severe climbs.

Such warnings often act as incentives, and in 1939 Dave Brower, Raffi Bedayan, John Dyer, and Bestor Robinson set out from Berkeley for Shiprock. Well versed in the new

Yosemite techniques, they were armed with all the latest gear, as well as a secret weapon: a bolt kit. Their ascent up the crazily skewed basalt columns to the fragile and bizarrely shaped tuff-breccia of the upper part of the route was a wild and historic multi-day adventure with difficult aid and free climbing. Avoiding the dangerous Ormes Rib, the team instead rappelled down a gully in the tortured landscape and traversed into the massive interior bowl of the decaying volcanic plug. From here they scrambled easily up to the final crux, a steep, 200-foot step to the summit. After many pitons and a scary lasso over a horn, Shiprock was won. And the secret new tool was officially initiated into the climbers' repertoire: the men had placed four bolts. Aware of the controversial nature of what they had accomplished, the four Shiprock climbers self-deprecatingly called themselves "rock engineers," but this first North American use of drill and bolt marked the dawn of another new age in the history of technologically aided climbing, and new visions of the possible soared. Brower, now an internationally famous conservationist, helped set the precedent of fixing climbing anchors in the wilderness. Could he have known the future implications of his act?

John Salathé
and Yvon Chouinard
in Camp 4,
Yosemite Valley, 1964

Tom Frost

Yosemite Valley's Half Dome was once more the scene of the next big advance in technical climbing standards. The beautiful southwest face of Half Dome had been attempted as early as 1933 by Leonard and other Sierra Clubbers, whose attempts convinced them that it could not be climbed without excessive use of pitons. Leonard wrote that "the undefined borderline between justifiable and unjustifiable use of direct aid would have to be crossed." But in 1946 John Salathé and Anton (Ax) Nelson climbed the sloping face by a difficult 5.8, A3 route using a revolutionary new piton, one that could be removed easily and reused numerous times. With these, the team was able to efficiently manage the 150 placements required for the 900-foot route.

Salathé, a Swiss immigrant, was a blacksmith who had a mid-life spiritual conversion; this led him to devote his free time to ascetic meditation and the good clean life of the mountains. When he began climbing, in 1945, he found that the available pitons were too soft to be driven into narrow granite cracks without buckling, so he turned to his forge. In his San Mateo shop Salathé used high-carbon chrome-vanadium steel (the same high-strength steel that was used for Model-T Ford axles) to forge ultra-strong pitons that could be hammered

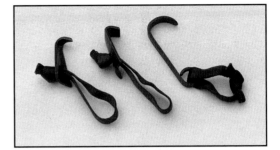

into the hard Yosemite granite—as well as hammered back out—without getting mangled. He also created a new tool that Nelson coined a "sky hook," the first hook for climbing Yosemite's granite edges.

Salathé's tough, thin pitons became locally famous after Salathé and Nelson's arduous 1947 ascent up a 1,200-foot chimney to the fantastic lonely spire of granite known as the Lost Arrow. With a rack of eighteen of Salathé's forged pins, twelve carabiners, and a few bolts, the two friends spent five devastatingly hot days on the route, a major psychological breakthrough in multi-day big-wall climbing. *The Lost Arrow Chimney* was a harbinger of the longer routes of the future, ones that would require hundreds of pieces of protection and aid placements, impossible without the kind of ultra-tough piton developed by Salathé. (Yvon Chouinard, a decade later, paid homage to Salathé when he named his similar pitons "Lost Arrows.")

Skyhooks (above), and a selection of Chouinard Equipment "Lost Arrow" pitons.

Tom Frost

Technology was developing on many fronts, and software as well as hardware changed drastically after World War II. Nylon, developed by the DuPont Chemical Company, was used to make strong and resilient three-strand laid ropes. Revolutionary in its time, this rope was ultra-strong but stiff and heavy compared to modern kernmantel designs. Nylon fabric, used in clothing, also allowed climbers to go to the cliffs more boldly, with lighter weight gear, than ever before.

Climbing gear was becoming more readily available by the early 1950s. Allen Steck, a Berkeley native who participated in several historic routes (including the first ascent of Yosemite's second major big wall, the north face of Sentinel Rock, in 1950) managed the Ski Hut, a Berkeley store selling all the latest climbing innovations, including Cassin pitons, aluminum army carabiners, and the new nylon ropes. (Steck spent many months climbing in Europe in 1949, introducing the first nylon rope to the Eastern Alps.) The Ski Hut also sold climbing shoes, which were becoming lighter and more sophisticated each year, and also the well-crafted aluminum carabiners of Raffi Bedayn (who had shortened his last name by this time). A typical rack of thirty-five carabiners, if they were aluminum, meant that the load pressing down on the climber's shoulder was now five pounds less.

Lighter equipment also meant that the remote ranges could be visited more efficiently. In the late 1940s Fred Beckey began ticking off routes in the Bugaboos and North Cascades. In Alaska he climbed the Devil's Thumb, Kate's Needle, and Michael's Sword, three spectacular granite peaks requiring huge loads of technical equipment.

The Modern Era

Audacious new climbing challenges in the Southwest, such as Spider Rock and the Totem Pole, were climbed by men with full arsenals of equipment in the mid-1950s.

Yosemite rocketeers were pushing standards throughout the West with the aid of the latest wide-angle pitons from Jerry Gallwas and knifeblades from Chuck Wilts.

It wasn't just North Americans setting the standards in the early 1950s. Another real breakthrough was the first ascent of the remote Patagonian peak of Fitzroy in 1952 by the powerful French climbers Lionel Terray and Guido Magnone. The Fitzroy climb, and the expedition of which it was the culmination, pushed the climbers and their equipment to new limits and was a triumph of the spirit facilitated by the latest lightweight and functional equipment.

The modern big-wall era began in 1955 when Walter Bonatti took climbing into a new dimension with his six-day solo ascent of a new route on the southwest pillar of the Petit Dru. Considered by many as the finest single climb of all time, this Dru ascent dramatically illustrated the potential of technology and technique combined with the power of an indomitable human spirit. The proof that a solo climber could self-belay up an incredibly difficult and technical steep route meant that there could be no more limits to the biggest rock faces in the world.

Above:
Yvon Chouinard,
Ventura, California,
1967.

Right:
Royal Robbins
racking up in
Camp 4 prior to
the second ascent
of *The Nose*
of El Capitan.
Yosemite Valley,
1960.

Photographs:
Tom Frost

In Yosemite, distinctions of the new style evolved. Few argued that pitons and bolts were not valid mountaineering tools. The inventive Royal Robbins, however, drew an aesthetic line, one that balanced the art required to find a viable weakness up a smooth wall with the minimum number of tools. He would return from each adventure with an exact count of the total number of pitons and bolts that his team had used. He also developed efficient techniques for living on the big stones, including the modern hauling system utilizing jumars (a Swiss-made rope-ascending tool designed for collectors of bird's eggs from cliffside nests), and his 1957 ascent of Half Dome's northwest face ushered in a new era.

Warren Harding, often thought of as Robbins's nemesis, was a world-class climber in all respects, though sometimes taking a different approach. Harding would choose his finest routes not by scrutinizing a wall's weakness, but rather for its strength and formidable location. His first ascent of *The Nose* of El Capitan was a testament to his tenacity and endurance. The climb required 125 bolts, specialized large pitons (made from the sheet-metal legs of a stove, hence the name "Stoveleg pitons"), and immense lengths of fixed rope.

Unlike Harding, Robbins rejected excessive use of bolts and fixed ropes and proceeded to prove to himself and the climbing world that a better style was possible. In *Basic Rockcraft*, the 1971 book that taught a new generation of climbers, Robbins wrote, "Like many of the technological wonders of modern man, bolts are at once a blessing and a curse. They make possible some of the finest rock climbs on earth by opening up stretches of blank and otherwise unclimbable rock. But they also diminish the value in climbing by making it possible for anyone to go anywhere if they are willing to drill." Robbins pushed standards with every major route and carried American tools and techniques to remote areas. His ascent of the direct west face of the Dru with Gary Hemming, and of the southeast face of Mt. Proboscis in Canada's Logan Mountains with Jim McCarthy, Layton Kor, and Dick McCracken (during which only two bolts were placed) were testpieces of the modern art of finding the most aesthetic weakness up a major wall and climbing it alpine style.

With airplane access, lightweight clothing, sleeping bags and tents made of new insulating and hydrophobic synthetic fibers, and tools and techniques developed on the walls of Yosemite, the best climbers of the 1960s tackled multi-day routes in other remote areas: the Bugaboos, the Troll Wall of Norway, the Ruth Gorge in Alaska, the Rocky Mountains of Canada, and the Paine and Fitzroy groups in Patagonia. All were arenas of the wild vertical.

Tom Frost on the first ascent of *The Salathé Wall* on El Capitan. Yosemite Valley, 1961.

Royal Robbins

165

Lure of the Impossible

In Europe climbers were taking Comici's concept of the direttissima to its logical limits, drilling their way directly up the overhanging walls of the Dolomites. The bolted "drop of water" line that was forced on many major faces culminated in absurdity in 1967 when Enrico Mauro and Mirko Minuzzo placed 340 bolts on the 1,500-foot Cima Grande north wall—on average, one every fifty-three inches!

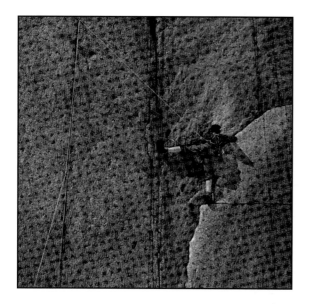

French alpinist Gaston Rébuffat pendulums on the *Bonatti Pillar,* the Petit Dru, Chamonix.

G. Ollive

In 1971 Cesare Maestri extended the logic of drilling the impossible to its ultimate limit; he and his mates hauled a 300-pound air compressor and pneumatic rock drill for his climb of Cerro Torre. In one spot, a place where a previous British attempt weaved up exposed, natural cracks, Maestri simply drilled his way across blank rock for 300 feet to stay out of the wind! Like Comici with his extensive use of pitons generations before, many climbers could not resist going "gonzo" once the technology was embraced. Resistance to the unlimited use of bolts was quick. Besides Robbins, legendary climbers such as Hermann Buhl, Walter Bonatti, and Reinhold Messner all spoke out over the years against the bolting mania. Not everyone joined in, however. In Gaston Rébuffat's 1968 edition of *Starlight and Storm,* an inspirational text describing his finest climbs, he includes a well-illustrated tools and techniques section. Although he gives detailed lists of equipment, he never mentions a bolt kit. A blind eye to the topic prevented the loss of the lure of the impossible.

Since the introduction of the bolt to climbing, its use has always sparked intense controversy. Perhaps it is temporal, as exemplified by a new route on the Dru. In 1975 Thomas Gros soloed the big wall (with his guitar!) in eighteen days, garnering disdain from the climbing community due to its unprecedented (though moderate by today's standard) use of sixty-eight bolts. The route, and the controversy, was erased in 1997 when a massive chunk of rock fell above the mid-way point.

The Clean Revolution

While the rest of the world nailed spectacular walls, British climbers were patiently learning a less brutal technique of climbing, involving a novel method of creating a unidirectional anchor. With tradition running strong in Britain, the sport had evolved slowly from the days of climbing exclusively with guides. Serious peer disapproval regarding unnatural aid caused climbers to surreptitiously hide any such equipment in their packs. Aid climbing was derogatorily coined "steeplejacking," and the piton was a last resort, placed only in emergencies.

In the 1920s top climbers began pioneering a pitonless craft on the numerous short crags in rural areas. The most inspiring outings of the day were the "pebble routes"—the first examples of clean climbing. In 1927, Fred Pigott experimented with placing and slinging natural chockstones (pebbles he'd picked up on the approach) for protection and aid on the east buttress of Clogwyn Du'r Arddu, or Cloggy, in North Wales. His partners, tongue

Clog Nuts, 1968.

Tom Frost

in cheek, excused his deeds as acts of Providence: the rocks from below were somehow accidentally finding their way into the cracks and wedging into the constrictions! Soon pebble protection became an art form, and expert eyes searched streambeds for the right combination of rocks. In the late 1950s, as paths to the crags switched from streambeds to railroad beds, climbers began using machine nuts found lying by the tracks. Drilled out and slung, these soon evolved into custom-manufactured aluminum affairs known as "chocks" or "nuts." John Brailsford innovated a synthetic polymer chock in 1961, and, though these "Acorn" chocks were adequately strong, climbers preferred to trust their lives to the "Moacs" he later made out of the more familiar aluminum.

Hamish MacInnes's ice ax collection.

Ed Webster

Soon climbers around the world discovered that with practice, patience, and cleverness, it was possible to climb exclusively with the new chocks. Royal Robbins, the leading proponent in the U. S. of the new tools, says of the late 1960s, "Climbers willing to choose a harder form of climbing brought themselves to a higher standard in deference to non-destructive principles. This was doubly good: chocks increased the challenge, and they weren't damaging to the rock." Customized shapes were soon produced to fit

more and more cracks, with the engineer-and-craftsman team of Tom Frost and Yvon Chouinard leading the way. Chouinard, whose heroes were John Muir and Salathé, began

blacksmithing chrome-moly pitons in the late 1950s, believing that removable pins were "cleaner," since they left less material in the mountains. In 1965 Chouinard joined forces with Stanford engineer Frost, who designed modern climbing pro-duction tooling, and Chouinard Equipment was born. The pair creat-ed the finest climbing tools ever made, including angle pitons, hammers, ice tools, and carabiners. During the successful climb of the south face of Annapurna in 1970, Frost got the idea for the first rigid twelve-point crampons while studying the tracks left in the ice by his mates. On his return, during a stop-over in

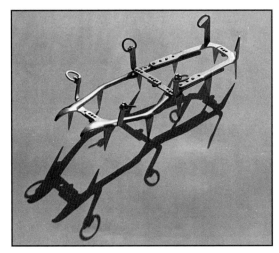

Rigid crampons and the classic grace of the Chouinard-Frost piolet.

Photographs: *Tom Frost*

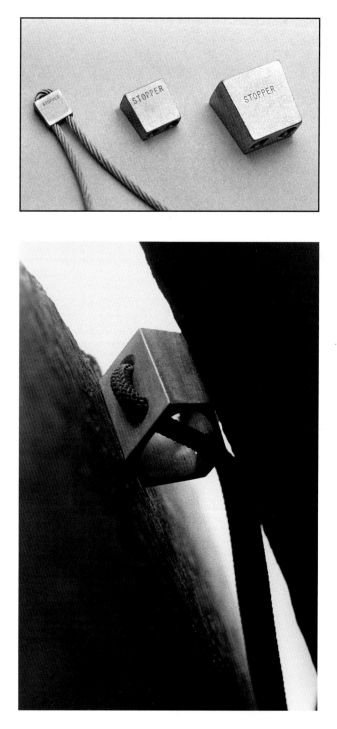

The tools
that started the
clean climbing
revolution:
the Stopper and
the Hexcentric.

Tom Frost

England, he climbed with his team on their home crags, using the Moac and Clog chocks, then available only in limited sizes. When he returned home, he engineered a set of eight chocks with optimal tapers, coined "Stoppers," the first clean tools available for a full range of cracks. It was a big risk for the company, but with a clear vision of the future, Chouinard and Frost redesigned their tooling for the new clean equipment. Their major contribution to the clean-climbing revolution was the invaluable Hexcentric, co-patented in 1971, which made protection available even in parallel-sided cracks. These new tools profoundly affected the future of climbing. The combination of the easy-to-use chocks and their ethical/environmental correctness led, in a relatively short span of years, to the almost complete disappearance of pitons from the free-climbing scene, and their relegation to last-resort status on aid climbs.

The first significant new route to go all nuts in North America was Royal Robbins's *Nutcracker Sweet* (5.8) on Yosemite's Ranger Rock, in 1967. But the clean revolution took some years to catch on, since ignorant or stubborn climbers used pitons on subsequent ascents. Most climbers who came to the game in the early 1970s didn't even own a hammer, and by 1975 only a few aid climbers carried and used them. Sensing that the willingness to bolt blank faces made the challenge of the mountains ring hollow, climbers took clean climbing to the limit. In the Shawangunks locals risked serious falls trying to avoid fixed pitons in order to earn a spot in the coveted "first clean ascent" registry at a nearby climbing shop. Here one could read tales of belayers perched on a tiny edge and anchored to a single lousy nut, with one hand gripping a carabiner poised to be clipped into the eye of a nearby fixed pin on the slightest sudden downward movement of the leader.

Meanwhile, other new tools were developed to make climbing more efficient. Ed Leeper perfected hook design with the invention of the arched base, and Clyde Deal, a park employee working in a machine shop in Yosemite, customized gear for the Camp 4 climbers, including the first "bashies," small blocks of aluminum with a hole for a sling or a wire. These cubes could be smashed into small pockets in the rock, but, unfortunately, once the sling or wire rotted or broke the piece was useless. Aid-specific software began appearing, too. With his state of the art sewn, fully-adjustable harnesses, vinyl-coated nylon haulbags, and single-point suspension hammocks (all design firsts), Bill Forrest pioneered technical ascents in Colorado's Black Canyon and throughout the Southwest. Forrest also evolved bashies to specifically sized "Copperheads," which enabled thin and shallow seams to be aid climbed without bolts.

Bill Forrest gear-testing at Sphinx Rock in Colorado. Forrest's many inventions also include the Pin Bin, the Daisy Chain, fiberglass-handled hammers, and the first ice tools with interchangeable picks—the Mjollnir ice hammer and Lifetime ice axe.

Bill Forrest collection

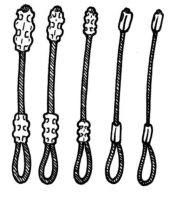

Copperheads.

The Far Ranges

Charlie Porter was another gifted aid climber who had a penchant for tinkering. He manufactured early versions of a two-part adjustable climbing nut, custom wall harnesses, a hammock with built-in padding, and a variety of specialized nailing tools. With his mastery of tools and techniques, along with his irrepressible spirit, he soloed a new route on the huge and remote north face of the north tower of Baffin Island's Mt. Asgard in 1975. After spending over a month ferrying loads thirty-five miles from the outpost town of Pangnirtung to the base of the route, Porter spent nine days alone on this fearsome wall in freezing conditions, and another week getting back to civilization.

Lowe Tri-cams.

Always reticent about his accomplishments, Porter never published an account of his route, the most significant big-wall climb since Bonatti's climb of the Dru. (Porter had a certain flair: once, when asked for a topo of one of his El Capitan first ascents, he drew a vertical line on a napkin, wrote "A5" next to it, and gave it to his bewildered inquisitor.)

That same year British climbers Joe Brown, Mo Anthoine, Malcolm Howells, and Martin Boysen took a similar spirit to the Karakoram, where they attempted the unclimbed granite face of Trango Tower. Their first attempt ended partway up, at what is now known as the Fissure Boysen. They had only one large angle piton, and Boysen had to run out eighty feet of unprotected offwidth, at almost 20,000 feet, before placing it to insure that he was protected for the rest of the pitch. On the next move his knee jammed and would not come loose, and he spent hours fighting to free it, cutting his pants off in the process. He prepared to die as the sun began to set, but, as he finally relaxed, he popped out of the crack and was lowered to his concerned team. After the emotional drain of nearly seeing Boysen die a cold death, and knowing they were running low on food, they retreated. The following year they returned and completed the climb. Boysen took a second bong and managed the offwidth without any problem. At 5.10, A2 their route was not as technically difficult as Porter's A4 adventure on Asgard, but it was the hardest and most impressive technical route completed at high altitude, and it opened the door to big-wall climbing in the highest ranges on earth.

The Secret Weapon—Spring-loaded Camming Devices

Greg Lowe.

Photos courtesy of Lowe Alpine Systems

The next profound equipment change was the development of crack-camming devices. After an incomparable career of first ascents dating from the 1930s in the various ranges of the Soviet Union, Vitaly Abalakov devoted his life to mountaineering instruction, equipment design, and the promotion of international good will. Scrounging surplus aircraft materials, he made a variety of imaginative tools, including the first hauling pulley, the first adjustable tube chock, ingenious rope clamps, and titanium pitons and crampons. His invention of the Abalakov Cam was the first application to climbing of the principle of a constant-angle curved surface, with a cam shape based on the logarithmic spiral. Designed so that a load produces a rotational force, the logarithmic cam shape allowed for a single device to fit a small range of crack sizes without a change in the loading pattern, making it predictable and stable. Abalakov shared his ideas with the world and freely distributed information on the cam's design and construction.

In 1973 Greg Lowe filed for a patent for a spring-loaded version of the Abalakov Cam, manufactured some workable single-cam units, and equipped his brother Jeff, who rapidly scooped some of the finest long routes in Zion National Park, notorious for its hard-to-protect, parallel-sided cracks. These early single-cam units had an elongated thirty-degree camming angle, which provided limited stability, and their use never became widespread.

Bill Forrest and Ray Jardine after an ascent of *The Yellow Wall* on the Diamond on Longs Peak, Colorado in 1969.

Bill Forrest

In 1977 Ray Jardine climbed *Phoenix*, Yosemite's first 5.13, with a new secret weapon. With an engineer's understanding of the principles of force and friction, Jardine designed a spring-loaded opposing multiple-cam unit with a more stable fifteen-degree camming angle and an innovative triggering mechanism. He kept his "Friends" cloaked in secrecy before his 1978 patent, and Yosemite was rife with rumors of Jardine's devices allowing for effortless protection placement on hard free routes. Before the commercial availability of Friends, a lucky inner circle of wall rats bought his initial limited production of the creative tools in the Camp 4 parking lot, subsequently saving vast amounts of energy on the taxing big walls.

As is the case with most technological advancements, the ethics of using Friends was a hot topic: did they make climbing too easy by taking the challenge out of placing chocks? Licensed by Jardine, Friends were mass produced in England and became instantly popular worldwide, to the point that soon there was no debate about their use. Indeed, for many climbers Friends, and their various descendants, became the very foundation of climbing protection and safety. And there is no question that spring-loaded camming devices allowed climbers to take a huge step forward in clean and safe ascents of both free and aid routes.

Evolution of the desert rack: Peter Williams at the base of North Sixshooter Peak in 1979; Ed Webster on the first ascent of *Star Dust Cowboy* (5.11), Castleton Tower, Utah, 1983.

Ed Webster (left) and *Chester Dreiman*

Mugs Stump relaxing in the first double wide A5 portaledge, Ruth Glacier, Alaska.

Steve Quinlan

A5 Bird Beak.

John Middendorf

Living on the Big Ones

Lightweight shelters have been the most recent advance in equipment for extreme multi-day routes. Evolving from Warren Harding's BAT (Basically Absurd Technology) hammock that could be anchored from a single point, the LURP (Limited Use of Reasonable Placements) tent was developed by Greg Lowe in 1974. Though lightweight, BAT hammocks were cramped and forced the inhabitant to lean against the wall, which in a storm ran with cold water. The precursor to the modern portaledge, the LURP tent solved the problem by adding a solid aluminum frame around the bed, keeping the inhabitants away from the wall. During its use on the first winter ascent of the northwest face of Half Dome, heavy winds and snow posed no problem—for the first time in the history of big-wall climbing. However, since it was initially considered a specialized tool rarely worth the weight, the device never made it past the prototype stage. Climbers seeking the comfort of a portaledge made their own. By the early 1980s portaledge use became popular with the somewhat more widely available one-person "Cliff Dwelling," manufactured by Mike Graham. Graham also produced a dozen two-person "Fortress" portaledges and equipped Hans Christian Doseth, Finn Daehli, Dag Kolsrud, and Stein P. Aasheim who made the first ascent of the spectacular *Norwegian Pillar* on the Great Trango Tower in 1984. (Tragically, Doseth and Daehli died on the descent when a rappel anchor failed.)

Portaledges allowed for a new level of comfort and safety on multi-day vertical ascents on big walls all over the world. Bigger and bolder big-wall routes are still being climbed without recourse to fixed ropes (and thus using less, not more, gear), and portaledges are continuing to evolve into more structurally solid, weatherproof affairs, such as the six-pound titanium A5 shelter used by Catherine Destivelle on her nine-day solo first ascent on the Dru in 1991. Modern shelters have allowed smaller and lighter teams to push standards of commitment on the world's biggest rock faces.

Today we see a continuation of the relationship between climbers and their tools. Helicopters have facilitated even closer access to the base of the big routes and have been used not only for the approach but also for the descent. Improvements in sticky shoe rubber have played a big part in changing attitudes toward free climbing on big walls. Improved insulating layers and lightweight weatherproof clothing and shelters have revolutionized climbers' attitudes toward bad weather. The adoption by climbers of the compact battery-powered masonry drill has sparked a huge advance in technically difficult free climbing, and the free-climbing skills so gained are being taken to the big walls.

Arguments about technology continue to rage. New equipment is invented each year, yet, at the other end of the spectrum, Lynn Hill's first free ascent of *The Nose* of El Capitan in 1993 proved conclusively that the route could potentially be climbed without any equipment at all. *The Nose* was originally ninety-percent direct aid, and Hill's climb was widely hailed specifically for its non-reliance on mechanical aids. But without the old piton scars, without fixed protection, without Hill's aid-climbing experience, without the extraordinary free-climbing ability she gained from bolted sport climbs and indoor gyms and competitions, would there have ever been a such a free ascent?

The relationship between technology and climbing follows a traditional pattern. As each new technology develops, there is initial resistance. Some tools are rejected outright as not practical (like the Dolt Cart, a wheeled hauling contraption used during the first ascent of *The Nose*), some of marginal worth fade into obscurity (like the tossed grappling hook), and others are used sparingly until accepted with the new standard that is created. Generally, the element of risk is reduced with each new technological evolution. Detractors will speak out against the new ideas and push themselves harder to prove the lack of necessity of new tools. But eventually new tools become mainstream. Climbing challenges have always seemed limited as a resource, but equipment and training advances enable new and bolder challenges to appear. Is there a limit? One thing is certain: no one can predict future technology and the limits to the human will.

The author would like to thank Yvon Chouinard, Tom Frost, Royal Robbins, and the three Ascent *editors for their advice and criticism.*

Xaver Bongard follows a strenuous 5.9, A2 pitch on the upper headwall of the Great Trango Tower during first ascent of *The Grand Voyage* (VII 5.11, A4+ WI4). Karakoram Range, 1992.

John Middendorf

SANDSTONE 101

Dougald Macdonald

I was afraid, but not afraid of falling. Six hundred feet off the deck, two and a half days into the climb, I hung dejectedly in my aiders. End of the line. "I can't see where to go," I yelled. "There's nothing but garbage above me!"

Half a ropelength below, Chris said nothing.

The wind rocked me in tiny arcs as I pondered what to do. To the left was glistening, bald rock; around a corner to the right, I suspected, a seam continued upward. But how to get there? Yards of crackless, lumpy sandstone intervened. Someone once told me uncertainty was the spice of first ascents. Fuck that. I wanted someone to tell me which way to go.

Leaning out to peer across the wall, I wondered yet again what I was doing here, over my head on an unclimbed wall with a partner I had known for only three days. He was young enough to be my son, and I had been afraid to climb with him.

I first spoke to Chris after reading a letter his father had mailed to *Rock & Ice*, where I wrote a news column. I didn't have a big-wall first ascent in mind when I called him, but it is doubtful he and I would have joined forces otherwise. We were unlikely partners.

The letter said this: Chris McNamara and partners had climbed *Wyoming Sheep Ranch* and *Sea of Dreams*, two El Capitan test pieces, in record times. He had scampered up the *Muir Wall* in less than twenty-four hours, also a record. In the past two years, he had climbed El Capitan around twenty times. He was seventeen years old.

I talked to Chris in August, intending to write a news report on the youth's El Cap ascents. We spoke about the climbs, and then I asked what he planned to try in the coming months.

"I want to go to Zion and do *Radiator*," he said promptly. *Radiator* is the fifteen-pitch south buttress of Abraham, one of the biggest sandstone walls anywhere. First climbed in 1990 by John Middendorf and Walt Shipley, it was still unrepeated, though one party had come close before snow drove them off. *Radiator* was said to be among the hardest aid routes on sandstone—a reputation Middendorf did nothing to dispel when he graded the climb 5.10, A4 PDW, the strange letters standing for "Pretty Damn Western."

Chris had never climbed a pitch on sandstone.

As it happened, I also had my eye on *Radiator*. I had climbed hundreds of sandstone pitches in recent years, including a new route and four other walls in Zion. I had no partner for Abraham, though. Half-joking, I threw out an invitation: "Want to do it together?"

"I have a school vacation at Thanksgiving," Chris said. "Let's do it."

By the time I hung up the phone, I was already thinking of bailing. I was excited about the route and the prospect of climbing with Chris, but the whole plan rubbed against my conservative grain. My ex-wife once called me Mr. Seatbelt, and she didn't mean it as a compliment. I was cautious by nature, shy around strangers. I preferred to climb with old friends, who, I believed, accepted my weaknesses. Now, in a glib aside over the phone,

I had signed up for the second ascent of the so-called hardest route in Zion with a partner half my age, whom I'd never met, and who had never touched sandstone. I could feel the seatbelt tightening.

Chris did not seem the least bit bothered by these circumstances. He had done *Sheep Ranch* with a friend from Alaska who barely climbed and was "cooked" by the intimidating wall. Chris got to lead every pitch. He felt El Cap's notorious A5 routes had been pounded out, fixed, and retrobolted to the point where they were "easy." Easy? "Well," he said, "nothing's as hard as people say it is."

In late September, Chris upped the ante in a fax: "The free time I have is Nov. 8 to 10 and Nov. 27 to Dec. 1. Ideally, I would like to climb *Radiator* in a three-day push with ropes already fixed Nov. 8 to Nov. 10 or Nov. 11. Then climb a new route Nov. 27 to Dec. 1. I realize this may sound improbable, but tell me what you think."

What I thought was this: either Chris was the greatest aid-climbing prodigy the world had ever seen, or he was a dangerously overconfident young fool who had just been lucky so far. Either way, I felt increasingly unsure of our plans. I told him I could only get to Zion once.

His response came via e-mail. "Do you really think *Radiator* is that hard? The topo says it only has one A4 pitch. I'd rather do a new route."

Oh, what the hell, I thought. So would I.

The trick with finding a new aid line in Zion is that such routes follow cracks invisible from the ground. Six months earlier, I had scoped a possible line behind the visitor center, but from my pictures at home I couldn't be positive the cracks would connect without a long bolt ladder.

"It's not like on granite, where you can work with tiny features," I explained to Chris over the phone. "When this stone is blank, it's *really* blank. You've got to have a crack." We agreed that I would go to Zion before him and scope the line again. If the route didn't seem promising, he would spend Thanksgiving in Yosemite.

Partway through the hour-long approach to my proposed line, I realized I was following footprints. When I turned the corner below the route, two young guys had just rappelled from an anchor at the end of the first two pitches. I was one day late. Even weirder, these two had found bolts in place, surrounded by fresh rock dust from a drill, indicating a *third* party had started the same new line and then abandoned it.

I began to feel a sense of panic, which was not eased by the sight of haul bags hanging from the fifth belay of *Radiator.* In the back of my mind I had been retaining Abraham as an alternative. I was extremely anxious to find another good line, one that I was psyched to climb, but also one I thought would look good in Chris's eyes. I was still apprehensive about climbing with him. He had so easily dismissed El Capitan's hardest, while I had done only two trade routes on El Cap. It's true that I had done some hard aid on sandstone, my ace in the hole, but I had no idea how these routes would stand up against Chris's Valley experience. Had I portrayed myself as a better climber than I was? I wondered, too, about sharing the strain of a new wall with a teenager and a stranger. What would we even *talk* about?

While I wrestled with these doubts, I did *Spaceshot* with a friend. This classic Zion wall did not feel as easy as I might have liked as a warmup for a new route with Yosemite's

The Angelino Wall, Zion National Park. *Drop Zone* ascends the unlikely blank left wall of the prominent dihedral on the wall's upper left section.

Dougald Macdonald

rising star. I felt slow and clumsy on the lead, and I slept poorly at the bivy. I even got pumped carrying my friend's bags into the airport after the route. My back hurt, and I had a strange knot on my left leg. Was it some kind of growth?

I hiked around the canyon and discovered two more good-looking lines the day after finishing *Spaceshot,* but I still had doubts about climbing with Chris, and I thought of lying and telling him there was nothing new to climb. When I called him, though, he was so hot for Zion that I didn't mention my ambivalence.

Chris said he would leave high school in the San Francisco area the following afternoon, drive all night, and arrive in Zion early in the morning. He asked, "How do I get there, through Nevada or something?" I laughed and suggested he look at a map. Then he said he had to borrow a harness. "Some guy has all my gear. I loaned it to a guy, and then he gave it to another guy—they're all my friends, so I know I'll get it back but...."

What had I gotten myself into?

Chris drove into my campsite at four a.m., stuffed one summer-weight sleeping bag inside another, and slept in the dirt until dawn. When he woke, we shook hands and I fixed coffee for me, cocoa for him. He was slender, with close-cropped hair; zits in various stages of evolution colored his face. He wore baggy blue jeans, a thin fleece jacket, and sneakers.

We scraped ice from my truck's windshield and drove through the shadowed canyon to look at routes. Chris was all agog:

"Has *that* been climbed? How about that one?" I wanted to show him both lines I'd picked out, so he could take some responsibility for the choice. But the first route faced northwest, and at that early hour in November it looked too cold to consider. We returned to the visitor center to examine the sunnier line. "It goes up that brown pillar," I said, pointing skyward with one hand and cradling my neck with the other.

"What happens at that steep section?"

I wasn't really sure. While scoping the line, I had spotted a water streak shooting through the cresting waves of rock 600 feet up, but I couldn't see if the streak contained a continuous crack. Based on my experience, I had decided the line might go, but I wondered if my faith would be misplaced. "We'll have to see when we get there," I said, trying to sound confident.

"Right on," he said, starting to sort gear. Before leaving, Chris checked in with his parents from the cell phone in the car he had borrowed from them. Then, shouldering monstrous loads, we struggled uphill for an hour through sand, cactus, and scrub oak to reach the base of the wall.

We flipped a can of chicken for the first lead, and I set off. The pitch ended with a scary hand traverse, with holds breaking and my feet scuttling on the wall in Guide Tennies. Pumped full of adrenaline, I was pleased to see Chris's eyes widen a bit when he popped the tiny piece protecting the traverse and swung under the belay.

The next pitch looked thin and spooky. Chris had said he wanted hard aid, and it looked as if he was going to get it. His first placement on soft rock was a Bird Beak, and, top-stepped on this lousy piece, eight feet above the belay ledge, he searched for a piton placement. He seemed to be ignoring an obvious horizontal slot.

"How about a Tri-cam there on your right?"

"I've never placed a Tri-cam."

Oh, man. "Well, you'd better learn," I said.

"How do you do it?" he asked, pulling the pieces off the rack.

"That slot looks like it'll take a Number 1, the one with the red sling. Put it in with the rails up and the point down, the sling coming over the top toward you."

"The rails?"

"Yeah, those rails on the sides.... No, put the sling over the *top!* Turn it over!"

The pitch got harder. A hook, some cams in creaky rock, scraps of steel, and then hooks again. Chris crept upward on edges and then stopped. "It's totally blank here," he cried. "I may have to put in a rivet!"

"Yeah, so go ahead."

He scratched around for an alternative, reluctant to place the bolt. Steeped in the competitive ethics of hard Yosemite walls, he knew that each hole we drilled would count as a demerit against our new route in the eyes of his peers and those he hoped would be peers. But there was no choice. The small bolt went in, followed by more hooks, another bolt, a loose roof, and then a bolted belay.

I was impressed. The lead was A3 or harder, among the most intricate sandstone pitches I had seen. I immediately dubbed it Sandstone 101, a class Chris seemed to be acing.

Chris, however, seemed uncertain about the route. He was disappointed in himself for placing the bolts and surprised by the loose rock and the painstaking nature of the climbing. "I'm not used to taking ten minutes for every placement," he lamented.

"Middendorf says 1,000 feet of sandstone equals 2,000 feet of granite."

"Do you think it will all be like this?"

In truth, I was worried about the line, which seemed blanker than I had expected. "I think the cracks will be better higher up," I lied.

But there was more trouble ahead. Our line followed a flaring slot choked with loose blocks. I belayed as far to one side as I could while Chris excavated the crack and bathooked around the worst section, but rocks still rained onto the belay ledge. I cursed him as one stone cracked me in the helmet and another struck a nausea-inducing blow to my knee. When I followed, though, I realized he had done a masterful job to avoid killing both of us. I jugged past stacked pillars of loose rock, then down-jumared to clean the crack from above for the benefit of anyone who might repeat the route. Thunderous crashes echoed past the park residences, where rangers were playing touch football on Thanksgiving Day; dust clouds billowed in the late afternoon sun. We called the pitch "Was A5, Now A1."

At his portaledge, Chris was horrified and thrilled by the dangerous lead. "Didn't you think that was the loosest pitch you've ever seen?"

"It was pretty loose."

He screwed open a big can of Beefaroni and said, "I mean, that must be one of the loosest pitches *anywhere.*"

McNamara on aid. *Dougald Macdonald*   179

I realized what was up. Among the aid-climbing aristocracy, looseness is one of the coins of the realm, like runouts and steepness. Chris was trying to attach a value to the experience, to quantify the fear.

"I thought this was the end," he said.

I mistook his meaning, thinking he believed the climb might be over, that the pitch might be impassable.

"No, I was thinking, 'So, is this what this sport's about? Is this where I die? Maybe so.'"

"What about me, down below? I was the one who was going to get creamed."

"Yeah, I guess it was bad down there, too." He asked again, "Didn't you think that was really loose?"

"Chris, that was an incredibly loose pitch."

"*Yeah,* it was."

Racking gear the next morning, Chris raised his eyebrows at my rigid-stem Friends. "How *old* are these things?"

"Older than you, maybe."

"How old are you?" he asked.

"I turn thirty-six on Monday."

"Right on."

We were quiet for a while. "Are you still seventeen?" I asked him.

"I turn eighteen in, like, a week."

"Does that get you anything special in California?"

"Longer prison sentences," he said. Tough guy. In fact, he expected to follow his father to Princeton in the fall.

I had stopped worrying about the long November nights in the portaledge. Chris slept most of the time—maybe his schoolwork was catching up with him—and he lay quiet and still on the cramped platform, a good ledge mate. He had entertaining stories about Yosemite, like the time he did *Zodiac* with his younger brother, Morgan, in his first season of wall climbing. A couple of Swedes had started up behind the two boys, and Chris overheard one saying, "Oh, no, the kindergartners beat us to it." But Chris and Morgan raced up the route in two days, with a couple of energy bars for food and wearing only light clothing. "We were *soooo* lucky a storm didn't come," he said now.

Chris was full of questions about climbing on soft rock. How much should you bounce-test the pieces? Can you trust the face holds? Is the darker rock always stronger? I was acting as a mentor, and I liked the feeling.

"I don't know if it's the sandstone," he said, "but I am *definitely* not as a bold as usual." Maybe, but he was rocketing up the learning curve. The unfamiliar stone had slowed him, but it would no more stop him than a penny on a track stops a train. This was my route, but I still felt like I was along for the ride.

And then, on the third day, eighty feet above the portaledge, I reached the end of the line. Twenty feet of junk-filled crack above and then blankness. To the left was more blank rock, and to the right was yellow stone that crumbled like dry cake batter. The water streak was over there somewhere, but I couldn't even see it, let alone tell if it contained a crack. Some mentor. I had dragged Chris along on a wild goose chase.

Why did I even bother with wall routes? These climbs rarely offered much fun in the doing; they only became fun in the telling. When I launched up a wall, was I searching honestly for something within myself, or just searching for another good story to tell? No answers. Only the wind and the jangle of pitons and carabiners.

I thought of Chris coming to Zion with nothing but borrowed gear and blind faith in my plans. Where did a teenager get confidence like his? Had he ever failed—did he even think about failure? I doubted I would ever enjoy such strength. But neither was I ready to give in just yet.

I looked to the right again and thought: the least I can do is give it a shot. I called for tension and pulled across face holds, hoping I could at least reach around the corner and see the elusive water streak. With the rope taut, I eased onto a hook and called for slack. The hook squeaked and popped and so did I, windmilling across the face. Now I was angry. Back onto tension again. The second hook bit and held. Slowly I traced a vector across the wall. Hooks in little divots, shards of steel in seams. Over and down, then up again. The rope stretched horizontally to the crack behind me. When I finally found a good nut placement, I leaned to the right as far as I could and peered around another corner. A knifeblade seam split an overhanging dihedral and surged up the water streak through three bulges.

"*Woo-hoo!*" I yelled. "Wait till you see this!" Immense relief. Vindication. The line existed.

Chris nailed up the corner, working his leg and back muscles expertly to step high in the aiders. The haul line swung in space. After fifty feet, he looked down and said, "This may be the best nailing pitch I've ever done. If I don't take a huge screamer, I'm going to love it."

In late afternoon I started the arching overhang we called the Sandstone Tsunami. When I lowered off partway up, I could see through the darkness that the hardest climbing lay ahead. I told Chris I'd like to take pictures of him on the lead if he wanted to go up in the morning. "No, I think you should finish it," he said.

It froze hard overnight and Chris was shaking our water jugs to break up the ice—*shucka, shucka, shucka*—as I equalized tenuous pieces in the overhanging rock. A knifeblade behind a block. *Shucka, shucka.* Beaks in a softrock bulge. *Shucka, shucka!* A dirty pod that blew apart when I tested the piece in it—oh-goddamn-it-watch-me!

Shucka, shucka, shucka!

Chris said: "Don't mind me, I'm just mixing margaritas down here."

I laughed and felt my shoulders relax. The pitch ended with thin pins in an overhanging corner. It was the wildest aid lead I had done, and I was standing proud in my aiders when Chris lowered out the haul bags. As he cleaned the pitch, I caught myself fishing for some kind of affirmation: "You think *that* piece is bad, wait till you see the next one!" Chris shook his head as he yanked out the gear and muttered, "Pretty fuckin' impressive."

Yeah, it was.

We bivvied just below the top. Chris merrily trundled boulders into the void to clean off the ledges. We were struggling with a name for our route. I was all for *8 Million Ways to Die*, because I remembered that terrible movie set in Los Angeles and the formation we had

Macdonald leading the "Sandstone Tsunami" pitch on *Drop Zone*.

Chris McNamara

climbed was called the Angelino Wall. But Chris had never heard of the movie. "Don't worry," he said, "when my mom hears we don't have a name, she'll come up with something." Then we thought of all the trundling we had done and settled on *Drop Zone*. We talked about other walls we might do.

"I've got February and April vacations from school, and I'm going to be right back here in Zion," Chris said.

Still riding high from the Sandstone Tsunami, I had taken the last two leads to the bivy ledge, because Chris was nervous about free-climbing on sandstone in sneakers. I expected to finish the last hard pitch, too, but in the morning he was ready to go, and with cold-numbed hands he boldly free-climbed and hooked a poorly protected slab to the top.

The descent was difficult and dangerous. I slipped on an exposed slab and self-arrested with my forearm, leaving a bloody streak on the rock. Near the end of the final gully, we tied a sling around a shaky tree and carefully leaned over the edge for a long rappel. At the bottom, we found another tree lying amid the debris from flash floods the week before. A faded blue rappel sling was tied around its trunk. I threw my haul bag to the ground and collapsed against a sandstone wall, rubbing a sore knee. I had surpassed myself on the climb, but the exhilaration of success was dissipating fast.

"I'm too old for this shit," I moaned.

Chris looked at me, eyes shaded under his helmet, and said, "Some people tell me I'm too young."

DO THE RIGHT THING

Dave Insley

I lit another cigarette and sank back into a musty couch in the dark, fetid living room. Beer cans and overflowing ashtrays occupied every semi-level surface. The only light came from an old console television, the kind marketed thirty years ago mostly as a piece of furniture. Often the house was dry, dusty, and deserted, but now it was swelteringly hot, humid, and crowded. The dust that had settled everywhere was now mixed with spilled beer, sweat, spit, and all manner of shedding disease, decomposed skin, blood, mucus, and urine. Black widows built their sticky webs in every unswept corner.

I was always kind of charmed by the ambiance and had lived there for three years because it was the only thing resembling a real home to me—an old ranch house with wooden floors and funky fixtures situated on an acre in the heart of the west's "Most Western Town," Scottsdale, Arizona. This house, built in the 1930s and suitable for condemnation, sat in squalid contrast to a mostly renewed, expensive, and thoroughly modern city. It was a tiny dab of rural bliss, a place where a country boy could feel relaxed and at home in an otherwise sprawling, character-less metropolis. Only a few of us called the place home on a permanent basis, but on any given night the back forty could quickly fill with Toyota pickups and sleeping bags.

Through the gates of that place walked athletes, artists, explorers, celebrities, raconteurs, students, con men, castaways and stowaways, to-be's and once-were's. There were rotting couches and chairs that people had left outside. Abandoned from "nicer" people's homes, these stylish pieces now provided comfort to weary climbers or kayakers or heroin addicts whenever they passed through town. Always there were cars and trucks parked in various states of service or repair; always the rooms were crowded, the toilet overflowing, newspapers and pulp novellas scattered among bits of dried fat and hairballs; and always there were people coming and going, leaving something to spoil in our refrigerator, or perhaps leaving a fresh disease to take root in the agar of our communal filth.

My god, I had sunk low! I looked around at the dank hole I was hiding in. Once I had such hopes and dreams; now I was fat with malnutrition, drunk on cheap wine, and sleeping in my own dirt. Across the room Mike Beres lay face down, snoring noisily through the upholstery of another of our stinky couches.

Dixie returned and brought a video, Spike Lee's *Do the Right Thing*. I watched with mild amusement, then nodded off. Mike and I alternately awoke to refrains of:

"Yo da man!"

"No, yo da man!"

"No, no, no, man, yo da man!"

When next I awoke, Moammar Bonswali was dragging me from the sensory deprivation of that room into the yard, gasping and sputtering in the dirt, wheezing, coughing. Blinking in the bright morning light, wiping the blood from my lip, cut open during the struggle, I cursed him once more.

"Come on," he urged.

"What are you doing here?" I asked.

He didn't answer but turned and walked toward his truck, got in, started the engine. It occurred to me that I shouldn't push my luck. I hurried to the truck and got in. Finally we were at Bowman's, eating breakfast. Moammar poured coffee into me and I began to stop hallucinating.

"So, what about something up in Siphon Draw?" he demanded.

"Sure," I muttered, picturing myself halfway up some ridiculous volcanic crud pile with loose blocks showering down all around me. I had done enough of the Siphon Draw classics to have some idea of what we were buying into. "How about the Invisible Tower," I said, more as a joke than as a serious suggestion.

Chuck Hill, Jon Colby, and I had once hiked up the drainage below the south face of the formation named North Buttress. Halfway up we found a delightfully steep and featured wall, split by a beautiful corner system with a perfect 150-foot dihedral as its middle pitch. We hiked up the other side of the gully to get a better view of the route, aiming for a high notch below an obvious gendarme. As we hiked toward it, the gendarme loomed larger and larger. Arriving at its base, I looked up at a perfect finger- and hand-crack that split the gendarme for about ninety feet, all the way through a roof system and out of sight above! Neither Chuck nor Jon seemed particularly impressed—they were pretty fixated on the route across the way—but I talked one of them into belaying me out of the notch so that I could get a better view of the wall below, on the other side of the notch. It was steep, and I couldn't tell whether or not there were any climbable features. My partners finally tugged me back in and we went over to the other wall. Chuck led a 5.10 pitch as the sun set, and we vowed to return to finish the route later.

I did return later, with Dixie, to climb The Crying Dinosaur. Afterward we hiked over to the wall below the gendarme, which we had begun calling the Invisible Tower because, while you could see it from the parking lot, on the approach hike it was soon lost, blending into the background so well that its profile could be discerned only from a few angles. Ever since our discovery a few weeks earlier, the hand/finger crack on the tower's upper portion had haunted me. We hiked along the base of the wall, a few hundred feet below my previous reconnaissance point. Several crack systems led through steep rock; it looked a bit loose near the bottom, but do-able. I was convinced that a climb starting here could be logically connected to the notch and the crack on the summit gendarme. All that was left was to find a victim.

Though I am certain that Moammar knew me well enough to doubt the honor of my intentions, and to question my fitness for the project, he quickly agreed to my plan. Later that morning, after a sweaty hike, we stood at the base of the wall discussing who would lead the first pitch.

"Yo da man," I said.

"No, no, yo da man," Moammar would reply, and we went on that way for a while. It looked as though two pitches would take us to the shoulder of the mountain through the cleanest part of the cliff. It would be an easy matter to then move the belay fifty feet or so to the base of the gendarme. The bottom of the wall looked a little loose, and Moammar really wanted to lead an overhanging crack that he could see on the second pitch. Foolishly, I agreed to lead first.

As was common for us in those days, we carried a bolt kit with half a dozen bolts and hangers for occasional face-climbing sections or belay/rap anchors; but we always tried to climb up weaknesses that featured crack systems and obvious natural protection. Bolts were expensive, both in terms of burrito money and in the sense that hand-drilled, fatty bolts required time and energy to place.

It is often assumed that a climb with long runouts or other marginal fixed gear resulted from the sheer boldness of the first-ascent party. Not necessarily true: sometimes it is simply a matter of economics. Bolts are expensive and climbers are poor. I can remember going climbing when it seemed as though every penny was spent and every favor called in, just to have gasoline and food and gear and smokes and all of the other details attended to. Then, on the climb itself, every spiritual and physical resource would be tapped out, three times as much gear would be required as you thought, the route would take days longer than you had planned, and, in the end, you reached the summit after toiling sense-lessly. Then you barely got off the mountain after leaving every piton and bolt and scrap of sling that you owned, crawling back to camp looking like a beggar in rags.

On this particular day we had only four bolts, and discretion would be called for in their use. Stepping high, off a boulder, I began the pitch. Moderate face climbing up dish-es led to a couple of huecos. Standing in the highest one, I drilled our first hole. Past the bolt the rock became steeper and crisper, and the holds started to make little creaking noises. I was aiming for a big, ear-shaped flake to drop a Friend behind to quell my creep-ing anxiety. When I got within reach, I placed the Friend, but as I climbed closer I decid-ed not even to touch the ear. It looked pretty bogus. I'd seen Stan Mish push a slab twice its size off a tower less than half a mile away, and that one had looked solid.

I wanted to place another bolt but didn't want to try to hang out anywhere to drill one. I certainly wasn't brave enough to hang from a hook on this crap! I also didn't want to use half our bolt supply even before reaching the top of the first pitch.

Above, I spotted an obvious and comfortable belay ledge at the base of Moammar's choice-looking overhanging crack, only twenty feet above me. Oh, but what a twenty feet! The only way was an obvious traversing line of holds, past a thin, bladelike flake, then up a lower-angle section. If all the holds had been good it would have been an easy 5.9, but every hold was questionable and crisp. At the blade I was faced with the option of not using it and creating a difficult boulder problem that I was sure to fall from, or of trusting it and keeping the climb within the range of probable—unless, of course, the flake peeled. I tapped the flake; it sounded horrible. I pondered my dilemma for a moment while energy drained from my arms and seeped toward my bowels. A fall would probably yank the Friend from behind the ear, or possibly take it completely off, and I would deck out. Crater. Fall all the way to the ground and to my death. No doubt the falling flake would then conveniently kill my partner and the cliff would have bowled a perfect strike. This was stupid and ridicu-lous. What was I doing here? Strength fading, I felt for the blade and gingerly pulled myself to the left. I brought my right hand over and momentarily both hands were on the flake. My left hand shot for a hold on the wall beyond. Then I began to move my feet, reached for a better left hand and finally got my right hand off the blade. I took a breath, my senses over-loading. Pulling up onto easier ground, I felt the weight of a thousand mountains slip from my shoulders, the knots of a thousand grannies slip from my gut. The metallic taste of burst-ing capillaries stung my mouth; a raw sense of reality burned lustily through my awareness.

I used a second bolt for the belay, for there were no natural anchors, and brought Moammar up. He cursed the loose rock, cleaning as much as he could along the way. He arrived grumbling but complimented my lead. His praise wasn't needed: I hadn't felt so good in a billion years.

He began his pitch but soon found it not as appealing as he had hoped. The rock was still a little loose and the crack a bit wide. He returned to the belay, cursing. Off to our right another crack system meandered up the cliff. "Moammar," I said, "forget about the left-hand crack. Do the right thing!"

More grumbling. Finally he went right. A little later the grumbling stopped, and the rope snaked steadily out, around the corner and up. "This is great!" I heard him exclaim. But a few minutes later he was stymied high on the pitch by a bulging section and a pinched-off crack. Natural protection looked impossible, and eventually he called for the bolt kit. With that one good piece of protection, he pulled through the crux.

I soon discovered what had stopped the grumbling. The pitch was excellent. Great rock, neat moves, good pro, and a spectacular position. I arrived at the belay in good spirits. From here we could walk off the climb or continue up the gendarme. I had my eye on the splitter I had spotted the year before, and hurried to its base.

Starting up the crack, I was impressed by the perfect quality of the rock. There were fingerlocks, sidepulls, and steep, high reaches. I took a short fall. It seemed hard. I climbed back to my high point and beyond, only to fall from higher up, near the roof. The crack had gone from fingers to hands, and now to off-hands at the lip of the roof. I asked Moammar if he would like to take over. He fired it, first try, and called it 5.10+ or 5.11.

"Hey, there's a fourth pitch up here, to the top of the pinnacle," he yelled. "It looks like a classic. You're in luck."

I grimaced. Moammar's idea of good luck was free corn dogs and a pair of great seats at a tractor pull. I seconded the pitch clumsily and stood beside him, breathless. Down the other side of the gendarme was a gully, probably easy fifth class. Above was a fifty-foot-tall, pear-shaped boulder that formed the summit. I placed a Friend in the crack between the pear and the main rock, then bouldered up on huecos to a 5.9 mantle onto the fat part of the pear until I was twenty feet above my pro with a last, short, difficult section between me and the summit. I pulled out the drill and began making a hole for my last bolt. Racing with the setting sun, I finally had the hole deep enough, but, reaching back into the bottom of the kit for the bolt, I was dismayed to find a frayed opening the size of a nickel. No bolt. I wanted to cry but cursed instead. After much bellyaching I pulled a standard angle piton off the rack, drove it as far as I could into the hole, and tied it off.

The sun was setting as I pulled through the final moves and heaved my body onto the summit. When Moammar arrived, we sat on the summit together, smoking and reflecting on our day and the climb. The route had been spectacular, bordering on the spiritual. Every sweet breath of air felt borrowed, undeserved, rich. I felt surprisingly close to Moammar. Before long his usual surliness would return and he would be dragging me back down the mountain, spiraling downward into our usual bacchanalia, downward to the decaying land below. But I wouldn't soon forget that moment of liberation and rest on the summit. No longer going anywhere, but not yet returning, we sat together like Krishna and Arjuna on an island of peace surrounded by bloodied soil.

tang of the fruit, the dappled light beneath the oaks, our sporadic comments, jokes, expletives, the lazy sweet labor of climbing together—I hope these will stay with me if I ever relinquish the sport. But these intangibles—flavors of food, wind fingers in hair, the taut blue sky, the drone of bugs and birds, the adrenaline pump of activity—doubtless will be lost. What will my older self retain, to visit on quieter, lonelier afternoons, somewhere ages hence?

We pack up, amble down the carriage road. Lagging behind, talking to Les, Lorraine is carefree, seems younger even than Kim. She laughs and skips, pointing out foam flower, lycopodium, wild ginseng. She scampers through the woods. Les is smiling, nodding over her botanical discoveries. Our necks craned to the quartzite wall, blotched yellow, orange, black, glitteringly white, I point and rattle off route names for Kim; she studies cracks and overhangs while we wait for the other two to catch up.

Lorraine and Kim have a different idea about climbing than I do, a luxury that borrowed gear and seconding tough pitches their first season affords them. They take extreme grades for granted, are looking ahead to more exotic moves. Les does our hardest leads, and I know what it takes out of him. For myself, I have sweated plenty on moderate rock, have caught and taken long falls. I can't see the cliffs as a playground, but rather as a place where tragedy lurks. Where joy must be earned and happiness arrives unnoticed, when you are contorted, struggling, intent on the climb; or, unexpectedly, at the top, amid the tangle of rope and gear, with bloody cuticles or a wasp-bitten shoulder as you watch a falcon plummet after a pigeon. It is too late for me to see it their way, and I suspect that I will not be with them when they are onsighting 5.12 in a couple of years.

Les and I tell them about the old days: *Dülfersitz* rappel—an arcane wrap of rope around back and legs before stepping off into the void; swami-belt tie-ins—as good a reason as there ever was not to take a lead fall; body belays with goldline rope; cowboy days of piton-and-hammer climbing. We tell them stories of the guys we've seen here: Romano, Bragg, Wunsch, McCarthy, Stannard, Barber—ascetics, fanatics, maniacs, prophets. A sense of the sport's past may prevent their becoming new-age climbers, shouting for tension, cursing and complaining, leaving garbage on the cliff. For me, a part of climbing is a reverence discovered in quiet moments, a pleasure that arrives only when voices are mute. Of this we say nothing.

If there is something of friendship in climbing, a solace and beauty the soul discovers in the inarticulate and immutable, a security in the ropes and knots, a companionable peace in the solitude of high windy places, then there is also something of climbing in friendship: we are like pilgrims seeking a vision, a holy way, each of us finding our own truth, transient yet recurrent amid the inscrutable and random intricacies of mottled stone. The evaporating path up those grades of 5.10 and beyond is somehow like the murmured clues of runes and relics embraced by the questing knight; like the words that go unspoken, not needing to be spoken, between friends, being of and about feelings that cannot be fully deciphered, feelings that grown men cannot comfortably discuss.

Les and I have taken our time to grow closer over the years the way men do when they are no longer young: without precipitation, always reserving something of ourselves. We take it for granted that some things remain private; somehow we know which questions not to ask.

We go over things carefully: movies we enjoyed, stories we read; we review placements and note the gear needed for each pitch in our guidebooks. Les designs circuit boards and I am a software engineer. I work meticulously, double-checking each instruction, each module, studying reams of code the way the faithful mull over the Talmud. Admittedly, I place and remove gear fastidiously. I never lose anything; sometimes I climb last or re-climb a pitch to pull the pieces no one else can get. We invent tricks and tools for retrieving cams and lodged stoppers.

We shake hands when we meet and again after a good outing. Les encourages me to climb harder, to do my best; he is not critical of my limitations, unable as he is to see into my heart. He has a strength that remains undiminished as others grow stronger. I amuse him with tales of my wild youth: fistfights in high school, car wrecks, scrapes with the law, affairs with zany women. I'm not sure if he realizes that the careful climber and the reckless kid are different halves of me; there is a past I haven't left behind.

In a way my commitment to climbing is improbable; I am like a piece placed wrongly on the game board that a practitioner's eye would catch immediately. I come to the cliffs, each time, by a new act of will, elements of lover and shell-shocked soldier in me; each voyage here marks me as a liar, and a penitent.

The summer I am fourteen a friend, Nathan, returns from Yosemite a graduate of some guide's course. He brings an endless leaden rope, seat-belt webbing, steel carabiners, a few beat-up pitons. He determines to teach us, like a missionary bringing true religion to the ignorant indigenous peoples, the skills he learned: how to tie knots, belay, set anchors; the art of climbing in sneakers or work boots. Larry and I, Nathan's misanthropic gang, fashion harnesses, practice bowline, clove hitch, grapevine. One day, girdled by our fathers' tool belts with purloined hammers slotted away, a lost crew of carpenter children from some Scandinavian folk-tale, we lug the gear to the hundred-foot wall at Arden, fawn-colored ancient granite streaked white and black, a mornings' sweaty hike along the Ramapo hills. It is there, after practicing verbal signals and dynamic belay, as Nathan shows us how to lodge cumbersome hex nuts into unaccommodating cracks, that I drop him. I watch him fall twenty feet to the ground, hear his leg crack like a gunshot one valley away, watch his face go through its transformations from lecturing show-off to startled surprise, and then to the frightened first awareness of bad pain.

Larry and I splint him somehow, despite his wriggling and cursing, using sticks and sections of tubular webbing we hack up with our jackknives. We carry and drag him over and through underbrush, rock walls, streams that I have no memory of crossing on our way in. We are scratched by prickers, soaked to the skin. Some of the time Nathan is screaming; some of the time he is passed out. It is almost nightfall when we lean him against a porch railing and ring the bell at a strange house. The woman who answers starts to close her door on us, two bruised and bloody bandits with their murder victim.

Though his leg mends, Nathan never climbs again. The gear we leave at the bottom of that wall is probably still there: moldy rope and rusty biners. I climb sporadically through the years, the way a once-bit kid occasionally pets a big dog he has been assured is tame. The memory of the fall fades as high-school acquaintances lapse and paraphernalia from wrestling matches and addresses of old sweethearts are lost. Larry makes the U.S. ski team and, one April, hiking Tuckerman Ravine in a long line of skiers, he breaks through snow and is sucked along a fierce hidden river; they don't recover him until late May. The last time

I see Nathan it is across a grave: like spies with half a postcard each we study one another, waiting for the other to reveal his part of a near-forgotten truth. Now, in my dreams, it is no longer me that drops him, but someone whose face I can't see, as I yell to him to watch out. It must be, when I meet Les, that the past is so distant that it occupies an unfocused space between myth and dream and reality where words can no longer reach it.

Did Newton realize that nothing could stay as it was? He believed that a particle, or a nexus of bodies, at equilibrium, could travel a predetermined path through eternity unless impacted by outside forces. I wonder if, like Sophoclean heroes and heroines, we each carry the seeds of our destruction within us.

Les and Lorraine are self-contained, independent. Their humor is for each other, as are special glances, the trailing brush of a hand. Lately, as we go humping down the carriage road looking for the last lost 5.10 we've never climbed, they trail behind, out of earshot; they dart off suddenly to climb something else. More and more frequently, I think maybe we should simply have planned separate trips: you need only two on a rope. Yet Les is religious with his invitations; I am perplexed until I meet his wife, Elaine, at a company party.

She is fashionable in a dark suit, impeccably made up. The smudge of blue near her eye, a hint of red accenting her fine cheekbone, remind me of the colors of Kim's sunsets, of Lorraine's dark lake. Les has told me Elaine is uninterested in climbing, regards it as a smelly, gritty pastime. I balance my plate of hors d'oeuvre and am awestruck by her pithy amusing chatter. She loves Dostoevski, Vonnegut, Toni Morrison. She sips wine, gestures grandly, explains in disconnected snatches the irreconcilable conflicts of the soul; the humor needed to cope with human idiocy; the miracle of joy retrievable from the ashes of suffering. I nod, eying the spiked punch bowl from afar. Elaine darts off to find a livelier companion. Intelligent and beautiful, she strikes me as the perfect wife. I look around the room but don't see Les anywhere. Remembering the brothers Karamazov, I think how love can drive us mad, the way innocence commingles with our basest impulses: jealousy, mendacity, betrayal.

Kim and I analyze the group's effectiveness as a climbing team, its inner mechanisms.

"She's taken some falls leading," I point out, thinking maybe they are falls that didn't need to be taken.

"Still," she adds, "he lets her lead what she wants to, what she needs to lead, to develop."

"You can lead when we climb, anytime," I counter, listing climbs I've arranged for her to lead. I am careful not to mention how I've calculated the odds for her, weighed out the rack, watched hairtriggered as she ran it out. Her determination seems to be offset by a matching insecurity; she often interprets a casual remark as an attack.

"I don't mean that," she replies, picking up my hand in her smaller one, studying the lines and scratches.

"They are... what's the word? Like school kids together, don't you think?" Kim sits on the bed, legs folded Indian-style, looking like a school kid herself. But her face is intent, serious.

"Giddy." Giddy with joy to be in the sunshine, on the rock, together. Sometimes I think I've felt that way for some girl. Sometimes I think I feel that way about Kim.

"They're giddy when they climb," Kim agrees.

Kim has told me she may go west next year, to Yosemite. "To be a climbing bum," she jokes, but I think she means to move past this, into what she thinks must be real climbing, away from what she calls "the hot-house Gunks variety." But this isn't about climbing. It's her rationalization as she looks to reformulate her life plan, having made a false start. There is a fierce drive in her, which I will never have for her, or for climbing.

I find myself wondering if Kim and Lorraine have a drive to compete against each other, or against Les and me, or even against unknown climbers. I wonder if this is what is wrong with me: I am content to reclimb old favorite lines, to follow someone else's lead on harder pitches. There is tactile pleasure in the rock surface, physical pleasure in the stretching shifting body; I have thought: I can't do the waltz or tango, but I can do this. I wonder if all along I have been wrong about what climbing is and how to do it.

All along I should have realized it was a mistake to plan a different sort of trip, eight hours travel in the car toward unstable weather, ten pitches of granite. The two-hour Gunks drive has settled on us like complacency; it is a deus ex machina that enables us to function. There is a security there that perhaps we shouldn't abandon: a safety in well-frequented routes, in the comfortable predictable responses of others to the demands of the moment. But something in climbers pulls their imaginations, their conversations, and ultimately, their bodies and souls, to bigger walls. I think: at least we don't live in Oklahoma. We'd be driving to the Rockies or Devil's Tower.

It's hard to get plans settled; everyone has different schedules. We pick one week, then have to cancel when work takes Les out of town. We pick another week. Elaine decides to come along with the kids to do some modest hiking in the Presidentials. Kim and I exchange a glance. She whispers, "The kids are too small." I whisper back, "Elaine doesn't like to hike." Lorraine points out that we'd need two cars, and adds, smiling, "Don't look at me. The whale is in the shop. I think they're rendering it down to lamp oil."

I keep my mouth shut, try to let things work out according to their own logic and, after a week or two, Elaine has decided to stay home. Miraculously, we all are in the car, headed north. In the back seat, Lorraine and Kim play that old string game, cat's cradle: one plucks strands from a starshaped pattern displayed by the other, then inverts her hands, spreads fingers, reveals an intricate net of angles. We watch clouds cluster then disperse; our forecasts run the gamut of gloomy to fine as we rotate through the seats taking shifts at the wheel.

We roll into Lincoln at dark, a touristy village complete with overpriced grocery, antique, and souvenir shops. We have agreed: we're not roughing it, and we find a motel. Lorraine has brought smoked oysters, croissants, Hungarian salami (made entirely of fat and garlic), Camembert soft and yeasty. We feast on this, acknowledging that it will probably not help our anti-gravity efforts tomorrow.

The pigeonhole problem of four adults and two beds is resolved while Lorraine is in the bathroom: Les pulls the mattress off one bed and slides it against a wall. He produces a child's sleeping bag that he unzips to make a flannel quilt. I take a pill to help me sleep and that, or the food, could account for my dreams: something with a boat, and a vast wobbling sea, icebergs or mountains, and then, in the darkness, the murmur of voices. I submerge into the depths of sleep that, like a weight of water or snow, press against me with great force, and then bob up onto a rolling surface where sleep and waking meet, like sea and sky at dawn, in grayness. Kim is awake and in the indeterminate predawn light we make love gently, almost without moving, with the cadence of lapping water or creaking ropes. I sleep again and do not dream.

The Gunks talus—a short scramble over mulch-covered schist—leaves us cursing and out of breath. We regard the Cannon talus as an insult deposited for out-of-towners, a daunting medley of awkward maneuvers: stumbling over, crawling under, bouldering up, blocks VW to tractor-trailer-sized. We sweat up the blazing rock field following the cairns and finally walk beneath the wall, eyeing possible lines of assault. Les stumbles, one eye in the guidebook, the other on the cliff, singing out route names we have never heard.

Maybe this is what we've come for: to feel these foreign names in our mouths as if we sing a prayer at dawn, facing the holy city; or to discover alien rhythms as we gyrate to a hollow drum, bare feet in the earth, below Kilimanjaro; to discover that ancient harmonies of sight, sound, movement, were always inside us. But each of us has come for something different. The Pleiades, weaving and twisting our fates, have brought us together to reveal very different truths about our lives.

We locate our climb and settle into a comfortable pattern: the second re-racks for the next lead while the pitch's leader belays the third. The grayish-white granite is fissured by long crack systems that snake up the face, stratified by seams and overlaps that distort the perspective. The face looks clean, featureless, though I realize this is partly due to the hugeness of it; I don't even know how to look for the next ledge. The pitches drop away behind us slowly at first, then suddenly the mountain transforms itself into that foreshortened apron that bespeaks great height. Looking down we realize that we are 500 feet up, on a big climb.

We shout suggestions across to two Welshmen on a neighboring route. They have no guidebook and don't know where to go. Their soft lilting voices reach us like scraps of some Celtic ballad telling of red-bearded lords and blond princesses, great battles fought, witchcraft and fairy tricks. Kim shouts pitch descriptions that are snatched from her lips and carried aloft by the wind. They wave to us and one of them moves up. Kim shouts our names and address in case they want to visit. "Aren't they handsome?" she asks, though how she could judge that of two helmeted figures a hundred yards away, I don't know.

On a pitch near the end of the climb, I have moved up and back a dozen times, perhaps more, too cowardly to take a short fall on a wretched cam placement. As bothersome as being stymied by the move's grade is my sense of exposure on the wall, my awareness of sheer fear itself. I move up again: it is a problem that eludes my tentative efforts at solution, like a piece of software that looks correct but wherein lurks a blemish that can blossom into catastrophe, or like a knot that appears sound but that unravels when load is applied. I try to clear my head of clutter but my mind forms webs among people, events; folds and refolds the strands, revealing new arrangements. I close my eyes for a moment, then blink in the rarified light: I try to focus the rock, the problem, to see the solution revealed like a check-mated king three moves ahead. But uninspired, I shift my weight clumsily, try a different nubbin with my right foot, retreat without having put my dubious arrangement of body parts to the ultimate test. It doesn't feel right, doesn't feel like enough. "Don't worry about it," Les shrugs when I'm back on the ledge. I untie from the sharp end as he rambles on about how finding good protection can be fatiguing. Still, I feel an overwhelming sense of failure. Kim tussles my hair and gives me a smile. I can't think of a thing to say. The cloud shadows sweep across the valley, then are gone, like the trace of spirits on the land, rushing away from us, scattering before cataclysm. The sun glinting on the lake below, on cars and people and rocks seems to telescope them toward me: a thousand feet from me they appear inches away. A quarter mile distant, yet close enough to whisper to, I watch a tanned woman in a halter top feed out rope as her partner searches for a way over a big roof.

Lorraine goes up, scampers almost, steps left where I struggled rightward, reaches up and makes a move I must have known before birth and needed only a Platonic nudging to elicit. I go up second and float across the scalloped face, unthinking, as if I am traveling a path I've journeyed along so often my body knows the way.

Today belongs to the others: Les is solid on the lead, intuitive about the route across acres of blotched granite. Lorraine has suddenly come into her own, passed me by; she makes astute decisions about what to discard from the lead rack, sets up clever anchors; she climbs with a new determination that will not be denied. "Great lead," Les exclaims, touching Lorraine's arm. She pokes him in the ribs, "You're going pretty well yourself, big boy." They squat next to each other, re-racking, chuckling over recent moments of insecurity or tension, cracking jokes about a stopper tightly wedged in a crack, a TCU that needed much tinkering to ease from a slot.

This is Kim's first time so high up and I can see it bothers her. Her climbing is ragged, her patience with the rest of us is thin. She glances at me, scrunched together as we are on a meager ledge. I know what she's thinking by her expression: they're at it again, giddy.

The last two pitches seem endless with premature congratulations, intimate analyses of everyone's technique. The trip to the motel seems endless, and Kim is silent, almost sullen. Mentally, each explores his or her private successes and failures on the climb. Kim and I go to a movie while Les and Lorraine go out for dinner and ice cream.

We plan separate climbs for the next day, Kim and I thinking to do *Whitney-Gilman*, Les and Lorraine deciding to try something harder. So we aren't there when it happens, though I can see them there, happy, in the sunshine, warm against the white rock. Distracted by something, the beautiful day, the climb itself, Lorraine has forgotten both to anchor herself and to tie into the end of the rope as Les leads off. He makes a long run-out, falls. Lorraine is jerked to the wall and several feet up loses the belay line. In that moment, I know, Lorraine can't believe what she is seeing and, in her thoughts, which move at the speed of light, Les seems to fall so slowly that perhaps it isn't happening at all, even as she realizes her failure to place an anchor without ever turning her stricken eyes to the bowl of tree she knows is there behind her, ungirdled by a bight of rope. She watches forever, the body turning against the azure sky like an astronaut on a space walk until, abruptly, the world stands still.

Les has told me the story twice at least, so that I can picture the event as clearly as if I'd been there. I can see it when I close my eyes; it is my own memory, too. Maybe accidents nestle like this, at some deep place in every climber's soul, burnt in by repeated imaginings, by dozens of scary lunges on tricky holds, from hundreds of tragic stories read, or laconic bar-room tales told over just-one-more pitcher of beer.

The way earthquakes and explosions realign the seeming permanence of landscapes and buildings according to a new underlying logic, we are subtly altered. "For some reason, I was watching the couple climbing next to us," Lorraine begins a too-intricate explanation that reveals nothing about what happened, rather something about what she has lost. As she speaks our eyes meet briefly, then both of us quickly look away. "We should have been signaling each other more carefully. Also, we need to check each other, check placements and belays." Les speaks at the ceiling, sounds like an instructor for an Outward Bound group. Away from them, Kim regrets the routes we didn't do: *Vertigo, Cannonade, The British Were Coming*—routes in which she showed no interest when she heard their descriptions.

Out of the blue, she gets mail from the Welsh climbers, at grad school in Pennsylvania, gearing up to go west. Careful of her privacy, I take phone messages for her. Kim has changed too, no longer needing to explain things to me or herself, some cornerstone of our relationship having been dislodged. More and more, she complains about her work, annoyed at being cooped up indoors, missing trips on nice days, missing the summer.

Before I can analyze the situation, before we've even talked about it, Kim has made up her mind about something: me, her life. She has packed up, decided to make a pilgrimage to Yosemite, hitching a ride with Owen and Tom, the Welshmen who, though they never materialize, seem always to have been here, moving about the apartment with us, along on our climbs, mocking me. Kim visits Les once in the hospital and then is gone. On subsequent visits I find I can't speak of her departure. No matter, the knowledge of it hovers in the air around us as Lorraine and Les and I recall past adventures or catalog our daily chores. I can feel our separate energies in the hospital room as if we are electrons guarding our orbits. Our words spin away from us, suddenly autonomous; like objects in a gravity-free chamber, they whiz and ricochet around our heads, take on new meanings, develop deadly power. There is a new politeness between Les and Lorraine like that between caged pacing cats, a space they now keep open between them that I am to occupy but cannot. If I have a word of wisdom or knowledge I should speak to them, I don't know what it is.

After a week Les is released, and I am relieved not to have to visit the hospital again. He returns to work in the first blaze of autumn, tottering along on crutches like one of those rocking, balanced, eternal-motion machines, the physical rigidity of taped ribs and plaster somehow suggesting a sternness or inflexibility of spirit. But perhaps it's just the impression one gets, seeing him wince as he turns to face his interlocutor. By winter the tape and crutches are gone, but he nonetheless retains a certain stiffness; maybe he was always this way and I never realized it.

No one has heard from Kim in ages but once in a while I find her name near the bottom of the rankings at some sport-climbing competition. Sometimes I see a lone woman running through the flurries or inhospitable winter sunshine. At the end of the day, I salute Les from across the lot, catch a slight movement that must be a nod. When on occasion I see Lorraine leaving work, I wave cheerfully and see an answering flutter from her, detect her fleeting puckish grin.

Each day the sun gains a fraction's strength; the likelihood that one of us will call another, plan a trip to a gym or a local crag, or even the Gunks, increases. It is at once both natural and impossible for me to call Lorraine or Les—natural if I had already done it, spontaneously; impossible since I have premeditated the act so long. I run opening sentences through my head and discard them; though genuine, they echo with false camaraderie. They are cloying, like the pick-up lines Kim and Lorraine giggled over. We languish like the scattered pieces of a puzzle or a game, waiting for some greater intelligence to realign us. The robins and wrens and bluebirds are back. The long winter must surely end soon.

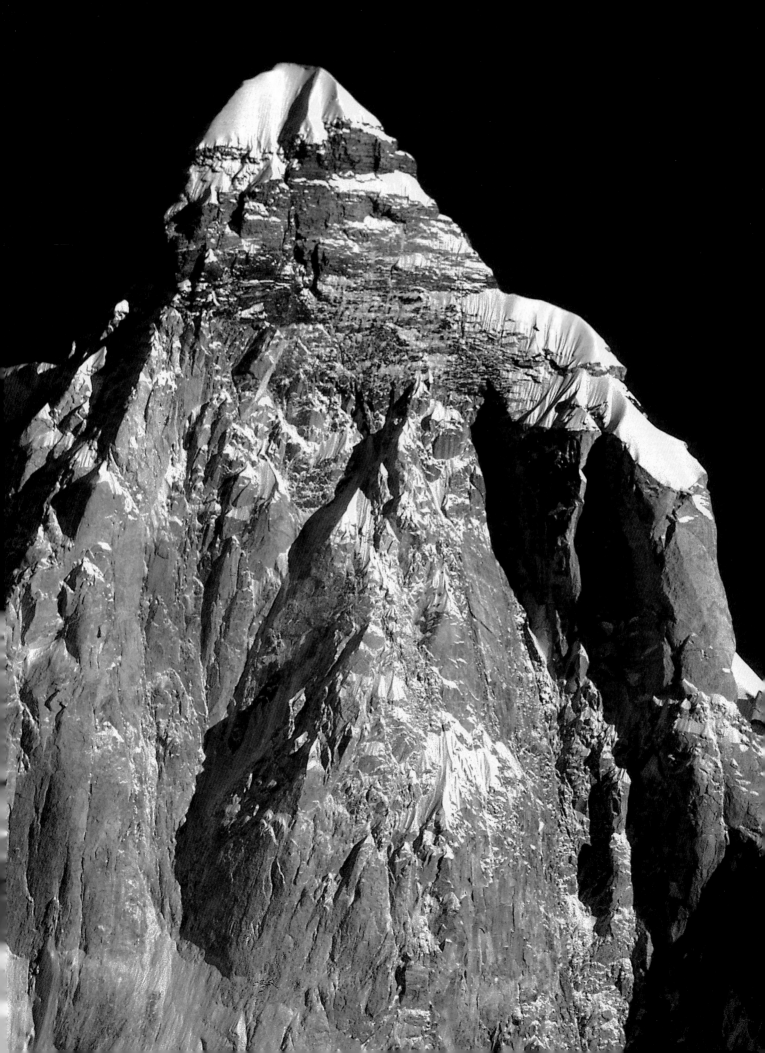

THE USE OF A MEAL
Alpine Style on Thalay Sagar

Andy Selters

Mostly we have nothing to do; in fact, the most important thing we can do is nothing. In four and a half beautiful fall days Kitty Calhoun and I have climbed seventy percent of a direct line on Thalay Sagar's north face. Now, for three days we've been waiting out a storm. We both have plenty of patience, and our portaledge is holding up fine. I do worry about the headwall a few pitches above us. There's been a lot of thin climbing, but this headwall might be the most intimidating piece of route I've ever seen: a 200-foot slab, sidewalk-smooth and essentially vertical, evenly glazed with thin ice. There might no pro on it, much less a belay, and the scary possibility is that we could get partway up it and certify the bad news. But as long as it snows there's no use in worrying. Every five minutes spindrift pours down the wall, easily powerful enough to wash off a run-out climber. So we just curl in our portaledge as the snow hisses over the fly again and again.

Our first priority is to save food and fuel, and this is best done by sleeping. At 21,500 feet it's easy to stay unconscious for almost sixteen hours a day. The remaining time is plenty to chip ice into a sack, melt it into two lukewarm drinks per day, pee a couple of times off the ledge, and hold a conversation or two. We allow almost no thoughts of

Left: The awe-inspiring north face of Thalay Sagar, Garhwal Himalaya, India.

Right: Kitty Calhoun leading a thinly-iced slab at 18,500 feet.

Photographs: *Andy Selters*

visiting the tiny food bag hanging at our knees. There's but one dinner in it, and that's not to be touched until we're moving again. For another couple of days we can have about an ounce of granola each day. Because of my greater size and metabolism, every other day I get a spoonful of almond butter.

Often the storm lifts, and we can peer down the route. It's been about twenty-five pitches so far, many as exhilarating as I've ever imagined. The last thousand feet has been a Glacier Point Apron steepened to sixty- to seventy-five degrees, with sheets of ice an inch to a foot thick. "Anchors, anchors," we silently cry, thirsting for gear placements like desert rats for water. Over the last eight pitches we've averaged one piece between belays. All our ice screws have their teeth bent over from bottoming into the granite. The wondrous thing is that the ice is plastic, and it holds to the rock like epoxy. Points go into it as surely as nails into pine, and it encourages you to step up and up, farther and farther from the safety below. Luckily, some sort of belay anchor has shown up about every 150 feet.

The delicate stuff began on the final lead on the third day. I approached a lower-angle section where, on a black and white print, Michael Kennedy had written "bivy?" I crested onto nothing more than a fifty-degree roll-over, nothing to bivy on. On the smooth, rusty granite, brilliant in the last sun, the only climbable ground was half-inch-thick panes of ice barely connected, and I had nothing between me and Kitty but screaming hope. I tiptoed across the panes, and, with about ten feet of rope left, providence delivered a quarter-inch chrome-ringed bolt (French?), and a groove into which I could pound an arrow. Please don't remind me, but that's what we hung the ledge from; that's all we had.

When I planned this venture, I had no idea we'd want a bolt kit, no idea we were taking on a "last great problem." The pictures looked like there'd be a solid apron of snow and ice, and then a few mixed pitches to connect with the last bit of the northeast buttress route. But the monsoon failed this year, and apparently July and August were brilliant day after day, so probably a lot of ice melted away. In Delhi we opened the log of expeditions that had tried this face, and I was surprised to see it was thick with experienced climbers, failed attempts, and words of caution. French, Spanish, British (with Joe Brown), Japanese.

Kitty didn't much care about the history, or the geography for that matter. Two weeks before we left the U.S. she couldn't come up with the name of the peak. What's important to her is "clahmbin," as she calls it in her forthright Southern drawl. You get her started up the route and

Andy Selters ponders the next lead at 21,000 feet.

Kitty Calhoun

she does just fine, especially since this is her first trip to the Himalaya. 'Course it's only my second, and we're the first team to try this direct line alpine style.

A few years ago a French guy took a huge tumbler somewhere above here, and he was lucky to get down with a shattered leg. Last year a Japanese fell the distance, and some of his friends showed up at our base camp. They came over shy and laughing and offering whiskey, then explained their mission. They pointed out an isolated tent and said it was the tent of their buddy's widow. She wanted them to ask us, if, on our carries to the base, we'd seen any sign of her husband. No signs, we said, as we looked off to her silent green tunnel, the door aligned toward Thalay.

This is Garhwal, holy source of the Ganges, the abode of the gods. When, the night before we started up the route, Kitty and I peeked out of our tent, we looked around at the dreamiest panorama I've ever seen. A layer of mist was half-filling the valley, and Bhrigupanth, Malla, and Thalay—massive apparitions of brilliant silvery moonlight—were floating on the vapors. It seemed we would need metaphysical transformations to rise into that world, not climbing gear. Now we are up there with the gods, scratching our crusty itches and just existing in wait.

Neither of us had slept in a portaledge before this trip, although I had hammock experience. The construction of this blue capsule began three months ago, when we lay down on the sidewalk in Bellingham. My friend Rick Lipke drew a chalk triangle close around our bodies. That was how it would be, my six feet two inches against the wall, Kitty's five feet two inches out on the apex. The lifeboat turned out to weigh only nine pounds, a fourth lighter than any other available. Now it's broken and sloping at the foot, the result of a stupid heave to get my pack up between the ledge and the wall, five days ago. We were hurrying to cut our morning prep time, and snap, there was this sickening drop toward forever. The tubing she'd bought at Boeing surplus was torn like cardboard. But that didn't concern Kitty.

"Where will we sleep?" I asked.

"We'll fix it," she said, which meant I would fix it. Indeed, at each setup I've been able to lash the joint together with cord, and the repair is still is giving us most of our foot area.

At the end of each climbing day Kitty will get cold and start shivering. I'll be trying to lash and fit the ledge's joints while they quiver in her grasp. The second night of this I whined, "Why didn't you bring that insulated one-piece suit you had?"

"It's too *fancy*." I guess her old homemade duds give her her own sense of comfort. She is determined to be determined; forging ahead is her strength and her vulnerability. During one of our first carries from base camp she started getting dizzy and moving really slowly. I saw she was getting altitude sickness, but she said, "Ah'll just keep goin', a half-hour at a time." I had to about wrench her pack off her before she'd go down instead of up. I wonder if she'd admit that a hundred pitches of 5.12 would be too hard. On her second thin lead her crampons skittered and she almost whipped, but she just let out a whimper and kept going. She learns quickly.

Day four of waiting, day eight on the route. Going light means you can move fast when the going is good, but when it's bad you live like a corpse. "Six" days of food had really been five, and I didn't even bring a toothbrush, much to Kitty's dismay. An acetone taste has begun to seep into my mouth, a sign that I'm metabolizing protein, consuming myself. We lie in our blue pyramid and dissolve deeper and deeper into an alpinist's virtue, knowing that hibernating with bad breath and withering shoulders is the best thing we can do to advance us. When the weather clears we'll use that last dinner to get us up a truly heroic route.

It looks like Kitty is wrapped around something. "Are you reading?"

"Yeah."

"What?" She produces a pocket version of the New Testament.

"We've been hauling a Bible?"

"Ah read it through once a year," she says in her native Carolahna. "Ah want to fahnd the truth," she says, as if in previous readings she'd somehow just missed the Truth passage.

Kitty Calhoun.

Andy Selters

Day five of The Wait; it's about three in the afternoon. I wake because it's warm and quiet; no snow has been pouring over us. I lean out and look around just in time to see a huge avalanche powering toward us. "Shit, Kitty, here it comes!" We sit up and brace out the fly with our forearms as the first blocks hit. We're getting pounded, it's getting dark, the ledge is creaking and straining, the darkness turns black and the pressure increases. Something is about to snap and we're going to be washed into a plummeting hell.

But the roar lessens and some light returns. Snow hammering onto the ledge has molded around our bodies. We sit petrified in heart-racing terror as thick as poison. Kitty will not be the first to speak of it. "We have to get out of here," I say, and she agrees.

A warm front is dumping wetter snow that sticks to the giant slabs above, so instead of pouring off in sugary waves it releases in one big train. We have no reason to think it won't happen again. I try to guess the strain on the minimal gear that we hang from. Our bodies and gear alone total almost 350 pounds. Does a big avalanche multiply that by a factor of three, four, or five? Yes, let's go down; at the bottom life will begin anew.

The next morning we suit up and ease off the ledge and onto front points for the first time in almost a week. We fold up the poles and I start the first rappel. Before I'm thirty feet down, the morning's first wave of powder sweeps over us. I look up sputtering and wiping snow off my neck, and another wave washes over. I pull myself back up to Kitty and another wave pours down. It's like living in surf. On the way up, in good weather, getting decent anchors had been our biggest challenge. With twenty-five rappels in this surf we would either make a fatal mistake or go too slow to survive. We unfold the lifeboat and crawl back in, shivering with all our clothes on. Now our down is badly dampened.

It takes a couple of hours before we can get warm—and for the musty smells to come back into the blue capsule. Now I feel the wire of my gut pulling tense as well as starving. We are so far from anything resembling security, and I care so little that this climb could put us in the league of famous climbers. This is total life at stake. I've never really known what it's like to have no options. I may have been in some jams, I may have thought I had no decent pro, or no capacity to earn a decent living, but those were simply games of relative necessity. Nothing except combat or a gulag can compare with the helplessness of being unable to go up or down a Himalayan wall. I grasp for solutions, and there are none. The only available move is sleep.

A few hours later I'm drifting in a sea of helplessness, clutching at imaginary twigs of influence as if they were rafts of reason. Somehow I or we must have done something to bring on this punishment. Maybe it's because we ate freeze-dried beef in this Hindu holy land. Or maybe there's something I need to clear up. That's it, I may have been misleading Kitty. We're being punished because I haven't been utterly honest.

After half an hour I get up my gumption and sort of tell her that I admire her, but if she's gotten an impression, well, I think I can't turn the partnership into a romance. She accepts this without much comment; I can't tell if it's with sadness or relief, or if she couldn't care less. In any case my words have the desired effect. By dusk the sky is clearing, the blue capsule is quiet.

Day eight of The Wait. I am in torpor extremis, starving and desperate. I gnaw on my long and oily hair, my teeth flexing in my loosening gums. I can feel my hip bones, fine and unsupported, much more prominent than two weeks ago. I had only eight percent body fat when I started the summer. Although Kitty is lean for a woman, we both think she's better equipped for this. Overnight the storm resumed, the pulsing hiss of sliding powder returned. There must be something more I need to say.

I pull out my history and breach things to her; I babble out stories that uncover wounds not healed, just scarred over. Climbing intensity, I realize, is woven in to bolster the masking tissue. Kitty listens, comments, shares in return. After two hours of this we are buddies, not just partners. And it worked. By late afternoon the clouds begin to clear. By dusk the surf has calmed. With tea I swallow my last spoonful of almond butter and go to sleep.

It's morning and it's perfectly clear and the blue walls are thick and stiff with frost and bitter cold like we haven't seen here. It's at least minus twenty Fahrenheit, and I have no fire to keep warm. It's time to make our break, but I can barely function. My hands cannot thaw; one glove has a small hole worn from the climb. Kitty has to take the lead down. When we finally get our packs on, we look up and see the summit brilliant white in the sun, 1,500 feet straight above.

"It looks great," she says as we both weigh the possibility of going up.

"I don't think we're up for it, Kitty."

"Yeah, Ah reckon you're right."

I yank myself up to extract the two cams from our anchor. Then down, down, wrestling the stiff rope through our rappel devices—yet still I can't get warm. Each anchor in this wall is so precious. Turning an old Chouinard screw into the supercold ice is enough effort to double me over for a breath. Often we go off of my retrieving Snarg, a custom device you slide into the tunnel of a removed screw. Without something like this we'd never have enough gear to get down. For retrieval we clip ascenders onto the stretchy seven-millimeter trail line and pull with all our feeble might, and the whole mass of rope and Snarg cascades onto us in yet another tangle. By evening we have made thirteen or fourteen rappels. We can see no sign of the tent we left at the base.

As the last shadows overtake the region Kitty yells up, "Ah cayn't fahnd an aynchor!" I rap down to her. Indeed, there is only a seam for a couple of knifeblades. Then, as she gets out our remaining headlamp, she slips and it bangs on the wall. It's broken, and now we're in total darkness. I have no thought of blaming her; our strengths and weaknesses are all one now, and it's apparent that some marvelous tie is giving both of us fortitude to take over when the other needs a break. But with the light went our last hope for setting up the ledge; from a band of ice we chop a ten-inch ramp to sit against. The night is mostly clear and warmer, and by feel I get the stove going between my knees while Kitty chips ice for that last dinner.

By the time I grip a pot of ice slurry, clouds have gathered. Then a quick flash. I see Kitty's surprise as she looks into my gaunt and hairy mug. Then thunder. She gets out the ledge fly just after the first wave of spindrift washes over us.

God, whatever you are, just give us this half a meal. So long have we waited to split this "dinner for one," and if we don't get it now I think I will cry, and we could die. It's sweet and sour pork, my favorite of our foil-entombed miracles, with freeze-dried bell peppers and tangy sauce. It's kosher in Garhwal. Kitty reaches over me with the fly, she can shield our torsos and the stove, but our legs are getting swept repeatedly with snow.

I dump the precious powdery lumps of food into the pot. It's barely lukewarm, but in a few more minutes on the burner it's edible. We chew it down in unfamiliar and mechanical gulps, while the fly draping over us collects snow like a garbage bag over two derelicts. As the powder wedging behind our backs threatens to pry us off our perch, we smear out the last sauce with our fingers and suck the flavor from our gloves.

We pull out a sleeping bag and jam in all four legs, boots and all. In the process waves of powder fill the bag and pack in around our knees. We wrestle and press to keep the tarp over us, even as our purchase on the ten-inch ledge disappears again. There's pressure in my groin, because we're sliding off and bearing on the knifeblades and it's cutting off my circulation. Soon my toes are numb, and I know if the storm doesn't stop we will not survive.

About midnight some stars return; the squall is moving on. The bag is a sodden sack, but it wards off shivering enough so we can clutch at hope. With the dinner stoking away inside us and the weather improving, we dare to feel a rush of relief. We lean against each other in renewed belief that life should be ours.

At dawn we reckon it's a dozen more rappels to safety. The route is unrecognizable with all the new snow hanging on it, or maybe we're in a different area. Out of reach, just twenty feet to the side, we see our chrome pot grips sticking into the snow. It must have been a week ago I dropped them.

At nine the blessed sun comes around, the burning so thankful on my face and the baking so good through my steaming down jacket. It's the first heat we've felt since that first lead ten days ago. Though Kitty and I are both skinflints, as we near the glacier we leave thirty-dollar anchors without a second thought. Our last desperate move is to go off our #3 Friend, rattly in an icy crack. After that, there's only a couple of bollard rappels to below the 'schrund.

On the level! It's so wonderful to walk after two weeks without even a stance, even if we have to heave through waist-deep snow. We can taste the world of life. We had fixed a seven-foot bamboo cane to the little tent, and, after wallowing around some, we spy it; only its top knuckle is sticking out. We can't remember if we'd left any food in the tent, but for the hope of it and for the tent itself we dig.

Calhoun
celebrates at
the base
of the face.

Andy Selters

Inside there's only a fuel cartridge and our books, so we shoulder the new weight and keep going. Blank and desperate, we plow down the glacier's lobes. Kitty stays determined until she discovers her north-wall hammer has fallen from its holster. Only then does she cry: it was her favorite tool. We make it to the moraines by dark and wrap our bodies around stones on the only level spot around, under a truck-sized boulder.

The next morning we march in slow, gasping pain to base camp. No one is there. Our cook, Muna, our liaison officer, Harbujan—have they abandoned us for dead? Among the trash there's only a couple of eggs and some noodles, and we boil it all. The blast of calories sends me into a coma, and as I lay in the sun with my shirt off, Kitty gawks at the way my skin sucks in around my skeleton. "Man, Andy, if Ah'd aknown Ah'd agiven y'all mah half of the dinner!" No one has ever said anything more gracious.

It's all too much; we had never imagined we'd be gone this long, be this hungry. It doesn't matter what sort of life we have now; there's just hazy and disbelieving thanks that we have life at all. The first step of return is to do nothing, and I lose myself into sleep much deeper than dreams.

THE BELAYER

John Hart

I start my strange and jagged walk
upon the limits of the rock.

Spreadeagled, hesitant and slow
athwart the shining stone I go.

Against its excellence command
my pale and dyslectic hand.

Below my feet the spaces turn;
the seventy black candles burn.

But from my harness swings a strand
in keeping of a human friend.

Small motions link us, rods away:
you know my fear by my delay:

you know the tremor and the talk
of a soft-bodied creature on the rock

for nothing can be hidden here:
the belayer holds you as you are.

I would not overstate the case:
all live by one another's grace:

we're not more bound together here
than a driver, say, and a passenger:

yet sometimes, going on belay,
I blink a comic tear away.

It seems no other link I've known
is so explicit and so sane.

A discipline attends our words:
this dance is done with real swords.

Friend, my life, a colored strand
lies in the stricture of your hand

by whose enablement I own
my place upon the solemn stone

the clean-limbed, ancient, powerful and tall
as beautiful as horses, and more still.

SOUTH

Photographs by
Gordon Wiltsie
Stephen Venables
Gregory Crouch
and Charlie Fowler

QUEEN MAUDLAND
Antarctica

Opening Page: Vern Tejas surveys the route up Mt. Vaughan in Antarctica's Queen Maud Mountains.

Previous Pages: Conrad Anker, Jon Krakauer, and Alex Lowe climb the summit spire of the Troll's Castle, Queen Maudland.

Above: Jon Krakauer and Conrad Anker skiing below Rakekniven Spire, Queen Maudland.

Right: Conrad Anker leads pitch four on Rakekniven Spire, belayed by Jon Krakauer.

Photographs: *Gordon Wiltsie*

John Roskelley approaches the west summit of Monte Sarmiento, Chile. *Stephen Venables*

Clockwise from Upper Left: The Cerro Torre group
at sunrise, Patagonia. *Gregory Crouch*

Gregory Crouch starting up the *S Crack*
on the *Compressor Route*, Cerro Torre. *Charlie Fowler*

Crouch at grips with the Headwall,
the *Compressor Route*, Cerro Torre. *Charlie Fowler*

A magnificent sunrise, seen from the
summit of Cerro Torre. *Charlie Fowler*

CERRO TORRE CAMPAIGN

Gregory Crouch

Cerro Torre is making us suffer again. Water drains from the snow-covered ledge above and pours down the crack where I jam my hands. The frigid waterfall soaks through my gloves and storm gear. Pounding winds drive sheets of almost-freezing rain at Alex Hall and me. Massive updrafts blow rain at us from below. Chill water runs down my arms, back, buttocks, legs, and fills my leather boots. My lips are blue.

Alex belays me from below with the end of the rappel ropes we control. The other end is stuck over our heads—for the fourth time. These sodden ropes are unmanageable. The wild wind launches them into space the instant we pull each rappel, and the eight-millimeter descent rope wraps around every imaginable rock protrusion. I curse myself for thinking a light rappel line would be useful in Patagonia. The wind *owns* the flimsy cord.

Alex and I have been fighting our way down from our high point halfway up Cerro Torre's southeast ridge, Cesare Maestri's infamous *Compressor Route*, for the last ten hours, and here I am, battered by the elements and run out from Alex's belay, freeing the damned rope again, section by section. Alex traps each new length under his boot in a wet crack, making sure it won't blow loose and get tangled elsewhere. Finally, I jerk the end of the thin rope loose and toss it down to Alex. He packs it into the crack and returns his attention to my belay. I climb down to him. "Only two more raps!" yells Alex as he rigs the ropes to a nest of rusty pitons.

"What was I thinking, bringing this fucking dental floss to Patagonia? It's useless!"

A crotch-fountain spouts from my belay plate as I descend. First down on the last rap, I topple down a cone of snow below the bergschrund and take myself off rappel. It's still raining and I'm still shivering, but all we have to do is rope up and stagger down the glacier to our sleeping bags packed in plastic bags at the Norwegian Bivy, a cluster of pseudo-caves and leaky rock walls in a moraine that serves as our gear stash.

We wade knee deep through a swamp of wet snow and eventually reach the bivy. It's nine p.m. when we crawl through a gap in the rock walls

Crouch at the Norwegian Bivy below Cerro Torre.

Charlie Fowler

beneath a shelter stone. The roof leaks. The floor is gritty, wet, and in no place level, but at least in the dank cave we're out of the wind and the driving rain. Alex stuffs his sleeping bag into a bivy sack, peels off his soggy storm shells and boots, crams himself into his bag, and begins to make a long-coveted brew.

I sit stunned, unable to summon the energy to remove my boots. Too exhausted to move, I stare at Alex as he fumbles with the stove. My swollen hands and feet ache, and I have had no food or drink in sixteen hours. For more than thirty days we've been trying to climb the mountain above us. This latest rejection has set a new personal record for alpine misery—for cold, wetness, thirst, hunger, exhaustion, and pain.

"Ha," I croak. A wry smile crosses my face.

Alex looks up from his labor. "What's so funny? We just got our asses kicked—for the sixth time."

"This is bliss, bud. This is exactly what I wanted—big Patagonian action—and it isn't as bad as what I did to earn this trip. I'd take a thousand beatings like this rather than go back into that hole in the ground working heavy construction or installing machines in McDonald's. Those jobs *really* sucked. I'm In Patagonia. How bad can it be?"

"Pretty bad," answers Alex, but with a big grin.

I started socking away money for this trip on a crew building a sewer-lift station for the city of Loveland, Colorado. After the heavy construction gig I took a job installing a machine in fast-food restaurants. I fiddled with tricky plastic parts in awkward corners littered with crushed french fries. I got hounded by hostile assistant managers who hadn't graduated from high school. I struggled to get the contraption working during all-night installations, then drove like a demon to the next job site in Texas, North Dakota, or wherever. Visions of Patagonia's perfect peaks sustained me through the grimmest hours. A Denver traffic jam could become a full-fledged Patagonian storm if I freed my imagination for a minute. Down south there would be no pneumatic tools, no bosses, no long drives, and no assistant managers. I wanted to be in Patagonia, letting the wind tear away the dirt of a tough year.

Alex said yes in a heartbeat when I asked him to join me for the Cerro Torre campaign. He's the guy you want reaching for you when you're neck deep in quicksand. Alex is strong and stout, even-tempered, and solid backbone—the perfect partner for a few months in the Patagonian crucible.

In the morning an atrocious wind pummels us back to base camp beneath the beech trees along the banks of the Rio Fitzroy. Long underwear, fleece clothing, socks, hardware, and ropes adorn the trees of base camp—relics of yesterday's epics. Alex and I ravenously descend on a tub of jelly, stuff crackers in our mouths, and savor hot coffee.

Base camp in Patagonia is the best place I've ever called home. I love every second of storm-bound base camp time. No bills to pay, no telephones to answer, no messages to return, no errands to run, no deadlines to meet—just hedonistic rounds of coffee, chow, card games, letters, writing, novels, sleep, whiskey, wine, and conversations with climbers and trekkers from all corners of the globe. It's an uncomplicated existence, and if it weren't for the power of the evil peaks lurking in the clouds, base camp would be the most peaceful place I know.

But the lure of the peaks is inescapable. Ten miles up the Fitzroy Glacier, the spires stand sentinel over the valley's head. Once caught by the long shadows of the mountains, which stretch across the landscape like shark's teeth, we cannot relax—and I cannot escape the fear. Soldiers waiting in England for D-Day probably felt the same.

Seven of us share a crude hut made of twisted logs and plastic tarps and barely able to keep out the weather: Thomas Ulrich and Stefan Seegrist from Switzerland; Charlie Fowler from Colorado; Jim Donini from Seattle; Jim's partner Stefan Heirmaier from Munich; and Alex and me. We're a merry group.

Another month passes. Five more times Alex and I trudge the ten miles up the Torre Valley and struggle upward on the slopes of Cerro Torre. Five more times sudden storms ambush us and slam the windows of opportunity shut, but only after we are certain to receive a good dose of pain. We never make it more than a pitch or two above the Col of Patience before storms blast us from the walls.

Alex finally runs out of time and returns to the States; his construction business and girlfriend require his attention. I'm stuck in the trenches with Cerro Torre—and now I lack a partner. I barge into Donini and Stefan's tent. "I'm climbing with you guys now."

Veteran Jim Donini is the survivor of four Patagonian adventures. He was blown off the summit ridge of Cerro Stanhardt attempting the first ascent in 1975, and the following year he made the first ascent of Torre Egger with John Bragg and Jay Wilson. Their success came at the end of a ninety-day battle. In 1988 he climbed an obscure spire in the Patagonian archipelago with Yvon Chouinard and sea-kayaked back to civilization. And here he is again, twenty-one years after his first trip to the range, in a dog-fight with Cerro Torre. Two months ago Donini vowed not to shave until he climbed the mountain, and now his grisly gray beard makes him look like a warrior from the Stone Age.

Stefan fell in with Donini during a desert cragging session and let himself get talked out of a winter of American rock climbing and into a season of action in Patagonia. He'd never had crampons on his feet before arriving here, but he's doing incredibly well at Cerro Torre's school of hard knocks.

Some days later the Torre comes out of the storm and stands calm and serene at the head of the valley. She's sheathed head-to-toe in an armor of ice, ready for battle. We trudge up into the shadow of the beast. In place of a sword, a coat of mail, spurs, and a war horse, I've got ice axes, Gore-Tex, crampons—and Donini. Wallowing through thigh-deep snow, we finally reach the base of the climbing leading to the Col of Patience. The route to the col was hard mixed climbing the first time Alex and I did it two months ago, and we belayed nearly the entire 1,600-foot distance. But with the familiarity that Jim, Stefan, and I now have, we simul-climb all but a few short steps and arrive at the col in the early evening.

Jim leads up the beautiful granite cracks above the col, skillfully avoiding patches of rime ice that cling to the stone. I jumar up third, with nothing to do but enjoy the spectacular view that stretches 100 miles north to Cerro San Lorenzo, shimmering pink in the last fires of the sun. Since we intend to climb all night, by sunrise we should be in a position from where we can forge on to the summit, even in poor weather. Because of my big push with Alex a month ago, I've got more knowledge of the route than Jim or Stefan, and they're going to let me lead through the night. I've spent hours mentally rehearsing each pitch; I'm sure I can find the route. So, as the peaks fade into darkness, I take the lead rope and climb into the night. There is no moon, just the pool of light projected by my headlamp, an oasis in a cold desert of blackness.

This is not a night for reflection; it is a night for action. The ice, snow, and stone unfold in front of my headlamp. I climb up and play the scene before me against my memory of a daylight passage over the same terrain. My crampons scrape over stone. Axe and hammer squeak into névé, crack into ice, and bang off rock. Sparks fly. Occasionally I yell instructions down to Jim and Stefan, but we say little at the belays. My world is ice and stone; no view distracts me from the pleasures of climbing.

Gray light seeps into the world from the east as Stefan leads across a bolt traverse. This is no spectacular sunrise, just the creeping gray of dawn. A layer of cloud that slipped in from the west during the night kills the alpenglow. Jim ties into the middle of the lead rope and we simul-climb across the line of bolts. I come over last, removing the quickdraws as we traverse up and right toward an icy chimney. The weather is deteriorating, but we push on.

Fear has the bile up in my throat; daylight has revealed the exposure. The wall under the bolt traverse is steep and plummets down thousands of feet to the glacier. This traverse is reputed to be the part of the mountain most exposed to bad weather—Alex and I took a tremendous beating here a month ago. The air is alive with a faint, cold, wet breeze as Jim grunts up the icy chimney, pounding at the ice and scraping over stone. Stefan belays. I have nothing to do but worry about the weather. We're in a race with it and with the two Swiss—Ulrich and Seegrist—who are hot on our tails and obviously as committed as we are to pushing through to the top.

Higher, at a belay stance, the three of us build an unbelievable confusion of ropes where we change leaders. The two Swiss blitz past us while we fumble with this rope-rodeo, and just then Cerro Torre gets hit by a charge of storm. Angry wind screams around us as we climb onto the Ice Tower, a battlement attached to the side of the peak. We're over halfway up the southeast ridge, climbing into the building fury of a Patagonian gale. Twisted gargoyles of rime ice, condensed out of the humid atmosphere, decorate the vertiginous walls. Clouds swarm around us. Visibility drops to half a pitch. Great rushes of wind careen through the rime formations with sharp gunfire cracks. The storm drives through the Col of Conquest between Cerro Torre and Torre Egger with the bass growl of a locomotive. These chaotic acoustic effects drive me to the brink of insanity. Cracks and booms heard in the howl of storm are comprehensible, but not the mumbled conversations, ringing church bells, and barking dogs that I seem to hear.

Then it's my lead, and I force myself to concentrate on the terrain at hand. Beneath a crust of rime, the ice is gray-white and solid. Crampons and axes hold me tight to the slope.

Cerro Torre welcoming the next storm. *Charlie Fowler*

Furious gusts attempt to buffet me free while I climb past a pair of bulges that push to vertical. The cacophony of sound gnaws at my confidence. Atop a bulge of ice I anchor and fix the rope. My shouts are drowned by the din of storm. Moments later there are exploratory tugs on the rope before Stefan commits to his jumars.

A scream sounds from a twisted gargoyle of neighboring ice, and suddenly I understand. The mysterious sound effects are noises produced by the ferocious wind as it crashes and rushes around the gnarled formations of rime. Understanding these "Patagonian organs" calms my fear. Laughing, I explain the strange acoustics to Stefan at the top of my lungs when he arrives.

Wisps of rime form on my jacket and bibs, grow on the ropes, and cling to the hardware and slings. Swirling winds hammer us from all directions. Updrafts fill my jacket with frigid air. With the storm as our constant companion, we encounter several bolt ladders between difficult sections of mixed climbing. In calm conditions these bolt ladders would be a breeze, but in this storm I fight a frenzied battle for control of my possessed étriers. The wind tosses them in all directions and updrafts sometimes stream them directly over my head. I have to pull them hand over hand out of the sky and hold them down before I can settle them with the weight of a cramponed boot.

I lead a pitch to the top of the Ice Tower. A gigantic chimney to my left divides the Ice Tower from the bulk of the mountain. Although the core of the Ice Tower is solid granite, ice adheres to the walls that jut out from the main mass of Cerro Torre. Updrafts sweep up the cleft to my left with the fury of express trains. Ice and snow particles roar upward in a grayish blur. After Stefan joins me, I traverse across the peaked roof of the Ice Tower on the side that slopes in toward Cerro Torre's headwall. My heels hang out over the gigantic chimney as I pick and kick my way horizontally along the roof, aiming for a small saddle. I traverse forty feet to the left, actually facing away from Cerro Torre as I look out over the top of the Ice Tower. The view would be spectacular in clear conditions, straight across to Fitzroy and Poincenot, but in this storm I barely make out the difference between the gray ice in front of me and the gray cloud beyond.

On the far side of the saddle a chimney rises up to divide the Tower from Cerro Torre's East Face. The saddle, at the confluence of the two chimneys, is a maelstrom. The architecture of Cerro Torre channels the chaotic air up to this confluence and magnifies the power of the storm. I belay Stefan, then Jim, across. Vertical stone soars up into the storm.

The route rising to our left is running with water. The feeble energy of the sun that penetrates the storm is just enough to melt the rime particles growing on the headwall. Later, I fix the rope to a cluster of Maestri's bolts on a ledge and hug my arms to my chest to preserve precious warmth. The struggle up the last eighty feet of tenuous mixed aid and ice climbing was the hardest lead of my life. While Stefan jumars, I pull the scrunched route topo out of my pocket. The pitch I just led is rated 5.7.

We lumber up the headwall bolts. Stefan leads, and Jim and I jumar. Rime ice grows everywhere. I belay Stefan from a stance high on the headwall and watch Jim push his ascenders up the icy rope below me. Winds swat him from side to side as he pulls up and shoves his top ascender higher. Jim hesitates a second, then his eyes widen to saucers as he slides ten feet back down the icy rope, neither ascender grabbing the slick rope until friction melts the ice clogging the cams. He cranks quickly up to my stance.

Swiss climbers on Cerro Torre's Headwall, with the notorious summit mushrooms looming overheard.

Gregory Crouch

"Jim, look!" A gray shape looms above us, barely visible through the clouds tearing over the top of Cerro Torre. "The summit mushroom. We're close!"

The two Swiss are above a blob of ice plastered smack in the middle of the headwall, on what must be the last rock pitch on the route. Stefan has hung a belay just below the blob and fixed the rope. A strong gust slaps me against Jim and we cuss, awed by the power of the storm. I fight to get my ascenders attached to the rope as it whips around in the wind. "We might make it," says Jim, "but we're moving so slow!"

Periodically cupping each ascender in turn in the hollow of my gloves and breathing on them to unfreeze the cams, I ascend the rope to Stefan. As I clip his belay, I see that the bolts disappear into the blob a few feet above. What is this chunk of ice—four feet wide, three feet thick and about eight feet high—doing stuck right in the middle of this vertical headwall of granite? One of the Swiss is standing on top of it, belaying.

I dangle below Stefan and shiver while I strap my crampons onto my boots at a dead-hanging belay. I smash into Stefan's legs as the wind screams and tosses us around. God help me if I drop a crampon. But soon I'm ready to tackle the bulging, overhanging ice.

"Be careful!"

My crampons get mixed up in my étriers as I make a few aid moves to reach the ice. The underside of the bulge overhangs the wall by two feet.

Suddenly, I can't see. The world goes black. I swing from a daisy, and my crampons scrape against bare granite. I cannot see. "I'm going to die"—the phrase flashes to my brain. The consequences of my eyesight calamity are brutally obvious. Yet there's a streak of orange in front of my eyes. Confused, I try to understand what is wrong. Panic rises. The orange streak tears open a bit. My God, my eyes are frozen shut! I rip my left glove from my hand. My axe and glove dangle from my wrist and thrash about madly in the storm. With bare fingers I yank out eyelashes embedded in chunks of rime.

Adrenaline hammers me. I get my gloves back on and top-step my highest étrier, bury my axe pick in the ice, shake my boot loose from the étrier below, and slam my second tool into the ice with no thought to placing protection, just to regaining the bolt ladder above this crazy ice patch. I crank up the bulging ice.

Maestri's compressor.

Charlie Fowler

I wiggle a tool free and see Thomas's grin above. "Hook the carburetor!"

"The *what?*"

"Hook the carburetor!"

Incredulous, I reach my tool up—and it clanks on metal. As I pull up, I come face to face with a large metal object. I heave myself up and stand on the thing beside Thomas. It's the only ledge big enough to stand on in the last 500 feet. The contraption, the size of a lawnmower, is Maestri's compressor, still attached to the headwall twenty-six years after the first ascent. I fix the rope and casually stand on top of the compressor, astounded that someone could bring this huge thing all the way up here. The ice of my last short lead was actually rime suspended from the bottom of the compressor like an upside-down ice-cream cone.

Stefan arrives atop the compressor. "Do you want us to fix a rope for you?" Thomas asks as he jumars upward.

"No," we shout in unison, since we are now only 140 feet from the top.

Jim joins us atop the compressor and I lead out five bolts—to where they stop. Maestri smashed his original bolts above this point to prove that the air compressor was essential to his ascent. When Jim Bridwell did the second ascent of the route in the late 1970s, he hand-drilled a rivet ladder to pass the section that Maestri had trashed.

A furry layer of gray rime about a quarter-inch thick covers the smooth, vertical granite of the headwall. I cannot find the first rivet. The two Swiss rappel past me on their way down from their topmost belay. They've climbed the last pitch of rock but not the gentle ice slope leading to the base of the wildly overhanging summit ice mushroom.

I scrape more rime from the stone but find nothing. Jim yells. I twist to look. His figure is indistinct, though only fifteen feet away. He's gesturing at his wrist. It's late. Just like that, I abandon the ascent and down climb the short bolt ladder to the compressor and join my friends. Suddenly, I am very cold—and a lot of cold, dangerous terrain separates us from safety.

The descent to the top of the Ice Tower uses the remaining daylight. We continue down in darkness, using headlamps. After each rappel the wind thrashes the ropes as they fall, but miraculously they never get stuck. Particles of ice whirl around in all directions. Rime grows inside my jacket, and I shiver at the anchors while I wait my turn. Communication is impossible, so we decide to rappel based on rope tension.

At the base of the Ice Tower I stand in an icy hell. A barrage of minute ice particles seems immune to the insane winds and exclusively devoted to swarming our stance. Jim and Stefan have their helmeted heads tucked back into their hoods like mutant turtles. We don't exchange a word as we execute the tasks essential to retreat. Past midnight, as I go down first on the last rappel of the traverse, my headlight flickers and dies. The struggle to maintain the traverse line with the ends of the rope whipping around unseen in the dark is utterly terrifying. At the next stance, below the traverse, I unweight the ropes, secure them, and try, unsuccessfully, to get my light to work.

Moments later, Jim appears out of the swirling darkness. "Stefan's headlamp's out, too. We'll have to bivy." He attaches the leftover slack of one of the ropes to the anchors and raps twenty feet. "These stances suck!" he roars up through the storm. "Send down the gear."

I slip the hardware down the rope to Jim. Stefan arrives and immediately switches to the fixed strand of rope and raps to join Jim. I pull the rappel ropes and go down. Stefan is wedged behind a flake and wriggling his way into his bivy sack. Jim is perched on a small ledge just wider than his skinny butt six feet to the left of Stefan. There must be fifteen pieces of gear in every available nook and cranny—the boys are gripped. But at least they saved the biggest stance for me. It's two feet by two feet, but it's covered in a layer of ice and slopes outward.

The only food left is a lump of cheese. I break it into thirds and share the pieces. Wind rips at my bivy sack as I fish it from my pack. I toss my cheese chunk through the mouth of the sack and worm my way in after it. The wind tears at the sack like machine-gun fire. There's nothing I can do to increase my warmth; every stitch of clothing is already on. I doze and nod and wait for daylight, nibbling at the cheese and shivering uncontrollably. Thankfully, I don't have a light on my watch, so I can't chart the passing minutes.

At dawn, fiery alpenglow shoots under the cloud layer and bathes the granite of the three Torres in an otherworldly orange glow. The fury of the storm is spent. Frozen but cheered by the sunshine, we break our bivy and rig for descent. The exposure from our emergency bivy, up until now obscured by darkness, is heart-stopping. In daylight, our seats look like good handholds.

We haven't slept in two nights and struggle to maintain focus for the ten rappels leading to the safety of the ice cave. Exhausted by fifty-three hours of consecutive stress, we rest in the ice cave for the morning and early afternoon. The day stays clear and calm. If we had retreated to the cave at the first sign of the previous day's storm and climbed today, we would have cruised to the top in perfect conditions.

Stefan and Jim are out of time. They must return to their lives. I have no such pressure—although I have no idea where I'll find the guts to make another attempt.

My gear is battered, much of it into uselessness. The soles of the new boots I brought to Patagonia two months ago are nearly worn off. My storm bibs are covered in duct tape. My gloves haven't kept my hands dry in six weeks. Even my crampon points are practically worn off by the mixed climbing Cerro Torre demands.

Donini gives me his equipment as he leaves for the States: bibs, a rope, gaiters, a tent, a set of Camalots, and a supply of carabiners—a thousand dollars worth in all. "Just get on top of the son of a bitch," he exclaims as he boards the bus. My equipment is rejuvenated, but I don't know where I'll find more stamina.

Charlie Fowler returns battered from Cerro Torre as Jim and Stefan leave. He has been getting hammered almost as long as I have, so, since we're the last two Americans still holding fort in this terrible war of attrition, we join forces. Charlie's casual attitude camouflages an intense drive. He has come to Patagonia often since the late 1970s and has a new route on Cerro Catedral in the Paine region to show for his efforts, in addition to several successes on the Fitzroy massif.

A morning of good weather lures us up to the Torre again, but a fresh rush of cloud stops us from doing any real climbing. We've got a new tactic—a tent, supplies, and a new bivy spot beneath a shelter stone on a moraine opposite Cerro Torre. With this high camp we'll avoid the ten-mile death march to and from base camp.

A serious storm lashes the range as we pitch camp, and now we must entertain ourselves during the wait for good weather—without the diversions of base camp. Horrified, we discover that *Moby Dick* is our only book. After dinner I jump to a forty-page lead while Charlie stares at the roof of the tent.

Gusts slap and claw at the tent fabric to wake us in the morning. For the first time in my life I willfully mutilate a book and hand the first chapters to Charlie.

Days later, Charlie and I are immersed in whaling. Sleet, rain, and snow whip our campsite as obsessed Ahab chases the White Whale around the world. Forty-page pamphlets of *Moby Dick* litter the tent, and the floor is sticky with food spills. Cerro Torre lurks unseen in the storms of Patagonia, as omnipotent and uncaring as Melville's whale.

One morning I snap. "Charlie, we gotta go down. I'm going nuts stuck up here. I need base camp. I need a real meal." Charlie shrugs his shoulders and soon we are marching down the valley, chased by the wind that hasn't stopped in a week. Four hours later we are laughing, joking, and eating with the members of a Polish expedition well-sponsored by Pepsi. Wine, whiskey, and stew warms my neglected stomach. It's past midnight when I stumble off to my tent, intending to sleep until noon.

"Greg! Greg! Get up. We've got to go up. The storm's breaking."
"Oh God... you're kidding? What time is it?"
"Five in the morning, and no, I'm not kidding."

Steph Davis petting her horse at Campo Bridwell.

Charlie Fowler

I crawl out of my tent and walk to a clearing with Charlie. I stare dumbly at the mountain and pray for storm. Clouds drift through the range but seem to lack organization and purpose.

A cloud swallows the Torre. "Charlie, let's get some coffee and wait and see what happens."

"I'm sure this is good weather. Those are puff clouds. We should go up."

"I can't face this without coffee."

Charlie goes to his tent to load his backpack. In the hut I slump onto a bench made from a split log. The hut is dank and dreary, and the ashes in the fireplace are cold.

My mind and body are numb. This isn't the hangover from a single night of swilling whiskey with the Poles. Sixty-seven days of physical and mental strain have precipitated this hangover. I have tried to climb Cerro Torre thirteen times. With great effort I fire a stove and set a pot of water on to boil.

I did Ranger School when I was in the Army—fifty-eight days with an average of two and a half hours of sleep a night and one meal a day while doing patrols designed to simulate the stresses of wartime. My Cerro Torre campaign makes Ranger School seem like Boy Scout camp. A great weight burdens my limbs. The energy to try, one more time, to climb this evil mountain eludes me.

The water boils furiously on the stove; jets of stream rise out of the pot, just out of reach. I stare uselessly at the bubbling pot as the minutes tick away. One tremendous sob wracks my exhausted frame. I cannot summon even the strength to make coffee.

With a groan that shakes the foundations of my soul, I lurch forward and grab the pot of boiling water. Desperately, I want this fool's quest to end, but my only escape is over the top of Cerro Torre.

Charlie returns to find two steaming cups of dark coffee on the stone table in the center of the hut. He'll never know how close our project came to failure over the making of those two brews. We drink cup after cup of coffee and check the weather every time we have to leave the hut to relieve ourselves. By nine o'clock I cannot deny the reality of the situation—the weather is good. We need to go climbing.

My mantra is "Please let it end... please let it end... please let it end," as I stagger over rock rubble on the approach up the dry glacier. The breathtaking scenery of the Torre cirque makes no impression.

Some hours later we load our assault packs with hardware and food at the Norwegian Bivy. A fleecy white cloud hides Cerro Torre. Consciously, I am amazed we persist, but at some deep level I feel Charlie is right—the weather *is* good. These puffy clouds are the clouds of fair weather. Two European parties nearby will wait to see what the weather does.

Charlie and I hardly speak as we deal with the climbing to the Col of Patience—there is nothing to discuss. It is late afternoon when we arrive at the ice cave in the col, where we will spend the night. Enough daylight remains for us to fix our two ropes above the cave to speed progress in the morning. Two Poles from the Pepsi expedition join us and fix their ropes alongside ours. Zbigniew speaks pretty good English, and the four of us arrange ourselves comfortably in the ice cave. I settle into my sleeping bag and eye the roof of the cave. "Zbigniew, how do you say 'good luck' in Polish?"

"*Powodzenia.*"

I chant "*powodzenia, powodzenia, powodzenia, powodzenia,*" as the Poles rock with laughter.

Zbigniew fishes a handheld radio from his pack and babbles in Polish on the radio from the opening of the ice cave. Conversation over, he stashes the radio and goes about preparing dinner. "What was that all about?" I demand.

"I talk to Polish television."

"*What?*"

"Yes, I radio to base camp where we have satellite link. Satellite link goes to live Polish television for Pepsi commercial."

I am astonished. "What did you tell them?"

"That we in ice cave with two crazy Americans, one who chants *powodzenia* like lunatic. That storm is raging. That we have no food. No fuel. That if we do not climb mountain tomorrow we surely die."

"Zbigniew, that's a total lie!"

"Yes, I know… but it does not matter."

Worried about the fickle weather and my fading strength, I pass the night listening to the others snore. Pale starlight filters into the tunnel from the outside world.

Crouch at the start of the 90-meter traverse, Cerro Torre.

Charlie Fowler

Neither Charlie's nor my headlamp will work when the alarm detonates pre-dawn. Trapped in blackness, we wake the Poles and send them off while we wait for first light.

In pale daylight I stand in the col. The stark spires lance into the southern sky. The morning is clear, cold, and *windy*. I wear two hats under my helmet—and all my clothing. The cold wind snaps at my storm shells. Charlie and I battle the wind up through chimneys chock full of ice, over faces of golden granite, and up ridges of snow. A cold blast of spindrift fills my face and glasses.

Charlie and I are curt with each other; we are tense and afraid. As we approach the bolt traverse, the part of the slender peak most exposed to the capricious Patagonian weather, the wind suddenly drops. A broad grin spreads across Charlie's weathered face and he risks a jinx: "Yeah, man, goin' up." Our tense mood breaks and we redouble our efforts.

Clouds drift around the peaks and fill the valley but don't seem threatening. We climb and watch in wonder as gentle clouds pour around the sides of Cerro Torre, one minute enveloping us in mists before disappearing entirely in the next. Once we're above the Ice Tower and onto the headwall, the clouds clamp around us completely. But the mists are still. As I change a roll of film, a scream of pain and the *whoosh* of an object falling unseen through the mist shatters my concentration. Two agitated voices shout back and forth, echoing down from the murk above.

"Someone's hurt," Charlie hollers down. We continue up the bolt ladder toward the mishap. Suddenly the ends of two ropes appear, and the Poles join Charlie at a stance above. I have no clear idea of what is happening. I cannot hear the conversation. What's gone wrong? Do they need help?

The Poles are indistinguishable in their matching windsuits covered with Pepsi logos. They pull their ropes and prepare to rappel again. Charlie helps them rig and tries to stay out of the way. A Pole raps past me. It's Zbigniew. He stops and tells me that he was leading up the ice to the top of the compressor with his partner belaying fifteen feet below. Zbigniew topped out on the compressor, clipped himself off, leaned back, and kicked his left foot out to the side for balance. His foot dislodged a flake of yellow granite the size of a tabletop—four feet long, three feet wide, and three inches thick. The tabletop fell and smashed the elbow of his partner and then disappeared into the mist below. His friend's elbow is useless, Zbigniew tells me, but there is no blood. They refuse help, rappel, and are soon swallowed by the mist, doing the reputation of Eastern European hardmen proud.

Crouch approaching the base of the Headwall.

Charlie Fowler

Shaken, we continue upward. Thank God that chunk was tabletop-shaped so it could frisbee off into space instead of plummeting straight down to crush us.

The massive bulk of Cerro Torre's summit mushroom looms out of the cloud. Charlie straps on his crampons and leads the ice-cream-cone of rime pegged to the bottom of the compressor. I jumar to join him. The only two pitches of this mountain I haven't previously climbed are now before me. Charlie hands me the rack and sends me out onto the last pitch of rock climbing. "Slay this white whale," he urges.

Up I go into the cloud, stretching between rivets. Some hook moves, a few funky pitons, rivets, and a free move get me to the last anchor, within easy distance of the top. Charlie jumars to join me; his crampons grind against the granite. Charlie leads into the cloud for the last pitch of low-angled ice that ends on a small plateau at the base of the

Crouch praising
the weather gods,
Cerro Torre.

One happy climber:
Crouch at the
summit bivy.

Photographs:
Charlie Fowler

summit mushroom. There is not a breath of wind. I ponder our coming night descent and spontaneously yell up at Charlie, barely seen in the mist, "Let's spend the night on top!" My idea seems crazy and impossible, but there is no wind—we could light a match in this calm. I fight to get my crampons on as Charlie establishes a belay, then I climb to join him, overwhelmed with relief to have accomplished what I set out to do sixty-eight days and fourteen attempts ago. Charlie and I hug and laugh and grin and vow to spend the night in a foxhole-like crevasse we soon discover at the base of the summit mushroom. The mushroom itself doesn't look possible: a five-foot overhang of rime—looking like the eaves of a roof—blocks access to the absolute summit. It stings not to be able to stand on the true top.

As we prepare our ropes and backpacks to insulate us from the ice beneath, I cannot force the grin from my face, despite the horrible risk that a storm will rage ashore and catch us at the maximum distance from safety. We squirm into our bivy sacks with nothing but a few cookies and a pint of Tang to share. I shiver without a sleeping bag, but the outrageousness of our aerie warms my soul. We laugh and talk and doze and wait for the dawn while gentle breezes waft the clouds from the sky.

Shivering, we emerge from our icy nest as the first streaks of red and orange color the eastern horizon. My eyes sweep the dark skies—stars everywhere, twinkling in the velvet night. Not a single cloud mars the vault of the southern sky. Mountain shapes form in the black-gray light before dawn. I fumble with crampon straps by the light of my headlamp, struggling to secure mobility. Pure cold pierces my fingers as I fasten the straps to my boots.

In awe and anticipation I stagger to my feet, grab an ice axe, and thirst for the sunrise. In this alpine world of dreams I have no link to the modern world below. The orange stain spreads along the eastern rim of the world. Nearly 10,000 feet below, desert steppes bathed in blackness stretch away and merge with the orange to the east. Color creeps into the sky, and the black vault overhead lightens to reveal a deep purple. Behind us, to the north, west, and south, lies the vast expanse of the southern Patagonian ice cap. Great mountains rise from the sea of flat ice. The approach of dawn tints the peaks pink, light purple, and blue. Just north of the rising sun the peaks of the Fitzroy group color brown

Charlie Fowler enjoying a perfect morning and view from the top of Cerro Torre.

Gregory Crouch

then yellow then pink. My connection with the world of campfires and conversation, sleeping bags and warmth, food and sustenance, lovers and friends, is lost. I have passed from the civilized world into a world of raw power, boundless possibility, infinite sky, impossible color, tremendous size, and utter, overwhelming, silence.

Only our giddy laughter and the crunch of our crampons on the frosty crust breaks the vast silence—discordant noises swallowed without echo by the great beautiful void.

A touch of yellow washes the orange east. A pause. For one precious instant the world catches its breath. And then, with a flash, the sun breaks the horizon. Vibrant, pulsing gold bathes the peaks, ridges, rock, ice, and snow as the first rays touch the spires of the Patagonian Andes. A crown of gold shimmers on the mushroom of rime ice over our heads. In a brilliant instant I fuse with the wondrous light of the sunrise. My future and past compress into the crystal sunrise. Ecstasy, beauty, and awe overwhelm me—and with outstretched arms I greet the sunrise. The glory lasts but a moment. The sun loses its tenuous hold on the eastern horizon and lifts free. The golden hues vanish. The sun pales to yellow and rises into the morning. A new day is born and the Patagonian Andes regain their stark daylight contrasts: black, gray, brown, yellow, and brilliant, piercing white.

Mortality returns. Charlie and I are a long, long way from our futures. Fortune has blessed us with eleven windless hours on the summit of Cerro Torre, but we cannot forever remain. Storms lurk under the western horizon. We organize our descent. One last time I tromp over to the western edge of the summit and gaze down onto the ice cap. The black shadows of the Torres are etched like dragon's teeth onto the white ice below.

On the way down a circling condor shares our celebration. We rappel through three parties of Europeans; six of the seven climbers are on their way to the summit of Cerro Torre on their first attempt. I am incensed that they can climb the Torre so easily, when I have suffered so monstrously for the same end. Then my anger mellows. I may have put my soul on the line for sixty-eight days and made fourteen attempts to climb Cerro Torre, but I accomplished nothing significant in the larger scheme of mountaineering. Maestri's route has been climbed dozens of times. The only importance of this ascent is its importance to me, and I have my reward. And my Cerro Torre will never be the same mountain that it is to those who make the summit so easily.

Julian Fisher imbibes the local brew. *Cameron M. Burns*

INSIDE THE BEECH FOREST
A Patagonian Sojourn

Cameron M. Burns

After three weeks of sitting in a smelly tent that looked like the interior of a broken washing machine, I finally learned that mountaineering in Patagonia has little to do with climbing. Oh, sure, sometimes the sky dawns bright and the wind stops howling for a few hours, and you can run out and snatch a summit if you're very, very lucky. More often than not, you climb about half a route, then retreat empty-handed in the soggiest, windiest blizzard you can remember. Then you sit and wait a couple of weeks for the sun.

Nope, I'm convinced that climbing in Patagonia is about something else, something other than scurrying halfway up a massive granite spire before turning around and being blown back to camp on your hands and knees. You see, while everyone's planning to climb a massive granite spire—always talking about it, always dreaming about it—not a whole lot of climbing is getting done. The hundred or so young men who dwell in the beech forest below the world's most spectacular peaks for the four months of the austral summer are really just looking for something else to do.

When my British companions, Julian Fisher and Charlie French, and I wandered into the Rio Blanco base camp one recent December for a six-week go at Fitzroy, our first thought was that we'd stumbled onto a refugee camp. Dozens of scraggly climbers, clad in filthy long underwear and sporting patchy beards, moped about a cluster of ruinous shacks that looked like piles of construction debris. Prisoner-of-war camps; Jonestown; William Golding's classic *Lord of the Flies*—these all came to mind at once. It was an anarchic society outside society, a fringe civilization dwelling somewhere between Neanderthal times and the present day. Scary monobrows and descending hairlines contrasted with the latest in high technology. Gizmos of all kinds adorned the scruffiest of Missing Links.

With every patch of blue sky that floated overhead, wrists were bared and excited consultations with barometer watches ensued. Everyone with a watch—even if its most advanced feature was an alarm—became an instant meteorologist, and speculation on what the weather would do next ran the gamut from full-blown optimism (for example, packing up gear and strapping on boots) to downright disgust, which was expressed, for the most part, by crawling back into a tent. All this excited speculation would last only until the next throng of clouds floated overhead, then everyone would sulk back into the weird daydream of being in a lush wilderness, thousands of miles from home, with no real purpose for the day.

Finding a non-climbing purpose became the point. Take Gunnar, a clockmaker from Germany, for example. Gunnar spent the first two weeks of his visit to Argentina hauling seventy pounds of potatoes between the village of Chalten and the Rio Blanco base camp. Hauling seventy pounds of potatoes can be done in a couple of days, but Gunnar felt the task needed his full attention for about fourteen. On several clear mornings, as Julian, Charlie, and I began humping loads to Paso Superior for a night in a snow cave and a crack at the mountain, we'd encounter Gunnar.

"Gunnar, aren't you going to try some climbing?" we'd ask, curious about his plans.

"Oh, no," he'd say, dropping a sack of potatoes on the ground near his tent. "I must return to Chalten to pick up some more potatoes. I think if I go down again tonight, I can bring them all up by the end of the week."

Gunnar spent the bulk of his time transporting his precious potatoes, counting them, then recounting them, scrubbing and peeling, boiling and baking. The "Fitz" was reportedly his climbing objective, but apparently nothing satisfied as much as having spent a day washing and priming a dozen potatoes.

When he wearied of potatoes, he'd start cooking other things. Gunnar could charm the socks off any gaucho, and about once a week he'd wander into Rio Blanco with a lamb he'd extracted from one of them. Then he'd set about arranging a party. Gunnar loved parties. He organized a party for Christmas, one for New Year's Eve, and random parties just because he was bored. But his real coup de grace was his twenty-eighth birthday party, a wild feast held in a farmyard outside Chalten, where he took reservations and a six-dollar contribution from any climber who wanted to attend. Needless to say, potatoes were the featured side dish. Gunnar was happy—he'd found his purpose and he cherished his role as party host-cum-restaurateur-cum-chef.

Then there was Jim. Although he was in Patagonia with one of Europe's best-known Patagonian climbers, he felt he hadn't the skills or experience for serious mountaineering. He'd never even walked across a glacier. Jim, with his introspective misgivings, allowed us all to play psychologist and gave us the platform from which we could offer thousands of tidbits of wisdom and hundreds of positive thoughts. He was the patient and we were the doctors, nursing his bruised mind back to health without losing our own stable mental ground.

Whenever we ever woke up in the morning and wondered what the hell we were doing, it was simple to focus on Jim. We'd arise, have our morning coffee and oatmeal, and casually sprint over to Jim's tent to offer observations and insights.

A typical consultation went something like this. Jim: "I don't think I have the skills to do Fitz's *Casarotto Pillar*."

Scraggly, bored climber-turned-psychologist: "Umm, well, I think you've got to look at it in a more positive light. If you have the confidence, you'll have the ability to climb the Pillar. Look deep within your heart."

Jim: "I don't even know how to put on crampons."

Unemployed climber-turned-psychologist: "Well, no one really knows how to put on crampons. The important thing is that you let the crampon know who's boss. Mind over metal, so to speak. Anyway, your partner will likely short-rope you across the glacier."

Jim: "I don't think you have any idea of what you're talking about."

Unemployed climber-turned-psychologist: "Yes, but doesn't my smooth, rambling voice have a calming effect?"

It was never a problem if two of the camp's budding psychologists arrived at Jim's tent at the same time. Most of us in the newly formed Rio Blanco Medical Association seemed to be in agreement, and so double-teaming Jim was merely a case of second opinions. I remember one time when disagreement did occur, but a third psychologist happened to be wandering back from washing his underwear and was able to break the tie fairly promptly. Like Gunnar, Jim—in his own way—had a niche.

Home Sweet Home,
Patagonia.

Gregory Crouch

Others found their own roles to play. Julian, a dentist from Newcastle, became the local news service. He had both an irrepressible restlessness about him and a knack for chatting, so he'd spend each day wandering around camp gathering news and distributing it in one fell swoop. Charlie and I would grill him into the wee hours on what the Italians were doing, or how high the French had placed their fixed ropes.

Harry and Kari, trying to make the first Finnish ascent of Fitzroy, were the Finnish version of the Two Ronnies. Harry, a bricklayer, told us about "working" their government, from dodging taxes to getting unemployment benefits, even if you didn't qualify. Kari, who worked for the government, explained how it was continually developing new techniques for catching tax evaders and welfare cheats.

Jay, a professional climber from the States, had so much experience actually reaching the summits of these Patagonian monsters that he became, essentially, a consultant to every other Rio Blanco resident, an expert in a sea of virgins, a Yoda among pubescent Jedi warriors. His tent—a bright yellow North Face version of a circus tent that we called "the big top"—only confirmed his massive status.

We'd all escaped to Patagonia—but we seemed to need an escape from the escape. And so, as the weeks dragged by, everyone slowly settled down into a role of some sort, no matter how ill-defined. Present were gourmet chefs and carpenters, gear repairmen and wine stewards, photographers and videographers, message carriers and dishwashers, and, of course, entertainers of all sorts.

Base camp was a man's world, usually. But shortly after New Year's, a Swiss woman strolled into Rio Blanco. That really shook up things. Although she arrived with a male friend, she sent the tribe into an unruly scramble. Scissors, soap, shampoo, razors—items never before seen in Rio Blanco—quickly emerged from haul bags. Filthy fleece was hurled into the nearby stream for washing. Secret stashes of highbrow Mendoza wines appeared, and guided trekking trips around the main peaks were offered by the dozen. With a woman present, no one was content with just one role. Every climber suddenly became a gourmet chef, a published author, a talented photographer, an entertainer—all rolled into one. The Neanderthal gang was, en masse, skipping several thousand years of evolutionary development, aiming straight for the Renaissance.

After a week the young lady left, with boyfriend in tow, leaving a wake of romantic hopefuls behind. Emotions settled back into place quickly, but the experience made us all realize how vulnerable we were to both society and nature's odd, powerful quirks.

By the end of the first week in January, I had spent nearly a month mulling over my own set of skills, wondering how I could put them to community service. Then it came to me: my saving grace was my ratty collection of guidebooks, topos, maps, and the spiral notebook I'd bought for eight dollars in Rio Gallegos. The topos, photocopied from the pages of Buscaini and Metzeltin's famous work *Patagonia*, held precious information that every Rio Blanco resident wanted to know. It didn't matter that the topos were a decade old and printed with Italian ratings, or that a zillion new routes had been put up since. All that mattered was that the topo looked partially like a mountain someone was thinking about climbing.

With each curious visitor to my tent, I'd hem and haw over the request, then dig through my reams of Xeroxes, finally pulling out the desired topo and a clean sheet of paper onto which it could be plagiarized. I felt vastly satisfied every time a would-be ascensionist wandered away from the tent, paper in hand, ready to take on Patagonia's finest.

My pile of information became my domain, my tent the one place within base camp I ruled supreme. I had nautical maps showing the Patagonian coastline, books about trekking around the mountains, informal sketches of the peaks copied from tourist maps, and Xeroxed pages from every *American Alpine Journal* published in the past decade. For special requests I would hike down to Chalten, where a popular pub had a vast collection of notes on routes. I had become something of a nerdy bookworm.

While Jay offered advice based on personal experience, I quoted published literature and accounts. While he spoke of subtle nuances in routes and descents, I methodically copied topos, grades, and rappel-anchor advice. I'd never liked the label "nerd," but being tentbound at the end of the world made me the ultimate bookworm.

Of course, in Patagonia, the weather alters everyone's life. When it cleared up for a couple of days in mid-January, Gunnar couldn't sit around base camp peeling potatoes. He had to go climbing. Jim couldn't sit around feeling out of place on a glacier after a hundred eager psychologists had found him fit for mountaineering. He had to go climbing.

We all did, and, with varying degrees of success, we managed to become Patagonian climbers for one great historical day. One day, and one day only. Then the skies turned gray on us, and moisture of all classification sputtered out of the heavens in a month-long drizzle.

Everything in camp received a thorough soaking, and my precious library was reduced to a fetid heap of pulp. The Dewy Decimal System took on a whole new meaning. As each day dragged toward our imminent departure, I spent sad afternoons picking out the most destroyed maps and tossing them into a fire pit.

The three-man "Anglo-Australian Patagonian Expedition" was over. On our last day in Rio Blanco, I handed the intact books and pages to Kari, who promised to take over the role of camp librarian for his brief stay. With the text in English and Italian, and the ratings in French and Italian, the Finn had a daunting chore ahead of him.

Eventually, we all went home. Julian returned to England and his dentistry; Charlie went back to his computers and winter climbing in Scotland; Jay packed up and went back to his professional climbing adventures; Harry and Kari returned to Finland, probably arguing about their government on the plane; and Gunnar went back to Germany and his clockmaking.

I returned to my newspaper work, with its deadlines, headlines, and high stress. For a few precious weeks I had been the best librarian in Patagonia. Able to pull information out of a disorganized heap of paper at the drop of a hat. Able to steer a disoriented climber to the foot of his proposed goal. Able to shed light on the mysteries of the peaks around us.

Maybe mountaineering in Patagonia really isn't about climbing at all. Maybe it's about something more basic. Escaping from an escape. Finding a role, no matter how trivial. Pretending to being a contributing member of society. If I had the time, I might try to solve the mysterious lure of Patagonia's famed peaks—why they prompt young climbers to fly halfway round the world to loiter about in a boggy beech forest. Unfortunately, I've got to start digging. An Italian friend wants a topo of the Casarotto.

SENSATION SEEKING
Psychological or Genetic?

John Thackray

Climbers are increasingly forced to justify their recreation to courts of law, or to government bureaucrats in charge of access policy, or in the broadening debate about mountain rescue and its cost allocation. Motives for climbing hardly mattered when it was a marginal quasi-Romantic pursuit. But lately the swelling number of climbers and accidents, the publicity in the news and advertising media, and the effects of our litigious society have introduced the notion that climbers should face some reckoning and accountability for the risks they incur. The public wants an explanation of why people pursue this dangerous sport, no matter how reductionist or absurd the sound bite. Climbers' habitual evasions, don't knows, or self-serving rationales like "the call of the wild" just won't cut it. Although there is no getting around the fact that climbing is self-centered and without redeeming social significance—unless you subscribe to such hoary myths that it is "character building"—climbers must nonetheless present a plausible rationale if their freedoms are to be preserved from the shackles of social control.

Outcries about the senselessness and irresponsibility of climbing are multiplying. In the U.S. the forces of meddling paternalism are circling our wagons. Fifty people die on the Mont Blanc massif every year and Europe shrugs. Here such carnage would be a heaven-sent opportunity for some political hack to declare that climbers need legislation to protect them from themselves. This is why the climber in the dock— or facing the bereaved parents of a partner who has bought the farm—needs to demonstrate evidence that climbing is the consequence of psychological factors and brain chemistry. These explanations, which I shall come to shortly, need to be better known in the climbing community.

Mallory's famous *obiter dictum* was forced out of him by the American temperament, at the close of a lecture in Philadelphia to raise funds for a forthcoming Everest trip. The phrase "because it is there" was said to a newspaper reporter whose editor recognized that some sort of explanation was what the American public wanted. Climbers owe him a debt: even so hollow an explanation is something to fasten on to. (The reporter may have touched a raw spot in Mallory, who was ambivalent about signing on for the next Everest venture. He eventually chose to go, according to Robert Graves' social history, *The Long Week-end*, to advance his career as a schoolmaster.)

Illustrations:

John Svenson

245

Many of the popular theories about climbers' motives rest on some imputed flight and escape—a noble savage's reaction to some stressful aspect of modern life. Take your pick: industrialization, urban crowding and decay, breakdown of the family, the growth of technology. It is not hard to imagine Mallory and friends pipe-sucking on these. Of course, this reaction-formation machinery is a magic carpet anyone can jump on. Every human deficit, pain, or yearning could be interpreted as the seed of the climbing impulse: sexuality (too much, too little), sociopathologies, materialism, frail ego.

Although mountaineering writing has become more subjective in the last few decades, it is no less psychologically myopic than the old stiff-upper-lip school. The furious nightly scribbling by expedition-eers suggests that many of us climb in order to have something of significance to say to Dear Diary. Drunk on metaphysics and oxygen deficits, we freight the act of putting one foot in front of the other up a mountain with over-signification. Eric Shipton, a famous scribbler of the old school, once observed that climbing is a form of philosophy—though he failed to explain why it was preferable to staying home and reading Plato or Kant. Climbers will recognize what he was trying to convey: that one of climbing's attractions is that it can yield an exhilarating sense of what feels like meaning—an indelible Eureka effect, a purpose uniquely fulfilled, a nearness to some vague yet powerful truth, which at times can even be detected in the narcissistic ravings of Reinhold Messner or Marc Twight.

Explanations of the essence of climbing change with time and fashion. Between Geoffrey Winthrop Young's pursuit of "the spirit" and the appearance of the "adrenaline junkie" of the seventies, climbers' self-image altered. The spirit stuff comes from the twilight of the Victorian's worship of the sublime. The junkie metaphor reflects the culture's taste for the "high." Instead of staying on the ground and ingesting narcotics or hallucinogens, the climber embraces risk in order to trip out on internally gen-erated endorphins. Neither concept is really any improvement on "because it is there."

Nietzsche, an avid hillwalker, urged man to a life of "self-overcoming." But it was Sigmund Freud, a weekend hiker, who mapped the psychology of self-overcoming, showing why some people are drawn to risk-taking rather than to the norm of avoiding it and why, too, they experience a thrill from situations that provoke fear and terror in average humans. The most thorough explanation comes from a disciple of Freud's, Otto Fenichel, who dubbed this phenomenon "counter-phobia." Why is it, he wondered, that "a person shows a preference for the very situations of which he is apparently afraid."

As children grow up they experience many triumphant overcomings of fears, or a least a diminution of earlier terrors. Each such conquest brings on pleasure and elation because of a remission of anxiety—and the knowledge that at least this particular fear will not be repeated. But there remains within all of us a vibrant, unconscious reservoir of anxious fears that have not been overcome. These, Fenichel writes, may be "warded off more effectively by *seeking* situations in which [anxiety] usually appears than by *avoiding* them." A counter-phobic attitude "may really be regarded as a never-ending attempt at the belated conquest of an unmastered infantile anxiety." Whereupon the cession of the underlying discharge of anxiety is experienced as a triumph. Drained of this undertow of fear, climbers at the summit experience joy and relief and perhaps, if they are like Shipton, a sense of some precious knowledge gained.

Counter-phobic triumphs do not exhaust the individual's underlying reservoir of anxiety. The medicine must be taken again and again. Yet Fenichel says that "when we see that many people with counter-phobic attitudes nevertheless consciously feel a good deal of pleasure... and can avoid becoming aware of the anxiety still operative in them, we must admit that they are relatively well off." Fenichel believes that "the entire field of sport" is an "outstanding example" of the counter-phobic phenomenon. "It will generally hold true that the essential joy in sport is that one actively brings about in play certain tensions which were formerly feared, so that one may enjoy the fact that now one can overcome them without fearing them.... People for whom a sport or at least certain kinds of sport (as for example mountaineering) is not a mere occasional relaxation but a matter of significance in their lives, are true counter-phobic subjects."

Another of Freud's disciples, Helene Deutsch, believed that people could relieve themselves of fear by displacing the inward knowledge of danger onto the outside world. "It is perfectly possible," she wrote, "to convert neurotic into real anxiety and to create for oneself the pleasurable situation of a game instead of the painful situation of a phobia. Once the anxiety-object is located in the outside world, the need for mastery over it is directed at some opponent in the game or the element that has to be mastered—such as mountains, water, air."

Here perhaps we have an important ingredient in our species' love of conquest and mastery over nature: the projection of underlying anxiety onto the natural world. Everyone has counter-phobia to some degree. Climbers either have more or it, or they have learned to manipulate it in some gratifying way that produces psychic rewards. But it is important to recognize that counter-phobia is far from automatic, even in hard men. Most climbers have known moments of sudden panic at the sight of a mountain or halfway up a difficult peak—evidence of counter-phobia's unreliability. Many climbers have bailed out when they were unable to control the imagery of the grotesque and demonic mountain. Indeed, the way climbers typically contemplate some difficult challenge seems to be, first, to release feelings of phobia in the imagination, then quell them, then release a little more dread, then again check it—a rehearsal of counter-phobic prowess.

Non-Freudians are inclined to believe that climbers crave danger, stimulus, excitement, and contrast for their own sake—not to discharge fear. About thirty years ago, behavioral psychologist Marvin Zuckerman created a personality inventory of the sensation-seeking personality, of which climbers are a classic representation. Sensation-seeking is not an abnormal quality, and sensation-seekers are not intrinsically psychopathological, antisocial, or abnormal. Unlike a simple trait like sociability, sensation-seeking, a psychobiological model on which individuals can be scored after completing a brief questionnaire, is ambiguous and complex.

Zuckerman's summation, in his 1994 book *Behavioral Expressions and Biosocial Bases of Sensation Seeking*, is this: "[Sensation-seeking] is defined by the need for varied, novel, and complex sensations and experiences and the willingness to take physical and social risks for the sake of such experiences." He is emphatic in believing that risk is not the magnet: it is the uncommon experience, which just happens to entail risk. Zuckerman has broken sensation-seeking down into four factors or components, each reflecting an aspect of the whole: thrill and adventure, novel experience, disinhibition, and susceptibility to boredom.

Zuckerman's scale has been widely used. More than 500 studies have been published in which it has been applied to different groups, and it has been translated into a dozen languages. Climbers have scored at the top of the range among the high-risk sports like scuba diving, car racing, or hang gliding—but not by much. High sensation-seeking scores are characteristic of many populations, from drinkers and sexual experimenters to depressives and druggies.

What determines sensation-seeking incidence? Studies of twins have found that genetic factors probably account for about half of this cluster of characteristics (the rest being attributable to some vague set of environmental causes, presumably anything from diet, to TV, to early upbringing). Heredity, then, links half of this type of behavior to our ancestors, the hunter gatherers of the Pleistocene, when it may have had survival value during the hunt. Nor are humans its only possessors: some animals can be said to have an analogous structure of personality. Across species an "approach" system, or an "expectancy" system, has been observed, which one group of writers in a recent *Journal of Personality and Social Psychology* says have at least three core processes. The approach/expectancy system consists of "an internal, subjective state of incentive-reward motivation; forward locomotion as a means of supporting goal acquisition; and cognitive processes [that] increase interaction with the environment." (These seem to have a remarkable similarity to the narrative template of the *American Alpine Journal!*)

These same processes are strongly associated with the presence of the neurotransmitter dopamine in animals and in the midbrain of humans. The so-called "pleasure" or "reward" mechanisms of the brain involve synaptic dopamine and norepinephrine, which are regulated in part by monoamine oxidase (MAO) in a complex chain of interactions, in which MAO makes neurons more active.

A number of researchers have tried to find a relationship between high sensation-seeking scores and low amounts of MAO in the blood. According to Zuckerman, nine out of thirteen studies have established some correlation. Although the relationship between MAO in the brain and in the blood is undefined, this seems to be a pretty good biological marker for a lot of traits. One study did find climbers high on sensation-seeking and low on MAO.

Nearly ten years ago Robert Cloninger, of Washington University, suggested that variable scores on his "Novelty Seeking Scale" (very similar to Zuckerman's) were mediated by genetic variability in dopamine transmission. But it was not until 1995 that a group of Israeli scientists established the first-ever association between a normal personality type and the genetic locus of a neurotransmitter. On January 2, 1996 the front page of the *New York Times* carried a story about Richard Ebstein and his team at the Herzog Memorial Hospital in Jerusalem: they had discovered that "novelty seekers tend to have a particular variant of a gene that allows the brain to respond to dopamine, an essential chemical communications signal. The gene encodes the instructions for the so-called D4 dopamine receptor, one of five receptors known to play a role in the brain's response to dopamine. Novelty seekers possess a version of the D4 receptor gene that is slightly longer than receptors in non-novelty seekers."

This breakthrough experiment, however, only points the way; Ebstein is nowhere near finding a "thrill-seeking" gene. The particular receptor he studied accounts for no more than ten percent of the difference in novelty seeking between one individual and another. Ebstein predicts that four or five other genes, when tracked down, will each exert about the same influence.

Scientists have come very far in a brief period. "Ten and even five years ago," Zuckerman told me recently, "nobody would have believed that you could find a single gene that had any relationship with a personality trait. Now it looks that is where the action is going to be."

No matter how keen and vigorous the hunt, it is unlikely to soon lead to an incontrovertible explanation of the causes of sensation-seeking and its analogues, in part because of serious problems of definition and measurement. The sensation-seeking scale is a seine net with some very large holes in it—as might be expected with a self-administered yes/no questionnaire. (Examples: "I sometimes like to do things that are a little frightening." And: "The worst social sin is to be a bore.") Something built from such bricks is a pretty crude tool, but crudity seems endemic to any inventory of behavioral traits.

The good news for climbers is that Freudians, behaviorists, and biologists all perceive climbing to fall within normal parameters—that it is part of a much larger pattern of human behavior and is therefore not deviant or pathological. They emphatically contradict the popular stereotype of an irresponsible risk junkie, as once propounded by the Polish psychologist Zdzislaw Ryn. In the 1972/73 *Himalayan Journal* he claimed that climbers are "a separate group of sportsmen with profound mental and biological peculiarities." In his study of thirty Polish alpinists, two-thirds exhibited a predominance of "schizoidal personality. The whole group was characterized by weak sexual adjustment, weak social adaptation, uncooperativeness." A Dream Team, if ever there was one.

That it can be shown that climbing has psychological and biological utility will perhaps distress those climbers who believe the sport exists to pump up their self-images of the rebel. For nonclimbers who come into contact with us, however, this research should be reassuring. Many climbers will object that none of the above explanations *feel* right, that they don't mirror "truths" about climbing and its subtle relation to the self. But no generalized explanation of such a widespread behavior as climbing is going to do that. Nor does it exclude the validity a more personal narrative of motive. Even if Dr. Ebstein succeeds in tracking down the four or five "thrill-seeking genes," they are unlikely to reveal a case of behavioral pre-determination. Their relationships to one another, and interactions, may, many theoretical biologists believe, be influenced by exogenous factors.

From the point of view of climbers, the very possibility of a genetic source to risk-acceptance is a favorable development, because we must recognize that climbing is today an interest group that must seek legitimacy and public acceptance by fair means or foul. Like any other interest group, it must use public relations and image management to secure its future. And if science or pseudo-science can help, so much the better. Joining in the scrum of interest-group politics seems a long way from the sublime pursuit of the freedom of the hills. But that freedom will be protected only if we ensure that the community has a good opinion of our sport.

DEAD MEN'S GEAR

Jeff apple Benowitz

On the Appalachian Trail one January I learned from some hikers that a man had recently died in the lean-to where I planned to spend the night. When I reached the lean-to, I convinced myself it was not yet time to stop, and later, lying under a tarp in a cold rain, the reason why the hiker died—hypothermia—crossed my mind. I did not sleep well.

While packing for a Valdez ice-climbing trip, my partner showed me his ice-axe holster. It was weathered leather and looked as if it were designed to hold a carpenter's hammer. He told me it was a dead man's holster. Looking at the holster in this new light, I saw many walls and waterfalls. Funny how that old holster went from a ratty piece of gear to an object of stories and lore when the term "dead man's" was added to its name.

In Talkeetna, following my first attempt on Denali, I visited the ranger station to sign back in. I listened to two rangers and a climber divvy up clothes and hardware. The gear had belonged to a Japanese climber who had died of exposure high on the mountain. I wondered if I would wear a dead man's shirt. Hitching back to Fairbanks, I also wondered if the stuff was jinxed. Did it hold some vestige of the man's juju, or was it simply stuff?

A week after I climbed Foraker, two people died on it in an avalanche. The wife of one of the dead men, looking for answers, asked a friend of mine how climbers deal with death. My friend responded with a statement to this effect: "It's time to divide up the gear." A dead man's gear is obviously useless to its former owner and is often considered communal—up for grabs. Is there some solace in the knowledge that one's gear is still going to the hills even if one is not?

John Svenson 251

One of the participants in the ranger-station gear divvy after my first Denali attempt died climbing in the Alaska Range. Somehow, during the great gear sort that followed, I ended up with one of his stuff sacks. He was one of the greatest alpinists there ever was, and for a bit I felt like some of his climbing ability might rub off the stuff sack onto me. Yeah, it was a silly idea, and after a short while I thought of the green sack as just a green sack.

The Hayes Range is a harsh place. Summits are rare in the summer and ethereal during the dark of winter. A winter climb of McGinnis Peak demanded a price my partner and I were unwilling to pay, and we abandoned gear haphazardly on the way down. Among the things left behind were a green stuff sack and a weathered hammer holster.

Trying to climb the east face of the Thorn in winter was a no-go. We climbed nothing, numbed our fingers and toes, and ignored personal hygiene. The pilot who came for us when the weather cleared told us that three Fairbanksians had died on a glacier system west of the one we were on, and once again I found myself thinking about dead climbers' gear. We missed the gear sort on this one and I'm glad. I had lent a pair of crampons to one of the three. I know that they are just hunks of metal. That they can't be jinxed. I think I also know that my friend's smile and dance steps are not now an intrinsic part of the crampons. Thing is, I really don't know what I think I know. All I know for sure is to be careful—and that I have another pair of crampons for sale that come with a story of walls and waterfalls.

Early in the season, two German climbers were swept off Hunter. The skis they left at the bottom of their route were buried by numerous slides. Later in the season, two American climbers dug the skis out and used them to approach one of Hunter's unclimbed spurs. They were also swept off the mountain.

EXPOSURE

John Hart

The faces change. The utter honesty
that's forced by the proximity of space:
try telling here there's no such thing as choice:
it matters what you do.
For here is real error, actual pain,
and death is present in the honored stone.

Danger is not the object. Nor is fear,
not ever, as a guide to actions, decorous.
Yet it surrounds us in our best desires
and all the borders of our strength
abutt that country where the risk is pure
the gap of strangeness open in the air . . .

If I read the law correctly, we endure
through no one's ransom and at no one's door.
The hand is excellent as it is odd.
We know ourselves lame animals, but here
the sun like three stones piled to be our guide
affirms that we are royal, and afraid.

WHERE THE GODS LIVE
Everest
May 10, 1996

Patricia Farewell

One mountain holds

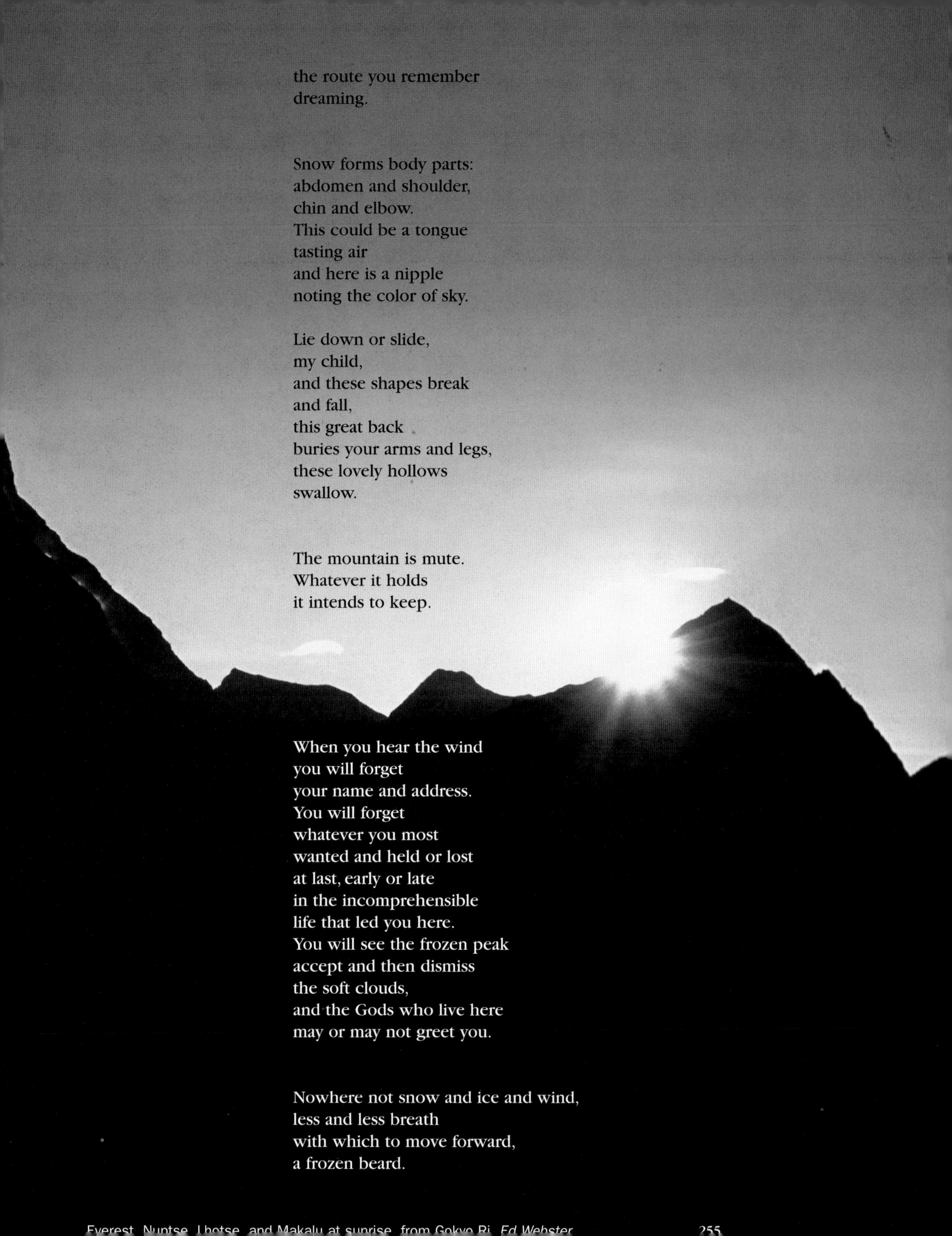

the route you remember
dreaming.

Snow forms body parts:
abdomen and shoulder,
chin and elbow.
This could be a tongue
tasting air
and here is a nipple
noting the color of sky.

Lie down or slide,
my child,
and these shapes break
and fall,
this great back
buries your arms and legs,
these lovely hollows
swallow.

The mountain is mute.
Whatever it holds
it intends to keep.

When you hear the wind
you will forget
your name and address.
You will forget
whatever you most
wanted and held or lost
at last, early or late
in the incomprehensible
life that led you here.
You will see the frozen peak
accept and then dismiss
the soft clouds,
and the Gods who live here
may or may not greet you.

Nowhere not snow and ice and wind,
less and less breath
with which to move forward,
a frozen beard.

Everest, Nuptse, Lhotse, and Makalu at sunrise, from Gokyo Ri. *Ed Webster*

If the eyes fail, the man falls
and will never be found,
the sound of breaking bones
will go unheard.

I chose to descend without the others.
It was well past our turn-around time
and I knew what I needed to do.

I chose to wait at the summit.
The others would arrive any moment
and all of us would head back down together.
I chose to become a stone
at last, to let all that was small in me
be me, kneeling on the mountain
then collapsing forward,
my back arched to support the snow
that would fall and bury it,
my sleepy face set in my folded arms.

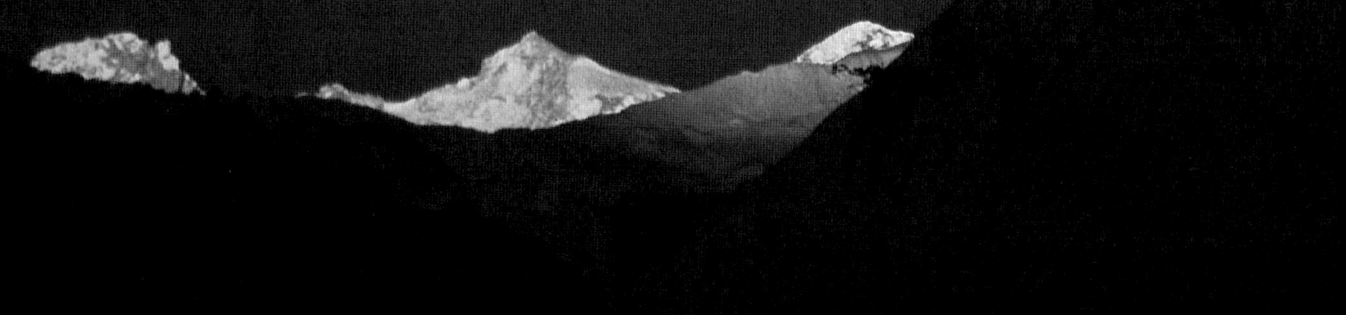

I chose to stay with the other.
It was he who led me
before I led him.

I chose to descend without the others.
I had some air and

at the top it was like being under water.

Before I see tents
I see blue rocks
sky
     and water
in my one good eye,
the left one.

Twice
I did not die,
though certain I was gone
you returned to the heart of the wind
and your late descent.
                    Here
is the hand I will lose,
the right one
                with which I wave,
no, salute, whoever moves toward me now,
stunned I'm alive.
This is my face adorned with white bulbs of ice,
my body armored in ice,
but stumbling, stumbling to life.

Where the Gods live
no birds fly.
No trees or flowers flourish.

Snow shifts its position
under the sun and moon
but does not melt.
Time keeps to itself.

Where the Gods live
all promises and secrets are broken.
Every obligation is forsaken.
No tent stands through the night.
No memory enters a quiet mind.
No laughter reaches the other.
No eye opens after closing.

Where the Gods live
the climbers lie
listening to the wind and the snow,
and all that they have seen
remains with them.

Makalu at sunset, from Ama Dablam. *Ed Webster*

NO OTHER ANNAPURNAS
Paragraphs Written in a Hospital

John Hart

When I was young and getting the mountain itch I naturally read Maurice Herzog's *Annapurna*, the story of the first-ever ascent of an 8,000-meter peak. I was haunted by the page where Herzog, drunk on altitude and victory, comes lurching toward his companions, waving in the wind his gloveless, perishing hands. But the famous passage at the end of the book never satisfied me. When Herzog, his career ended by frostbite, declares, "There are other Annapurnas in the lives of men," it didn't ring true, somehow.

In due course I became a climber of sorts. Twenty years later, a rock bounding down an ice couloir in California shattered my right knee. I'm writing this in a hospital bed. Thanks to modern orthopedic surgery, I won't lose the leg. I can hope to walk. A little light hiking might not be out of the question. But climbing, as I have known it, is plainly not in the cards. I'm not a Hugh Herr or a Mark Wellman. If my body is no longer suited to climbing, in the conventional manner, I probably won't climb.

Some of my gear came in here with me a month ago, and I have taken an odd pleasure in using it to furnish my curious campsite. Various useful items hang from carabiners. When a cord in my traction system broke, I insisted that it be replaced with five-millimeter perlon. To stabilize my body at night against the traction, I wear a sit-harness, clipping in to the head of the bed. And I try to digest the fact that this well-loved paraphernalia will never be used, in earnest, again.

I've had time to think some more about Herzog after Annapurna, and to feel more keenly that his self-consoling words were a little too easy and not quite convincing.

Not that climbing is the most important thing in the world; surely, by any rational measure, it is among the least important. Not that it has dominated my own life: I never did it enough to get genuinely good at any aspect of the craft. Not that other activities, maybe better ones, won't replace it: I even feel a certain relief at the release of time for things I need to do more.

No, climbing is not very important. The things I will undertake in its place are arguably richer, worthier. But they will not replace what is gone.

Human joys are not fungible, not interchangeable, like silicon chips or soybeans. Climbing is one of many possible occasions for effort, or the exercise of skill, or ambition, or wonder. But it is also *climbing*, the thing itself, unique.

Whatever else I turn to, I will not find there the struggle to wake and move in appalling cold at the foot of a mile of ice-bound hill. Not again will I feel the hum in the blood after mounting a rock pitch I had thought beyond my limits, or the unearthly peacefulness of a series of night rappels. Nowhere else will I know the end of the bivouac, the striding toward me of enormous dawn. Nowhere else could I have seen, in a windblasted tent, the uncanny floating ball of St. Elmo's fire.

Every climber has these moments. Mine, the yield of a mediocre, sporadic, low-altitude "career," are remarkable only to me. But they hold a place—in my memory now—that nothing else can fill. In some quiet corner of my mind, I will not cease to grieve.

In the lives of men and women there are joys and struggles far more significant and poignant than the arbitrary job of getting up some cleavage in the granite, some volcanic pimple, some crumbling heap propelled by plate tectonics to the top of the troposphere. But there are none that are just the same.

There are different things, better things, higher things.

There are no other Annapurnas in the lives of men.

260   Sunrise, Mt. Kenya. *Ascent Archives*

TUOLUMNE GRANITE
(First climb after convalescence)

John Hart

At first it made me think that I could climb
its gray and lifted wing of silicon,
in hardness an alternative to Time,
its Elemental beckoning me on.

And then it made me fear that I would fall,
perched on my hooves, with safety far below,
the bootsole sliding and the handgrip small,
the balance wrong, and gravity to go.

And then it caused me shame that I had been
so much less brave upon it than I knew
I had it in me to be, now and then:
so slack, so unconsenting, so untrue.

And then the hope and fear and shame were done.
You did not see me stop to kiss the stone.

PICTURES FROM KYRGYZSTAN

Steph Davis

I'd barely heard of Kyrgyzstan, didn't even know where it was until we got there. But after a storm-filled season in Patagonia it took only the words "Good weather! Big granite peaks!" to get me fired up.

The trip to the new republic, bordering on northwestern China and once part of the Soviet Union, was complicated from the start. Assembling the team took on all of the drama and complexity of planning a high-school dance. Topher Donahue and his girl-friend, Patience Gribble, had organized the trip, so they were definitely going. Kennan Harvey, my boyfriend, seemed to want to go, but was waiting to see if I'd go. I, of course, wasn't going unless he was. The other issue was Kennan and Topher's tradition of part-nership. That, coupled with Patience's lingering elbow tendonitis, made me confused about who my partner would be. No one really seemed sure who would climb with whom. There was a vague and general feeling that if no one decided anything, it would all work out once we got there. I wasn't convinced.

I thought I'd solved the problem by asking Doug Byerly to come along, until Patience and Topher suddenly announced that they were both injury free and would be climbing almost exclusively together. Doug solved the new problem by inviting Jimmy Surette. Chaos was held in check, if just barely. I began to think it might be best to go with the flow on this trip, a suspicion reinforced when we tried to leave the States.

Kennan and I found ourselves four days behind the rest of the crew, because Delta couldn't get us from Salt Lake City to New York. When we finally landed in Uzbekistan, at a dilapidated airport that was either in the process of being renovated or falling apart, we were relieved to learn that Topher and Patience had also been delayed and were here in Tashkent. Doug and Jimmy were already in the mountains, and we four hoped to join them at base camp in about four days. The journey was starting to seem more like an Asian trav-el adventure than a climbing trip. At the very least, I thought, we'd come home with some good photos. But a picture is only worth a thousand words; sometimes a pen works better.

Driving

We are driving, sort of, up a long and winding hill on the way to Katran, one of the last towns before our goal, the towers rising above the Ak-su Valley. The boxy minivan doesn't like carrying six people with expedition gear and food up steep passes. Travel is slow. The land is big and arid. In our frequent stops to tend to the radiator I get a chance to look at the scruffy goats and donkeys, and at the women selling melons, honey, and sour-milk balls along the roadside. The women wear gauzy dresses shot with multi-colored foil threads and filmy, sparkly scarves on their hair. I immediately want a sparkly scarf.

A canvas yurt perches on a slope beside the dirt highway. A small boy has been sent down to the road to fetch water from a pipe that sticks out of the hillside. Perhaps it is this pictur-esque tableau that inspires Patience to play *National Geographic* by propping her eyeglass-es on the faces of a small, ragged girl and her naked baby brother. Topher clicks his shutter.

Steph Davis rope-coiling. *Kennan Harvey*

Talking with
Kyrgyz women.

Kennan Harvey

Semetei is our interpreter, guide, and cook. He is nineteen, toothy, and will start attending the university in Kyrgyzstan's capital, Bishkek, after this trip. His English bursts forth in quick phrases that get halted by hesitations and an Asian accent. The van jolts. I ask Semetei if he's ever been to the Ak-su Valley. No. I ask what kind of food he usually cooks. He admits to never actually working as a cook. In fact, he's never slept outside, he tells me, laughing happily.

Heavy machinery sits idle by the roadside as cars and trucks steadily roll on. Occasionally, we pass a run-down trailer fronted by a table displaying the ubiquitous Fanta bottles and milk balls, presumably for sale. Small children peek through faded curtains, but their parents never emerge as we rattle past. Kennan spots a police car coming and asks Semetei if the police often stop drivers on the road. Semetei says cryptically, "Some people give money, then there is no trouble. Our driver has given money twice today." The driver does appear rather tense. Semetei remarks that the minivan is not permitted on this road but can't seem to explain why. We try to look nonchalant as the police car passes us.

Evidently this is a twelve-hour drive, perhaps not counting radiator stops, although it should take only half that time to drive from Tashkent to Katran. But Tajikhistan pokes into the middle of Kyrgyzstan like an unfriendly porcupine; it has been at civil war for years. Semetei and the driver look alarmed when I ask why we can't just drive straight through Tajikhistan. Semetei makes vague and ominous references to guns and Tajikhs. He fires off a stream of Russian to the driver. I stop asking questions.

Trekking

The trail is steep and rocky. We are hot. The Kyrgyz horseman are wearing the national hat—tall white wool felt with a black velvet brim and black filigree patterns stitched on front and back—and torn, navy-blue Adidas warm-up pants. I walk behind a horse, watching the horseman's rubber flipflops slide as he pulls on the frayed bridle. I ask Semetei why we need seven men to lead seven horses on this three-day approach trek. He looks at me in surprise. "They will not trust their horse to another man. Horses are valuable. Forty dollars is how much they can earn in one year."

I feel a bit cheated. Couldn't we pay one man three or four year's salary to lead all the horses and tip their owners?

As night falls we lay out our blankets and sleeping bags, then sit in a circle with the horsemen. They produce a plastic soda bottle of champagne-colored wine that tastes of apples. We converse through Semetei as the wine goes around. "How old are you?" he says to me.

"Twenty-five."

"You have children?"

"No!" We all snicker. The horsemen look puzzled.

"You and Kennan are married?"

"No!"

Most of the horsemen are about my age, and all of them have at least three children. They are curious about our jobs. They think we are rich.

The next day we stop at noon. Semetei is exhausted. He's never walked this much in his life, and he looks a bit bedraggled from his first night on the ground. Only after we'd had tea and packed all the horses were we able to pry him from his sleeping bag this morning. I sit in the shade beside a nomad hut, tentatively touching my tongue to a dried sour-milk ball an old woman has given me. It is dingy, rock hard, and smells faintly of horse manure. They are supposed to satisfy thirst somehow, but I can't see these things satisfying anything except a desire to throw them away. I slip it into my bag, smiling appreciatively as though I'm planning to savor it later. Kennan hucks his into a bush when the nomad woman isn't looking.

Davis
and horsemen.

Kennan Harvey

265

Semetei and Topher watch the horsemen; they have been drinking yogurt and tea at a distant hut for almost two hours now. The packs and baggage lie beside the horses in a large meadow. Perhaps the men are discussing improved strapping techniques. The packs have been falling off the horses regularly for the entire trip. "They look like a bunch of construction workers on strike," says Kennan.

Semetei goes over to investigate. The horsemen are indeed on strike, wanting more money. Topher looks around the nomad settlement. "They might have the right idea with the strike," he says dryly, "but they probably shouldn't have decided to do it in a field full of horses. I bet these nomads wouldn't mind earning some extra money."

Semetei gets worked up; he takes his job seriously. As he shouts at Serohzdeen, the chief horseman, his face darkens and saliva sprays from his lips. The horsemen crouch on the ground nearby, listening. I see their eyes tighten as I try to help Topher and Kennan in the negotiations, and I look at them in disgust. Twenty minutes earlier one man had seen me take a bottle of ibuprofen from my pack. He pointed to his head and grimaced, then pointed at the medicine. The other six suddenly developed headaches, too, and I reluctantly emptied most of my only bottle. Now, after accepting my gift, they are turning on us.

What about last night's wine drinking and chatting? What about our agreement? I feel betrayed. If I were earning a year's salary in three days, I'd be ecstatic. I walk away as Semetei and Serohzdeen shout. Kennan gestures and jokes with the horsemen as though nothing is happening. For the first time I realize how delicate this trip is. In five minutes we could find ourselves stuck at the foot of the mountains, equally far from our destination and our starting point with more baggage than we could ever carry.

Descending

I'm feeling the altitude as Kennan and I simul-climb to the summit of Peak 3850—the Center Pyramid; after all, it's more than 12,000 feet high. From start to finish, we've left nothing on the route but some urine and four bolts avoiding the crux aid pitch. Yesterday Kennan found a short, difficult slab traverse that led into a good crack system—and this was the key to freeing the route. We realized today that my last lead was the final aid pitch marked on the topo. It went free! Now we are indulging in satisfaction as we cruise over easy terrain to the top.

The weather is still perfect ("Six hours of rain in forty-two days," Kennan will repeat to friends when we get home), and the lichen-covered granite glows in the afternoon sun. The summit ridge is in sight, and our goal now is to get down before

Kennan Harvey on on the *Blue Moon Variation* (5.11) during the first free ascent of *Yellow Moon*, Center Pyramid.

Steph Davis

Davis topping out on *Yellow Moon,* Center Pyramid. Behind are Peak 4810 (left) and Peak 4520.

Kennan Harvey

dark. Soon we are greeted by what appears to be a piece of laundry line looped around a projection. Far below, a loose gully winds tortuously down the back of the peak. We look into it with trepidation. "We could scramble further along the ridge and check out the other end of the peak," Kennan suggests optimistically.

I look down again. I don't want to traverse the length of the ridge only to realize we need to come back here again. Someone has rapped from here before—and presumably made it to the ground. "Let's just start down," I reply.

The irresistible Russian Tower.

Kennan Harvey

The gully is gravelly and treacherous. I hold my breath as we pull each rap line, waiting for it to get stuck in loose blocks or tug them off. Stones come hurtling down sporadically as we creep down loose, wet scree between rappels. I feel like a pin in a bowling alley, and I also feel silly rappelling the steeper sections, which really aren't very steep. But the idea of scrambling unroped down these gravel-covered shelves is horrifying. I resign myself to being totally gripped. Annoyingly, Kennan doesn't seem bothered.

As night falls, we reach a cliff at the bottom of the gully. We rappel into the dark, swinging in to place nut anchors in fractured rock. It's a relief to reach the talus and coil our ropes. We pick and slide our way down, ford the river, and arrive at camp. "I guess that was the wrong way," I say sheepishly.

The next day Doug and Jimmy return from climbing Russian Tower, the peak beside 3850. With shudders they recount their descent. Their topo encouraged them to rappel near a water streak. Despite their better judgment, they obeyed and ended up setting fifteen anchors, leaving most of their rack. It took them almost as long to get down as it did to climb the seventeen-pitch, 5.12 route. Evidently it was the wrong water streak. Before doing Russian Tower, they'd climbed Asan Peak in the neighboring Kara-su Valley. That descent had taken them down a death gully that randomly loosed showers of blocks around them. Purely by chance they hadn't been hit.

So far everyone has returned from climbs bearing horror stories of epic descents. We are like cats climbing trees and getting stuck, but there is no fire department. Our topos, in French and Russian, with vague line drawings, mainly serve to lead us astray. Doug and I begin to reminisce fondly about Patagonian descents, doing countless rappels down the same routes we had climbed up, fearing only stuck ropes, failed anchors, and storms.

A week later Topher and Patience climb 3850. Sufficiently dissuaded by our tales of the gully, they go on to the end of the ridge and make a few raps to a pleasant grassy slope. As they describe the convenience of their descent, I glance at Kennan apologetically. He politely refrains from commenting.

At Ak-su Base Camp: Doug Byerly, Steph Davis, Jim Surette.

Kennan Harvey

The next week, as we climb Russian Tower, all I can think about is the descent. After hearing Doug and Jimmy's story, and remembering Greg Child's account of his descent with Lynn Hill, I am braced for an experience that will make getting off of 3850 seem like lowering off a sport route. As we come down from the summit, we continue past Doug and Jimmy's water streak and end up gently scree-skiing and hiking for a few hours until we finish with a couple of short raps. It's almost anti-climactic—and the easiest descent yet.

Socializing

Sometimes it's too hot at base camp; other times we huddle by the fire. A constant stream of local nomad hunters occupies the plank benches by the cook site. They bring their own bread and yogurt and drink tea for hours with Backet, our new cook. Semetei is in Bishkek starting his first semester, probably impressing university girls with tales of his mountain adventures and crazy American climbers. On his last four days he hiked about ninety miles to bring messages and prepare for Backet's arrival and Doug and Jimmy's early departure. His month in the mountains has turned him into a ridiculously strong hiker, precipitated by his preference for carrying messages and buying bread from the nomads, rather than cooking it himself.

Backet is older and knows much less English. He does, however, seem to know how to cook, and even, on occasion, to want to. The locals like him more than Semetei, and they linger around camp regularly now. Sometimes two or three days go by before they leave. I wonder if their families notice their absence. Not much hunting happens. What could be so exciting in our base camp? "I think they just like to get out of the house," Kennan says.

Davis leading on the first free ascent of *Yellow Moon,* Center Pyramid.

Kennan Harvey

I grow weary of trying to communicate with Backet. It's hard work. Someone somewhere seems to have taught him to say "little little" for "very little," and as this is one of the few English words he knows, it's not long before I feel like I'm in a Little Caesar's pizza commercial. Kennan, however, has endless enthusiasm for breaching the language barrier. When he talks to the Kiwi trekkers, he says "mate" and "glay-see-er." When he talks to the British climbers, he says "abseil." He is indefatigably flexible. He spends hours with Backet before he triumphantly imparts to me one piece of news he has deciphered. When we get a chance to check the information with a local who speaks more English, the news is totally inaccurate.

Today Kennan is engaged in another elaborate discussion with Backet. He changes the words in his phrases and nods and gestures enthusiastically, trying to coordinate our departure. He points to imaginary donkeys. "One *ishik*, two *ishik*, three *ishik*, four *ishik*. Everybody happy!" Kennan repeats this several times while Backet thumbs through a Russian-English dictionary. Their talk dodges in circles, bumping and conjoining at random points that neither can perfectly ascertain.

The Kyrgyz visitors have noticed my interest in their bread-making technique. Backet breaks off from the donkey discussion to point at me and announce, "Bread study!" The young men smile at me invitingly from the fireside. One boy holds his hands out and another pours water over them. He puts a few inches of water into our red plastic bowl, drops in two lumps each of salt and soda, and stirs with his finger. Then he reaches into the flour sack with cupped hands and adds two loads of flour. As he starts mixing with his hands, Backet leans over to tell me, "two breads." The other men sit in the shade and point to me, wanting me to take a turn kneading. I shake my head and look at the breadmaker.

"His bread," I say firmly.

On the moraines.

Kennan Harvey

The breadmaker kneads for almost ten minutes until the dough is as white as plaster. He calls for more water and dips his hands in it, punching wet fists into the dough over and over until it can get no smoother. As the iron pot heats, he rubs a piece of goat fat around the bottom and adds some sticks to the fire. He presses the dough flat, punches holes in the top with a twig, and lays it in the pot.

We all smile at each other and wait for the bread to brown. It turns out crusty and chewy. I am impressed that the men make their own bread, but then, I guess they have no choice when they don't go home for days on end.

That night a hunter offers Kennan some of the green powder we've seen them chewing. It smells like dried pond algae. Gamely, Kennan puts a pinch in his lower lip while Topher, Patience, and I goggle at him and question him on his state every thirty seconds. He starts to feel a head rush and burning in his lip and quickly spits the stuff out.

"No throwing up," I say sternly.

Patience observes Kennan's face. "You're not a very good color," she says. "I'm looking at Topher and Steph, and you don't look the same."

"You do look a bit haggard," I observe.

"I don't *feel* nauseous though," Kennan says and then immediately puffs his cheeks, lunges past me, and vomits into a bush. We all look at each other in shock but are unable to keep from laughing hysterically. We are saved from callousness by Kennan's own laughter between heaves. The Kyrgyz men watch him inscrutably and tuck more powder into their lips.

Soloing

Kennan and I have climbed four routes together and have taken two exploratory trips away from the Ak-su. The end of this trip is becoming real; we have about two weeks left. The days are getting shorter, and I can tell it's September. We get only about six hours of sun at base camp now, valleyed in as we are by peaks on both sides of the river. Some of my voracity is subsiding. I'm starting to think about work and home.

I walk to the river to wash my hair and look up toward the glacier at the head of the valley. A few yaks graze in the distance, looking like ottomans with their short-haired backs and fringed bellies. I remember hiking up there a few days ago, seeing flat, platinum rocks that gleamed in the sun and granite boulders perched like mushroom caps on ice stalks that rose from the glacier.

I look the other way, just behind camp, at Peak 4520. That and 4810 are the only major formations that Kennan and I haven't climbed. The latter is beginning to look cold and icy, although Doug and Jimmy managed to sneak in a route before they left. I scan up the right shoulder of 4520, trying to pick out the route that Topher and Patience, and then Doug and Jimmy, climbed. It looks fast and low angle. When it steepens, the route finishes with a beautiful crack system that I can see clearly from here. Topher and Patience spent three days on the route, Doug and Jimmy took one and a half. They did thirty pitches of climbing—with only a few pitches of 5.10—and thirty of rappelling.

Behind Davis rise
Peak 4810 and
Peak 4520.

Kennan Harvey

I stare at 4520. If I gave myself three days, four liters of water, maybe I could do it. I could go really light—a bivy sack, some candy bars and jerky, a tiny rack, jumars, clothes. I can see a huge ledge about two-thirds of the way up; I could bivy there, and again on the summit or on the ledge on my way down, depending on the time.

Once the idea is in my head, I can't get it out. I'm reenergized.

A week later, at 4:30 in the morning, I slip out of camp. In the dark I'm glad I made the stash of ropes and water yesterday since now I only vaguely recognize parts of the grassy slope in my headlamp beam. As I start climbing the first easy pillar, I feel familiar handholds.

At six I reach my ropes and water. It's still dark and cold, and I'm at the end of familiar ground. Carefully I repack my bag and flake out my ropes at the base where it looks easiest to start. I have a tiny French topo, but I'm still not sure if I'm even starting where they did. The sky is lightening. I shoulder my pack and start to free-solo for a while.

Hours melt as I lead pitches, belaying with a Grigri, then rapping down and jumaring back up with the pack. I'm incredibly alert. I've gone off route once already, and the panic I felt as I suddenly found myself doing irreversibly hard slab moves on a slack self-belay has inspired me to scrutinize my path anal-retentively as I move. All day I manage to avoid rope snags and dead ends. In the back of my mind is the conviction that if I can get to the good bivy ledge today, I can actually do this route alone.

As night falls, I make it to the ledge. It's getting cold fast, and I waste no time flaking out my ropes and crawling into the bivy sack. The top is much closer than I'd expected. I realize with a start that I've done twenty two-hundred-foot pitches today—two thirds of the route. Unless something goes very wrong, I'll summit tomorrow and start rappelling.

The bivy is cold and long. Wishing for a sleeping bag, I try to curl into myself. As dawn falls, I try to move fast. Off route again, in my frosty morning stupor, I climb unprotected across a slab for a full pitch until I gratefully get into the final crack system. Now I can spend my time climbing instead of worrying about the route. The cracks are splitter and fun. I start to get excited. I pull around a roof thickly hung with icicles and leave everything on a big ledge. Unfettered, I climb a sharp ridge to the very top, where I can see into both the Ak-su and the Kara-su valleys. It's odd to be here all alone. I feel my solitude forcibly and get back to business.

The rappelling is endless. After I regain my bivy ledge, I switch directions and rappel to the side of my route, aiming for a gully I've gone down before as part of another descent. As night falls, I continue robotically, detangling ropes and thinking of my warm sleeping bag and tent. Despite my efforts to stay on track, I get lost in the dark and find myself dangling free from a cliff when I should be hiking down talus. Ultimately, luck is on my side, and by midnight I make it down to the river. The dark shadows of 3850 and Russian Tower loom from the other side. I'm relieved and satisfied, and kind of amazed. I'm really done now. I'm ready to go home.

Peak 4520. Davis's solo ascent of *1,000 Years of Russian Christianity* ascended the lower and upper right-hand pillars. *Kennan Harvey*

THE CLIMBING MAGAZINES
Read, Skim, or Ignore?

John Hart

I'm an odd person to be talking about the major climbing magazines, because I don't read them. Oh, I see them, all right. I scan them for entertaining letters and certain kinds of news. I shake my head at the photographs of scary, paradisiacal places. I browse the openings of the major articles, daring the authors to pull me in. But then each magazine finds its way into a stack of items for later attention and—sooner or later, snowed under by newer arrivals—gets squeezed, like old glacier ice, out the door.

Surely these hardworking publishers deserve better? But I wonder if I'm alone in finding these products both successful and unsuccessful; sophisticated, yet somehow unengaging; dazzling, and yet not far from dull.

Did the modern climbing magazine take a wrong turn somewhere? Is it climbing itself that has changed? Or am I simply not part of the audience for which these products are now intended?

Fortunately, not every subscriber has been so quick as I to discard the evidence. Thanks to Allen Steck and others, I've been able to look over a century's worth of glossy climbing magazines in English: ten years of *Ascent*, twenty-four years of *Mountain,* twenty-eight years of *Climbing*, fourteen years of *Rock & Ice*, and twenty-eight years of the *Canadian Alpine Journal*

The modern climbing magazine, as a species, has evolved several times, not quite from scratch, out of a sort of primordial soup of much more modest publications: newsletters, amateurish regional magazines, and lightly edited club journals.

The first venture into the zone of large formats and lavish photographs was *Ascent*, by Allen Steck out of *Sierra Club Bulletin*. In the mid-1960s the Sierra Club was transforming itself from mountaineering club to conservation powerhouse. In 1966 it decided that its annual *Bulletin* would no longer give space to climbing reports. Worried by the loss of a place to track events in the Valley and elsewhere, Yosemite climber Steck proposed that the Club begin publishing instead an annual devoted to climbing and to climbing only.

David Brower, the Club's executive director of those days, was initially cool. But he couldn't resist a climber-to-climber invitation to Steck's Berkeley home: to see slides of his host's recent trip to Mt. Logan. Gaping at an image of Hummingbird Ridge, Brower said abruptly: "That's your cover. Print it in color." "Great," said Steck, gulping at the two-fold assent. A color cover? In those days it was an extravagance, and he wouldn't have dared to ask.

And so, with Hummingbird Ridge aforefront, *Ascent* 1967 appeared: the first English-language mountain publication to break away from the staid or chattersome club mold, the first to give coated paper and breathing room to fine photography. On the writing side, *Ascent* seemed to have tapped into something amazing. It was if a world of climbers had been carrying well-wrought pieces in their heads, or stuffed into desk drawers, waiting for a market like this to open up. Beginning with Lito Tejada-Flores's "Games Climbers Play," perhaps the most-anthologized climbing essay ever, piece after piece now looks like a classic.

Ascent soon had company, and competition, from the Old World. In 1968 English photographer Ken Wilson became the editor of a journal called *Mountain Craft*, described by Audrey Salkeld as "respectable, established, conservative and dull." Wilson set out to change that. First he devoted the whole of one issue to Patagonia, an area not much publicized at the time. Next, in January 1969, he changed the journal's name to *Mountain*, giving the issue not a date (though you could find that if you looked) but a number: *Mountain* 1. A photograph filled the cover from edge to edge. There was early clumsiness but also a run of beginner's luck. The third issue, for example, had Chris Jones on the southwest buttress of Fitzroy, Doug Scott on the Bonatti Pillar, and Tom Patey musing quotably on "Apes or Ballerinas?".

Mountain regarded itself above all as a newsmagazine, and the first block of pages was always given over to reports of notable ascents worldwide (if a little heavy on the British Isles). Early numbers were peppered with the mocking humor of Ian McNaught-Davis and the ethical scoldings of editor Wilson, who didn't hesitate to spin the news: "John Allen free-climbs Great Wall but uses chalk." "Maestri rapes Cerro Torre with 1,000 bolts."

Ascent, meanwhile, seemed to be losing steam. Its seventh issue, in 1973, somehow lacked the edge of its predecessors. Its eighth contained some interesting experiments but only a handful of satisfying pieces. Its ninth issue, which took two years to produce, seemed on some pages to be scraping the bottom of the barrel. Then *Ascent* ceased appearing for a while, only to start up again, in 1980, as an occasional anthology, "the mountaineering experience in word and image." It had found its niche but—with years between its appearances—can't any longer be counted among the magazines.

Its replacement, on the American side of the water, was already emerging. In 1975 a five-year-old regional rag in Colorado began its pursuit of higher standards and a larger audience: *Climbing* magazine. Its editor, Michael Kennedy, would recall: "*Ascent* had a very nice literary quality and clean graphics, while *Mountain* had a tremendous information value. I wanted both." It took him a decade to approach this goal, but by 1987 Kennedy was exulting, "*Climbing* has finally become a real magazine. It's no longer a dip-shit little magazine about a dip-shit little sport."

The nip of competition may have helped it along. In 1984 there appeared the first issue of the next new publication, *Rock & Ice*, published in Boulder, Colorado, just over the main hump of the Rockies from *Climbing*'s offices in Aspen. *Rock & Ice* 1 was twenty-four pages long and published on newsprint. But self-taught publisher George Bracksieck was determined to beat *Mountain* and *Climbing* at their own game. The new publication seemed to aim at a younger readership, with a jazzy, jagged look and a sharp nose for trends. For instance, *Rock & Ice* picked up on competition climbing sooner and more enthusiastically than did either of its peers. It also published more fiction.

So now there were three.

In 1986 a colorful new climbing magazine, *Polar Circus*, came on the scene in Canada. Though it only published two issues, it seems to have administered a useful shock to the good, gray *Canadian Alpine Journal*. That annual magazine had expanded its format in 1970 and started publishing much black-and-white photography, yet had remained implacably pedestrian. Now the magazine took a public look at itself ("Why hasn't the *CAJ* attracted such quality in photography and writing?" it asked on the editorial page) and brought in a new editor, David Harris. His arrival in 1987 placed the journal among the ambitious climbing magazines, if not in direct competition with the bimonthlies. Now there were four.

By this time *Mountain*, the surviving elder of the tribe, had been through some changes. Founding editor Ken Wilson withdrew in 1978; Tim Lewis took over until his death in 1984; Bernard Newman carried on from there. Under Wilson, the magazine was almost all hard news. Lewis widened its range a bit, running, among other things, some notable short stories. Newman retained the softer focus, but seems to have been struggling with declining readership and U.S. competition: *Mountain* shrank as *Climbing* and *Rock & Ice* grew.

In 1992 Newman decided he had had enough. *Mountain* 148 was the last. (Some of the magazine's imprint remains in the purely British publication *High*, whose editor, Geoff Birtles, had done a stint at *Mountain* with Lewis.) So today again there are three quality English-language mountain glossies, all North American, two of them frequently published, and those two based in the state of Colorado.

Rock & Ice and *Climbing*, once quite different, seem now to have converged. Both are fat, sassy, full of ads, and "perfect bound" (with a flat, glued spine). Both have given up on the clear, uncluttered look that editors once sought: we have instead a cheerful jumble of departments, subdepartments, colors, typefaces, screens, and omnipresent ads. *Climbing* used to be the patrician of the pair, with smoother layouts and more reticent graphics and design; comparing recent issues page by page, I was surprised to find that *Rock & Ice* now has the edge in accessibility and gracefulness, once you get past the atrociously busy cover. (I do miss the classy covers of *Mountain*: logo and number floating diffidently in a corner, staying out of the way of the photograph.)

As for content, the magazines differ subtly, if at all. In each, feature articles have a shrinking place: the bulk of space actually goes to regular departments. *Climbing* now lists twenty of these in its table of contents, *Rock & Ice* sixteen. Even the "departments" have many components, and the reader quickly loses any sense of overall design. Each magazine carries one equipment column devoted to puffing new gear; *Rock & Ice* at least has the decency to label this segment "advertorial."

The *Canadian Alpine Journal* can't be compared with the Colorado magazines. It is annual; it's mostly about Canada and Canadians; and it lacks ads (though it experimented with them briefly). It is serene, reserved, a little pale: ineffably *northern*. Editor Geoff Powter, who succeeded David Harris in 1993, is continuing the Harris line; he favors evocative, somewhat confessional work over the older, just-the-facts style, and prints a good deal of verse. You get the impression, though, that the mails aren't bringing him quite enough to work with.

Why read a climbing magazine, anyway? There seem to be three reasons: to find out what's happening; to glean practical information; and to take part in a sort of celebration of the craft and the places in which it is practiced.

News: we find out about new routes, the fortunes of expeditions, the outcomes of competitions, the latest casualties, and other history-in-the-making. *Ascent*, *Mountain*, and *Climbing* each intended to maintain a comprehensive list of new activity, but only *Mountain* kept this effort up indefinitely: the job grows overwhelming. What you get now is a sampling. At the moment, the closest thing to an international logbook of ascents appears to be the *American Alpine Journal*. I keep wondering if an annual publication devoted entirely to such data, without photos or fluff, might not support itself quite handsomely.

Besides the bulletins of who did what on what with whom, other kinds of news engage us: debates about ethics and style, controversies about credit and veracity, and (increasingly) matters of access and regulation. Cesare Maestri and Cerro Torre kept *Mountain* busy for several years: did the Italian "rape" the peak with bolts in 1970, and did he climb it at all in 1959? Ken Wilson's dogged probing of Maestri in a 1972 interview is one of the most interesting things the magazine ever published. *Ascent* explored the issue in its own manner by publishing David Roberts' novella *Like Water and Like Wind*, which has a Maestri-like protagonist. On ethical questions, *Mountain* usually took the most traditional, restrictive line; *Climbing* often seemed the most libertarian. Readers chimed in via letters columns, a constant source of entertainment. I laughed out loud the first time I saw the distinction drawn (in a letter to *Rock & Ice*) between chipping holds and merely "comfortizing" them.

As bearers of news, the magazines really seem to have done their job. Not every kind of news will interest every kind of reader; competition reports, for instance, are despised by many and devoured by some. But the scene is the scene, and you get a pretty fair picture of it, reading the American magazines.

I find that old magazines, scanned by the stack and decade, have a fascination that no single issue can match. Like frames in a film strip, they only tell their story—of a sport unfolding, feuding with itself, reinventing itself continually—when run at speed. Among other things, such a survey leads to a certain fatalism about all things "ethical." It seems that any practice that begins to be talked about, even by denunciation, will sooner or later prevail. Has a line finally been drawn at hold modification? Watching the steady retreat of the conservatives across the years, I wonder.

As the frontiers of climbing move outward—as 5.14a becomes the easiest new rock pitch worth noting, as routes and faces are climbed in batches, not one at a time, as competitions create a new kind of elite—the "news" of climbing must become more remote from the average reader. Surely not even one percent of the audience is operating on the frontier. I think part of the charm of climbing publications, in earlier days, was the feeling that, with a certain amount of dedication, one could go and do likewise. Precious few of us, now, can feel that. And few of us are going to be confronting the ethical questions involved in putting up hard new lines. Ordinary climbers (of which I am emphatically one) watch the actions and debates of the leaders from a growing distance, and maybe with diminishing attention.

Rock & Ice surveyed its readers in 1987 and reported frequent comments: "We're tired of the ethics debate, and we're tired of seeing climbs we can't do." The latter gripe has been around for a long time. A letter to *Climbing* in 1972 asked for more attention to the needs of 5.3 climbers: "You know, the type that's ruining the climbing for all the 5.9-5.10 acrobats." The numbers change, but the complaint remains.

Climbing and *Rock & Ice* have responded by providing generous servings of the second basic food group: practical information, stuff that climbers of all levels can use. This takes the form of area guides and route descriptions; reviews of gear; and lessons in technique, from building a home "campus board" to staying out of the way of avalanches. There is even an occasional attempt to cater to genuine beginners.

When the subject is access and regulation, the newsworthy and the practical overlap. Ordinary climbers have plenty at stake here; they are hit as hard as anyone when climbing areas are closed, for instance, or when aging bolts can't be replaced. They may also worry legitimately about some actions of their betters, for the controversial practices of a few can draw the wrath of the authorities down on the many. When those authorities call for public response to their proposals, whether it's banning fixed anchors in national forest wilderness or development plans for Yosemite Valley, it's in almost anybody's interest to know the issues, and to respond.

Have the magazines done their job as providers of practical information? It seems to me that they have. If I skip much of it as either too familiar or too abstruse, that's just my choice. And if I clip an article, as I sometimes do, it is probably going to be from this practical category.

That leaves the third and most difficult function of a climbing magazine: *celebration*. To present the sport, to savor it, to reveal it, to laugh at it. To give us vicarious tremors and appreciations. To deepen understanding. To make us wince and smile with recognition and wonder why we're out there, and suddenly remember.

The easiest route to celebration is through a camera lens, but here there seems to be something of a law of diminishing returns. The profusion of stunning images makes each one less stunning. How often these days does a photograph really make us stop and stare? Reading along through the early, modest *Mountain*s, I was dazzled by a two-page photo of Cerro Torre. Returning to it later, with newer images on my retina, it looked rather tame. Another early *Mountain*, reviewing an early *Ascent*, had already noticed the effect: "Though the pictures improve, their impact seems to diminish." We're spoiled. Here's another mile of exposure, another unblemished wall, another 5.13 climber bonded to the crag with chalk and fingernails: wonderful, truly, yet we've seen it all before.

One solution is to go beyond realistic photographs to images of other kinds. All the magazines except *Mountain* have used drawings from time to time. My favorite departure from the literal is still the cover of the 1974 *Ascent*, which looks like an artist's fantasy on K2 but turns out actually to be a microphotograph of a crystal: a demonstration, before its time, of the principle that certain "fractal" shapes turn up in nature at any scale you choose.

It's the writers, however, who are supposed to be the life of this particular party. Celebration is what the typical longer article, the feature, is there to provide. An expedition account, for instance, can communicate information for the next foray, and may even contain some news; but its purpose is to provide an experience: to put us in the physical and mental boots of the adventurers, to make it all real. Besides the realistic account, celebration can take place in essays, personal portraits, polemics, fiction, poetry. It can take place in cartoons.

But how often is this promise, or hope, delivered on?

Several obstacles get in the way of successful celebration of climbing through writing. The first is the obvious: inadequate stylistic tools. We can hardly be expected to respond when a story begins with barren information, like this recent piece in *Rock & Ice*: "The parking lot at New Hampshire's Pinkham Notch is nearly full of cars when Kevin Hand and I pull in. It's the end of March, and, after a week of stormy clouds and winds, the sky has lifted, baring the white summits of Mount Washington and the Presidential Range." Diagnosis is also easy when writers reaching for evocation come up with a fistful of clichés.

"We were highly adrenalized," begins an ambitious piece in the *Canadian Alpine Journal*. "Ominous dark clouds were moving in from Chilco Lake and howling winds confirmed that [we] would soon be immersed in the full violence of a storm."

(Editors, editors! Where are the blue pencils and delete buttons? Can't we lose some of these ominous clouds, these howling winds? Must rains always pelt or lash? When the weather clears, must the sun always bathe faces with light that is golden? Can't epic tales do something other than unfold? Must every avalanche be a wall of snow or a relentless tide? Is every death to be a tragedy? Indoors, must crowds inevitably go wild?)

Yet actively bad writing—the easy target—doesn't account for the lack of magnetism in the typical climbing article. Indeed, many pieces are quite adequately written; quality varies from issue to issue, but I think the general level is getting better, not worse. I've been surprised at how good some recent articles seemed—once I made it my business to read them.

Even the accomplished climbing writer, I think, is up against certain limits in the subject itself. Climbing, after all, is a little like sex. Each, as experience, is compelling, inexhaustible. Yet to each there is a certain sameness: vary the details though we may, there are only so many permutations. Like writing about sex, climbing writing tends to excite in the reader not the desire to read but the desire to do—to pursue our own story, however unremarkable, rather than to listen in on someone else's.

I've sat around enough campfires to suspect that climbers aren't really that avid to hear one another's stories, anyway. What they love is telling their own. Sitting through a companion's tale is the price we pay to get to the moment when we can start reliving, out loud, our personal experience.

Am I saying that climbing writing *can't* engage us? Obviously not. But more, perhaps, than writing on other subjects, it must seize our attention and reward it with something out of the ordinary. It must go well beyond the obvious. It must describe familiar things with extraordinary sharpness, catch them from an angle that makes them new, pack an uncommon emotional punch, or shed the sidewise, humanizing light of mockery.

Take these four bulletins from an ill-starred climb on the north face of the Matterhorn:

> We adopted that well-known psychological strategy—a kind of sleight of mind—whereby you know perfectly well you are lost and in a serious situation, but you try to pretend you're somehow still on-route by forcing implausible features to the guidebook in order to keep your confidence up....

> After that I held my breath tiptoeing through the manic moods of the mountain, across that self-absorbed, icy face that flung rockfall down upon us arbitrarily, like curses or tears of stone....

> Dawson had distributed an occasional Friend and hand-driven peg along the pitch—they wouldn't hold a fall, but they kept the rope from sagging....

> As if the force of his effort bent the ridge down towards him like a buckled chinning-bar, he pulled out to his amazement through a notch onto the summital section of the Hörnli Ridge.

These from "Letter from Zermatt," by Dermot Somers, in *Mountain* 84. Just a war story? Yes, but told to delight.

Over the years, plenty of creditable things have appeared. I think of Reinhold Messner's Nanga Parbat story "Solo" (*Mountain* 65); Jeff Long's haunting fiction "Cannibals" (*Mountain* 89); John Long's bouldering piece "The Welder's Gloves" (*Rock & Ice* 14); Alison Osius's "Risky Business" (*Rock & Ice* 14); Marc Twight's "Kiss or Kill" (*Climbing* 98); Greg Child's "The Trouble with Hunza" (*Rock & Ice* 18); and quite a few more.

Most of the memorable pieces are funny, at least here and there. Climbing writers have always had an eye for the absurd. Each magazine has seemed to have its designated wit. *Ascent* had, and has, Joe Kelsey. The early *Mountain* had Ian McNaught-Davis. *Climbing* had Jim Vermeulen. Tom Higgins turned up in all three. Mockery works best, by far, when it's directed at climbers themselves. To mock nonclimbers for their lack of knowledge is easier but can seem a little snide.

Not surprisingly, few of the best pieces of climbing writing are solely about climbing. They are about climbing and something else: climbing and an interesting character, climbing and a science-fiction future, climbing and a controversial opinion, climbing and a well-drawn personal conflict. In a few of my favorite stories, the physical act of climbing never occurs at all. The narrative stops, so to speak, at the bedroom door.

Do I speak for many or for myself alone? If I am less interested in climbing magazines than I used to be, it is partly because I am less interested than I used to be in the scene the magazines reflect.

If I had ever been anything other than a follower of other people's routes, I might be accused of nostalgia for my glory days. I am innocent: I had no glory days. But I may have been fortunate in entering climbing at that moment, in the early 1970s, when it was just emerging from its almost secret earlier existence into public view. The booted foot called *Ascent* had just tipped over the concealing rock, and what a swarming world it had revealed!

Yvon Chouinard recalls a remark by Sir Arnold Lunn: "There is a spontaneous and light-hearted quality in a sport which vanishes as the sport matures." Since 1967 this sport has well and truly matured. Participation, surely, has exploded. (Having been part of the explosion, I do not complain.) Since Tejada-Flores wrote "Games Climbers Play," several major new games have been added—the sport-climbing game certainly, the competition game, the casual indoor game. Climbing is no longer, as Michael Kennedy wrote, "a dip-shit little sport." The panorama is more crowded, more commercial, more sophisticated, more colorful, more noisy, more full of personalities and self-promotions. To some who follow the bustle through the magazines, it is undoubtedly more interesting than it ever was. I simply happen to be one of those for whom it is less.

Much has been gained but something has been lost as climbing has entered the mainstream. Much has been gained but something has been lost by the parallel professionalization of the climbing magazine, that process launched by *Ascent* itself some thirty years ago.

The modern magazine is like a coalition government. To keep up a critical mass of circulation and advertising, an editor has to keep the loyalty, if not the enthusiasm, of sport climbers and expeditioneers, rads and trads, newsmaking climbers-of-the-moment and armchair mountaineers. That balancing act might seem impossible, yet it is succeeding.

After years in which magazines were sustained only by free labor and personal sacrifice, they are now going concerns. That climbing can support two commercial magazines at once is actually pretty remarkable: the backpackers, supposedly thirteen-million-strong in America, are down to one.

No matter that most of any issue I receive may go unread: I remain part of the fragile, grumbling consensus that supports the modern climbing magazine. I continue, if only barely, to subscribe.

And if, to my great misfortune, somebody handed me a magazine to edit—as a business, not a subsidized labor-of-love—what would I, what would I dare to, change?

I would certainly try to simplify layout and design, to reduce the number of departments and subdepartments, and generally to lower the level of visual noise.

I would refuse to run "advertorials."

Recognizing that the essence of the climbing magazine is news and practical information, I might just set aside the job of celebration, making space for evocative features only when something came in that was extraordinarily good. For those occasional pieces, I would pay top dollar, or possibly offer awards (to be left in the bank if work of the requisite quality didn't appear). In photography, too, I would angle for the occasional piece that is spectacular in itself and not only because of what is shown. I would look for interesting art and non-realistic images.

And I think I would publish more rarely. It is anyway impossible, given the pace of events, to cover the whole climbing world in six issues a year, or even nine issues a year, the schedule *Climbing* has lately adopted. Why try? A slightly more leisurely clip would do no harm and might leave a little more room for quality.

I think I'd set up as many issues as possible as regional features, or otherwise tie them together by theme. This seems to add interest whenever it's done; if a magazine stays on my shelves, it is usually one of these.

On the whole, though, I'd rather go climbing.

IRONMONGERS OF THE DREAMTIME

John Ewbank

*Excerpts from the keynote address delivered at the Escalade Festival,
Mt. Victoria, Australia, April 23, 1993.*

When Lucas Trihey phoned me in New York to ask me to present my own twisted visions of some of the stuff that went down, or should I say that went *up*, back in the dark ages, he was modest about the scope of this event. In my mind's eye I imagined a small affair, a packet of crisps and a slide projector, with a few old fossils like myself circling our wheelchairs around the pie cart. To find it all so civilized and well attended is gratifying, especially with so many accomplished climbers presenting such a wide range of topics: Greg Mortimer, talking about his ascent of the north ridge of K2. Jon Muir, who climbed Everest without oxygen and had a cigarette on top! I like it! Greg Child, with his slide show of his recent route up the Nameless Tower in the Karakoram. Kim Carrigan, Mark Baker, and Malcolm Matheson—three truly exceptional rockclimbers. To witness how far Australian climbing has developed since I hung up my boots is quite amazing, and to be remembered for my contribution is most touching.

To paint a picture of the times gives me the excuse I need to speak of the people who were around then. Many of them may be names you've never heard of, but they meant the world to me. If I sound sentimental, it's because I am. Having grown up with no real family in any normal understanding of the word, and finding myself adrift in a strange land, some of these people became the first family I ever had. It may be true that I put my neck out quite a long way on several occasions; it may also be true that climbing saved my life.

I still find everything about the entire subject of climbing as exciting as ever. As soon as I felt nervous about presenting this address, I welcomed it as a sign of that excitement. Climbing, to me, was always a door through which I could enter into a place of serious, controlled excitement: a sweaty and dirty holy communion. If one does it well enough for long enough, it becomes an existential state of grace. The ironmongery I allude to in my title was in some ways the key, and the Dreamtime was the emotional landscape it helped open.

I am incapable of a blow-by-blow account. If at times I appear to be completely missing the point of my own address, believe me I'm not. Imagine we're on some cliff we've never seen, doddering around in all directions. We *will* find the connecting bits, and they *will* all relate, even though the line may wander at times.

For my first detour I would like to propose two points. The first is that by the act of climbing we externalize something within ourselves and make it tangible within a ritualistic framework that is then comprehensible, repeatable, and sharable, at least to some degree, and if only by other climbers. We could think of this first point as being part of that which we *bring to the cliff*. The second point is that if we try to alchemize the experience into words, we are asking for trouble, and then there is no end to it—the questions, the words, or the trouble. We could think of this second point as being part of that which we *take from the cliff.*

To continue the detour even further, here's a line from one of my own songs: "Each time I open my poor mouth, I cheapen my poor heart." To give the blow-by-blow account I referred to would cheapen whatever it was and in doing so cheapen my own heart. And it would be boring, probably to you in the listening and to my own tongue in the telling. Besides, all that stuff is in the guidebooks, and it's all there on the cliffs themselves for that matter—a few peg scars, a few rusty bolts. To capture the spirit and the ethos of the times with their attendant freedoms and restrictions, and the characters who were a part of them—that's what interests me here. But to capture that is like trying to take a photograph of a dream.

Most climbers know that to try to express the whole racket in words is to risk sounding like an absurd Monty Python sketch. Rather than risk the embarrassment, we go for the clichés and avoid the center that we can only hint at. Myself, I prefer the hints, however cryptic and however futile. *Conquistadors of the Useless* will probably remain the best title that's been given, or ever will be given, to any book about climbing.

Another thing I remain fascinated by is the manner in which climbing allows for tremendous individualism while simultaneously engendering an extraordinary level of collective tribal consciousness. Since we live in a fragmented and secular society, the act of creating this odd yet unifying Dreamtime of our own, however foolish and however minor, may be one of the most priceless aspects of climbing—an aspect that cannot be bought and sold, packaged and promoted through the mass media, then trivialized and sold back to us as this month's fashion accessory.

This "collective social Dreamtime" I speak of is epitomized by climbers grouping together in tribal fashion. From Camp 4 in Yosemite to the Heights in Llanberis to the Pines at Arapiles, the rituals and the totems of belonging remain the same. The guidebooks, climbing magazines, and a gigantic body of climbing literature have become the archive of its existence. However, the *personal* Dreamtime is to be found in a more savage suburb of the heart: on the climb itself. And to paraphrase a famous remark once made by a particularly self-serving and arrogant prime minister, *going walkabout wasn't meant to be easy.*

To create one's own Dreamtime is, of course, a contradiction in terms—the traditional Dreamtime carries with it the implication of inheritance. Nevertheless, the allusion is not entirely without basis, however personal. I still draw spiritual sustenance from pivotal moments experienced on various climbs; and if this sounds like a lot of mystical nonsense, be thankful you didn't have to listen to me in full spate a quarter of a century ago. My main reason for making this allusion is because of what I see as the connective power of climbing—the manner in which it can create a bond between the climber and the landscape. This bond to and with the earth is central to the Dreamtime.

I am not using this analogy of the Dreamtime simply because I am in Australia. Nor am I using it as small change in the cheap contemporary currency of those who wish to appear environmentally holy. And I certainly hope it won't be construed as one more simplistic championing of the old noble savage routine—an alienated and condescending construct if ever there was one. No, I am using it because it is the best example I can find to illustrate the aspect of climbing in which I am most interested.

I am now referring to a spiritual experience. I am using an Australian aboriginal model as opposed to a European model because in the case of the latter we are faced with a legacy of man-made structures, be they circles of stone in their most simple manifestations, or cathedrals in their most elaborate—in other words, monuments of belief placed upon a landscape. I use the Dreamtime because within it the focus was on the landscape itself, and has remained so to this day. All that is needed to create a sacred site on a landscape is ritual, belief, and tradition. Nothing has to be built or changed in any permanent way. *In fact, to do so would very likely be to destroy the sacred site.* All of this is by way of making the point that climbers have their own rituals for turning steep bits of the earth's surface into sacred sites.

Bruce Chatwin's *The Songlines*, while fanciful in places, is a wonderful book that explores some aspects of storytelling and songs within traditional Aboriginal culture. One line in particular struck me: "The songs become a blueprint for finding a way in the universe." I'm not for a second trying to imply that climbs have this same power, but the connection is there. I remember thinking as I read that section, "Yes, that's what the climbs were: steep dreams and vertical songs."

One of the interesting aspects of turning something into a sacred site by the act of climbing is that we then superimpose special values on it, even if these values are comprehensible only to other climbers. Another is the proprietary interest that the climbers involved often feel. This is why they are constantly fighting about each other's behavior: "You used two bolts, while I used only one." "But you scratched it—you scratched my sacred place." "Oh, I put chalk on it—but I didn't leave a piton!" "Piton! You chipped a foothold big enough to sleep on." Climbers are obsessed with an experience they wish to share, but which they do not wish to be altered or lessened.

I think it is important for climbers to see cliffs within the context of a broader landscape, and to accept that they may already be sacred to others. The rising popularity of so-called "wilderness experience" holidays points toward the desire to fill a need that is far more fundamental than merely wanting to see new places. Ergo, the increasing conflicts of interest worldwide, especially in the national parks. A large number of white Australians, since the first settlement, have generally suffered from a chronic and well-documented sense of dislocation and alienation from the landscape in which they found themselves. A similar sense of dislocation is now suffered on the European homelands of these settlers, and in many cultures throughout the world—a sense of alienation from the land upon which we live, a lack of spiritual nutrition.

In my opinion, for Australian climbers to follow the modern French and Spanish model of wholesale bolt mania, especially retrobolting, will be a disaster. When the cliffs have been transformed into something that resembles a repository for bolts, climbers will be immeasurably poorer for it. I visited some such cliffs in France last summer and my reaction was simply one of sorrow. There is the famous anecdote of the young man in California around the turn of the century who asked for advice as to where to invest his money. He was told: "Buy land." "Why?" he asked. "Because they ain't making any more of it," came the reply. The same applies to cliffs. They ain't making any more. Once the cliffs have been bolted to death, once they are no longer wild places in any sense of the word, we rob ourselves of the opportunity of entering a landscape where we can dream.

As an expatriate Brit, I reserve the right to make fun of my country of birth. But visiting some of their cliffs, one has to face the fact that they sometimes do get it right in certain respects. For those cliffs to have stayed looking good after so much use says a great deal about the approach the English have applied to developing their cliffs from one generation to the next. Would you put a bolt in *Clockwork Orange?* Would you pour concrete over *Uluru?* When the cliffs we cherish have been loved to death, climbers will not be able to lay the blame at the feet of some anonymous government agency, nor will we be able to point accusing fingers at some convenient scapegoat in the form of a big, bad multinational. The blame will lie fair and square with ourselves.

A sculptor was once asked how he carved the perfect elephant out of a chunk of white marble. "It's easy," he replied. "I just chip away everything that's not the elephant." There is a connection between this story and the act of climbing—especially the act of putting up new routes. As the number of climbs and the number of climbers increase, it is getting harder and harder for young climbers to find that chunk of rock out of which to make their own elephant. It is a lost cause for the old guard to try to lay down the laws of the land. In terms of climbing it is only the young who have the tendons and the tenacity (not to mention the power drills) to carry on the evolution of traditions, and the best that can be done is to gracefully suggest options. If each succeeding generation feels the need to outstrip the achievements of the past—which they must, for muscles are there to be used, not merely flexed—then I hope it may be done with a sense of reverence for the cliffs themselves.

The "Last Great Problem" that climbers have been forever trying to solve may in the end turn out to be thc ability to leave the unclimbable alone. I respectfully suggest that only the greatest climbers of the future will be able to develop the nerve and the confidence to exercise this ability. This is neither Zen nor New Age Wimpspeak. It is the hieroglyphics of the human heart feeling the ancient need to connect with the timeless beauty of the earth itself without damaging it.

So now, having deluded myself into believing that I can talk about climbing in a reasonably calm manner, I find myself staggering through the same minefield I did more than twenty years ago. At that time I became so embroiled in issues such as bolting that I felt I had to stop climbing altogether. Having placed hundreds of bolts and having also removed hundreds, my dance routine became confusing and enervating, to say the least. Of course, I was too young and too silly to see the difference between the beauty of an activity and the politics that surround that activity. I now realize this dichotomy exists everywhere, in everything—the gulf between music and the music *business*, for example. The most important thing I can say to young climbers today is that I personally lost the guideline between having an adventure and simply beating one more cliff into submission. And when that happens, everything becomes pointless.

To those who want climbing to be just another sport and nothing more—vertical billiards or overhanging golf—I find myself turning back into that abrasive teenager and saying "Whoopy doo!" And to those who want it to be something more, I say "Good luck!" When Bernard Shaw was accused of being too subjective in his criticisms, he replied, "I always try to be as subjective as possible." It is in this same spirit that I make no claims to any objective viewpoints. I was too close to it then, and I'm still too close to it now. The intervening years have done little to change the way in which I view the whole shenanigan of buggering about on steep bits of the planet. I still obsess about it every day, no matter where I am and no matter what else I'm doing. After countless gigs as a musician, I still find myself more at ease on a cliff than on a stage. Quite independent of the level at which one is climbing, I believe that the act has the potential of being a transcendental activity, comparable to so-called high art and the traditional spiritual disciplines: instability, foolishness, sheer hard *yakka*, and the occasional willingness to risk everything for moments of lucid, visionary awareness.

I'd like now to try to present an overview of the scene as it was, where it came from, where it traveled, even to some extent *why* it traveled in the manner it did, to where it now stands.

When my family immigrated to Australia I'd just turned fifteen, and to say I was pissed off is an understatement of Himalayan proportions! Immigrants were called "ten-pound pirates" in those days. That was the amount it cost to immigrate; the Australian government paid the rest, God bless 'em. There wasn't enough room in the baggage allowance for me to bring my rope, piton hammer, three pitons, three slings, and three carabiners. (Three must have been some sort of magic number for me.) For me, the decision to move seemed like a catastrophic blunder. I believed that the center of the universe was the gritstone outcrops of Yorkshire. I had a trip planned to the Isle of Skye, a hit list of Lakeland classics to get through!

All I knew about Australia was from the immigration pamphlets—it was always hot and sunny with lots of beautiful beaches. The people who wrote the pamphlets knew enough about the appetites of the prospective immigrants to emphasize the abundance of that which they would be willing to cross the world for—jobs and sunshine. The pamphlets certainly didn't show any cliffs. All I heard about was a flat land full of deserts and snakes and sheep and kangaroos and duck-billed platypuses.

We moved to Wollongong and I started at Mt. Kiera High School. Started is the right word—I only went once. Up above the town was Mt. Kiera itself, with cliffs on two sides, and that was the "high" school I was interested in. Every morning I'd set off for school and walk around the corner to an overgrown block. I'd disappear into the bushes, change into a pair of sandshoes and shorts, stash the uniform and the books, and then set off running to the top of Mt. Kiera. I'd spend the day doing boulder problems and scaring myself silly, then run back down, change into the school uniform, wander home, have a cup of tea, and invent another day at the office. I had a good imagination! This went on for three weeks before the letter arrived—but that's another story altogether.

One day I came across a group of scouts abseiling. They had manila ropes and slings and steel carabiners from Austria, which they told me they'd bought from a shop in Sydney called Paddy Pallin. I got very hot and excited and hitchhiked to Sydney a few days later, ending up at 201 Castlereagh Street, second floor. Forget King Tut's Tomb! At Paddy's there were piton hammers, hemp waistlines, carabiners and pitons from Austria—it seemed as if everything was Made in Austria in those days. His catalog was a beauty; a four-page black-and-white foldout sheet, with really good diagrams. I used to look at it for hours. To own a Paddy Pallin H-Frame Rucksack was to own the world. To have one of his sleeping bags as well was to be a master of the universe.

But the most important thing of all about that day in Sydney was that Paddy put me in touch with the Sydney Rock Climbing Club (the SRC). They had a reputation for drinking, womanizing, and always having the biggest campfire. Pretty heady stuff! The club secretary wrote back and put me in touch with one of the members, an eccentric young man named Peter Draffin, who in turn wrote and told me about an upcoming trip.

I made a pack called a Yukon Frame, from a design in a scout manual. It was made from wood and stretched canvas. Onto it you could strap a kit bag or whatever. It looked like the H-Frame of the village idiot. I got a Caltex road map, scaled at something like twenty miles to the inch, and set off hitchhiking to the Blue Mountains one Saturday morning to try to meet up with the weekend trip to Mt. King George. It was actually marked on the Caltex, so I thought I'd find everybody camped in a field at the end of the dead-end road marked on the map. I had no reason whatever for thinking any of this except sheer optimism. I arrived at sunset to find everything upside down. The dirt road led to the top rather than to the bottom, there was no climbers' pub, no campground, no field, and no farmer to ask directions from. After I'd walked the final three miles without seeing a soul, it occurred to me that this wasn't the Lake District. I looked down into the Grose Valley at more cliffs than I'd ever imagined and lit a campfire. A very big campfire. I didn't have a sleeping bag, so I put on my extra clothes and went to sleep. I kept waking up and throwing more logs on and wondering where all the climbers were. I found out several weeks later that they had been camped down in the Blue Gum Forest, 2,000 feet below. All six of them.

The next trip was held at a place called Narrow Neck. The SRC would hold these special instructional weekends every now and then, mainly to teach the basics to bushwalkers who wanted to go canyoning or to start climbing. I arrived to find maybe eighty people camping on every bit of level ground in and around the old Psyncave. There was a lot of drinking, a very large campfire, and a bit of womanizing going on, so I knew it was the right place.

Now, when Peter had written that we would be sleeping in a cave, I imagined something from a German fairy tale: an entrance hole, then a snug, deep, dry cave with a flat floor covered in leaves. I didn't realize that in Australia the expression "cave" can mean just an overhang of rock, so the fact that it was winter and I didn't have a sleeping bag didn't concern me at all until about eleven o'clock, when everybody started crawling off into their Paddy Pallin Hothams and Fairy Down Everests. It was one of those nights that seem a universe away from the same spot in midsummer. The wind felt as if it had just left the South Pole and was in a hurry to get to the tropics before it gave itself frostbite.

It's a funny thing how to be poor is a source of such excruciating embarrassment when one is young. To admit that I didn't have a sleeping bag became unthinkable. My Yorkshire accent was so thick as to be almost unintelligible. Then there was the Yukon Frame, which had created a minor sensation, and my lack of anything that resembled climbing equipment. To now admit that I didn't have a sleeping bag was impossible. I thought, "Bugger me dead. They'll never let me come climbing again!" So I decided to finish the half-empty flagons and keep the fire going all night, a demented case of death before dishonor. Luckily, a climber named Bob Ryan put two and two together and did a diplomatic whip around the site, collecting a huge pile of spare clothes. "Here," he said. "Put this lot on!" I went to bed looking like the Michelin man and I still hardly slept a wink, but I never forgot the way Bob looked after me that night.

The next day was cold and crystal clear. The wind was still blowing and a whole crocodile of us did a climb called *Giuco Piton*. When we got to the top we walked to a good lookout spot. In one direction was Dogface, the Three Sisters, Mt. Solitary, and, way off in the distance, the cliffs of King's Tableland. In the other direction was Boar's Head. Somebody was ranting about some great old volcanoes somewhere called the Warrumbungle Mountains. Just the name alone was enough to get me going!

The Warrumbungles! I think that may have been the exact moment when I decided that Australia wasn't such a bad place after all. It seemed like the whole joint was full of cliffs! Admittedly, a lot of the ones I was looking at were the wrong color: red, orange, yellow. Coming from Yorkshire, I imagined all cliffs should probably be black or white or shades of gray. But why hadn't the people who wrote the pamphlets mentioned this lot?

Something you need to understand is that there existed a strong link between climbing in Australia and climbing in England, not only through the climbing literature, but also through folklore and oral tradition as brought over by a small but steady stream of immigrants—two vastly different sources of information. The Rhum Dhu Climbing Club in Australia in the late fifties was in every respect typical of many of the clubs that existed in England, especially in the North, during the forties and fifties. It was started as a reaction to what its members perceived to be the stodginess of the SRC, and there was an emphasis on drinking, smoking a lot, not taking any of it too seriously, having a good time, falling off, and being willing to take a few risks now and again. This was all in the spirit of working-class Northerners who dominated the scene in England at that time, but the model was taken from the folklore, from the oral tradition that the immigrant climbers (Eric Saxby, Dave Tanner, Bryden Allen, Alan Gordon, even myself to a tiny degree) brought with them, *not from the literature*.

You must keep in mind that this was well before the publication of Joe Brown's *The Hard Years* or Dennis Gray's *Rope Boy*, books that give considerable coverage to aspects of climbing such as motor bikes, working in factories, getting drunk, falling off, and generally pissing about. In other words, climbing as a lifestyle within a workaday social context. So when I speak of the other link with English climbing, that is via the climbing literature, we're talking literature with a capital L. A lot of it was comfortable, cosy, rather proper, public-school-stiff-upper-lip adventure stories. It was too noble and smug, but it was the literature that crossed the hemispheres. It was usually written by people with double-barreled surnames or an entire mouthful of initials—sometimes both. Exceptions, such as the wonderful writings of Colin Kirkus and Menlove Edwards, just didn't seem to make it across the equator.

This is not to say that the men who wrote the books that were deemed worthy of export were not themselves great climbers. They often were. The trouble is that the style in which they wrote was often reflective of the English colonialist mentality as epitomized by Kipling. The tradition of nineteenth-century English peak bagging in the European Alps usually carried with it the symbolic gesture of unfurling an invisible Union Jack—however unstated—and long holidays on the continent were in any case the preserve of a small and privileged class. Early- and mid-twentieth-century Himalayan peak bagging had similar undertones of empire building. Not that the English were the only ones at it; far from it! Nor is this in any way meant to detract from the individual motives of the climbers themselves. Hell, in the old days, if they wanted to climb something big, they had to be on what amounted to a national team. The team itself, at least in England as late as the early fifties, tended in turn to be selected on a class basis, as much as on actual climbing ability. These asides simply point out the social and political climate in which these climbs were made.

Edward Whymper and a handful of others were exceptions to the rule. When Whymper climbed the Matterhorn it became front-page news, probably having a similar propaganda value for England as landing on the moon had for Americans. But the fact that Edward climbed it for Edward and not especially for England could hardly be a headline for the *Times* in 1865. After all, you did that sort of thing for King and Country, not to scratch a very personal itch.

But I really do digress. What I wanted to speak about was the pipe smoking! Of course! How could I forget? The pipe was the token taken from the capital-L literature. Virtually everybody in those books seemed to be smoking a pipe. And sometimes they even had photos of some brave nutter leading a desperate-looking slab with a pipe clenched in his teeth. And tweed jackets! But I don't think the tweed jackets ever made it over. I'm trying to think if I ever saw a tweed jacket disappearing up a hundred-foot slab. The woolly hats made it, though. I wore mine through an entire summer—I thought it was illegal to climb without it. One hundred degrees? Want to do a climb? Right! Let's make ourselves really miserable and put on the woolly hats! I even went so far as to buy a pair of leather shorts! The particular photo that prompted that purchase had probably been taken in Austria, home of the mighty Stubai factory. Such foolish innocence.

Of course, the same thing happened in the seventies after the visit of the brilliant American climber Henry Barber. Henry climbed wearing baggy white painters' pants and a white flat cap, and after he departed the cliffs were covered with young men wearing white pants and hats! And I'm sure there's a contemporary version occurring right now that I'm unaware of. So that Sunday night, as I hitched back to Wollongong I had a new dilemma. Should I be saving money to buy a sleeping bag—or a pipe?

That's a rough outline of how things were here in New South Wales in 1963. Dave Rootes and Russ Kippax, who had been the main men in the area and who had founded the SRC in the early fifties, were gone. To climb in the Warrumbungles might involve two full days hitching each way. Bungonia Gorge had only about four recorded climbs. The coastal cliffs were totally unclimbed. The Blue Mountains had hardly even been scratched, and the nearby townships were mostly in a state of disrepair, far removed from the trendy havens they are today.

The scene, nationwide, to the extent that it existed at all, was very regionalized. We were vaguely aware that some climbers operated out of Melbourne and climbed in the Grampians. We knew climbers were active in Tasmania. There were rumors about Brisbane and the Glasshouse Mountains. But each area was really quite ignorant of the other's existence. So it was like a tiny secret society of no-hopers surrounded by surfboards and footballs and tennis racquets and water skis.

Of course, Australia itself was a very different place back then. It's quite amazing really; it's been only thirty years, but the difference is staggering. There were no jumbo jets and the age of cheap airfares was still in the future. The cost of a round-trip airfare to London was the same as a rundown terrace house in the center of Sydney. To go to Europe was a once-in-a-lifetime luxury, except for the very rich. Most people still made the trip by boat, a six-week voyage. There was still a very real feeling of isolation from the rest of the world—the "rest of the world" meaning Europe and North America. To still be referring to the countries to the north as being in the Far East is the continuing measure of our mental disgruntlement! Greenwich is a funny state of mind....

I ran away from home and moved to King's Cross. Dave Tanner and Eric Saxby lived on the same street and looked after me until I found a job and rented a room of my own. We'd go away every weekend. Hardly anybody had a car, so we'd all go on the train or hitch. Some weekends there might be ten climbers, other weekends only three or four. If you wanted to climb regularly you didn't have much to choose from in the way of partners: you took whomever you could get. This would often lead to hilariously mismatched rope-mates.

Right from the beginning I kept hearing about Bryden Allen. It was "Bryden Allen this" and "Bryden Allen that" and "Bryden Allen every bloody thing." The stories were rampant. Death marches to unknown cliffs, getting lost and benighted (good fun!), running out of water (sounded serious!), tight ropes galore, lousy belays, and long runouts with poor protection. At least half the people who'd climbed with him said they never wanted to again. Add to this the fact that he wanted to climb all the time and you see why he was running out of partners. (I should add, by the way, that behind all these embroidered horror stories there were in fact quite a few grains of truth. I did the second ascent of some of Bryden's climbs, using more or less the same gear, and they definitely had the funny quality that makes you want to close your eyes and pretend you're not really where you are and doing what you're doing.) Bryden grew up in the hills outside Canberra and went to England as a kid. He returned to Australia, having become an expert rockclimber, to find himself transported from the extensively developed cliffs of England to a veritable treasure trove of untouched rock. He was like a shark in a feeding frenzy.

When I heard that he had published *The Rock Climbs of New South Wales*, probably the first real guidebook ever produced in Australia, I hurtled down to Paddy's shop and got a copy and read it two or three hundred times. That was it. I *had* to meet this guy. But the bugger was never around! I gave up all hope of a casual meeting on some windy clifftop and decided to simply phone him and offer my services. I dialed, but when the voice on the other end said, "Hello. Bryden Allen," I couldn't get a single word out of my mouth. I panicked, hung up the phone, and felt down for days afterward. It was an early lesson in what results when bravery and cowardice occur at the same instant.

A few weeks later I finally met him at Lindfield practice rocks. It was a scorching summer's day, and he was bouldering in just a pair of shorts. His arms were about the same thickness as my legs, and his legs—well, his legs made mine look like a pair of walking sticks. I used to look like a whippet that needed a good night's sleep and a dozen T-bone steaks. I watched him do a few hard problems, and I thought, "Jesus Christ! This guy must have muscles in his shit!" His consuming project at the time was to climb Echo Point, near Katoomba. He'd already used up five partners and was desperate for a sixth. I'd never even seen it, so when he asked if I was game I just tried to look cool and said, "Sure!"

We became something like the odd couple. He was twenty-five and I was fifteen—an abrasive, competitive, *combative* whippersnapper. Bryden was tolerant of my comic posturings but at the same time wasn't willing to just take all my crap without getting up to a few tricks of his own. When we got to Katoomba he said I wasn't allowed to look at our proposed route until we got down the track as far as the bridge at Honeymoon Point. When we arrived there he had this really smug expression on his face and said okay, I could turn around and have a look. I nearly started crying. I thought: this guy's even more of a nutter than they said he was. Then I realized he was joking. A few minutes later I realized he wasn't joking. Well! To admit that I'd lost all interest would be to miss my great opportunity to show him how fearless I was, yet to go ahead with it would almost certainly turn me into a gibbering wreck. I decided to take the gibbering wreck option and managed to control myself enough to say something like, "Mmmm. Looks good!"

In the end we spent five days on it, over three attempts, with two nights on a shale ledge and one night hanging in bosun's chairs. The method we used to get up is so hilarious in retrospect that it bears recounting. On the constantly overhanging top half Bryden would simply drill until his arms and hands were too tired to hold a hammer. Then he'd set up a hanging belay, tie everything off, and haul up the H-Frames and a length of flexible electron ladder—the stuff cavers used. To conserve carabiners he would only clip, say, every fourth bolt. My bit consisted of grabbing onto the ladder, unclipping, and flying off into space—a sequence I would repeat over and over until we were together again. We'd then get everything hopelessly tangled and confused, and finally repeat the whole process. My knuckles were white for weeks.

Bryden's and my birthday are only one day apart, and the weekend we got to the top happened to be those two days. Bryden had turned twenty-six and I'd turned about forty-two.

He and I climbed together regularly, even spending weeknights at Lindfield rocks, bouldering with pencil torches in our mouths. We also made a lot of our own gear. He had a workbench in his room near Sydney University, and we'd make hangers and file the bolts down to size. We made our own skyhooks as well, and when the first imported ones came over from America several years later, it was interesting to see that the design was almost identical.

The best contraption was the thing Bryden called the crackajack, which didn't work at all but was a great idea. It was made from two lengths of rod, each about three inches long. One piece was solid, about three-quarters of an inch in diameter, with an external thread. The other was hollow with a larger diameter and a corresponding internal thread. This piece had a winding lever attached to it, and both pieces had sharp teeth filed into the ends. The Inquisition would have loved it. The idea was to crank it up in any crack from three to six inches wide, hang from it on a sling and then place a bolt. The trouble was you needed two hands to get it started! Also, the lever wasn't long enough to exert enough torque to get the teeth to bite. None of this mattered to us. We loved it anyway and carried it everywhere in its own special bag made from green japara cotton. I favored wooden wedges. At one stage I was so crazy about them that a casual observer would have thought I was on the way to build a small bungalow at the top of the cliff.

Various people had experimented with expansion bolts and ring bolts of different types, but it was Bryden who came up with the bolt and removable hanger as it is still more or less used today in Australia. Aesthetically speaking, this is still the most advanced system in the world, and the fixed-hanger American/European version is a real eyesore in comparison. Bryden was a great champion of bolts (given the pitiful nature of what else was available this was hardly surprising), but he always made a point of using as few as possible.

One thing I couldn't figure out at the time was why nobody was using nut protection. I realize now that one of the reasons is because it didn't feature in the literature that crossed the equator. The pipes did, so everybody dutifully smoked them, but the awareness of nuts had only traveled across on the grapevine, so nobody used them. I'd seen them used a few times on gritstone and in the Lake District, and I'd even practiced putting them in down at the local quarry.

I have an image of hordes of scruffy boys, all unknown to each other, sneaking off to our respective quarries, placing our Joe Brown statues on top of a suitable boulder and then going at it like demented ferrets. It's not as dramatic as it sounds, of course. The quarries were often only thirty feet high, and looked like rubbish dumps, but they were important training grounds in their day. (I'm not talking Orders of the British Empire or knighthoods here. I'm talking about something much closer to the spirit and seldom-bathed body of William Blake and his visions of angels and dark satanic mills. I'm talking rusty bedframes, old car tires, broken-down prams and twisted sheets of corrugated iron. I was taken to see an indoor climbing gym last month, right in the center of Manhattan, and I thought it was very impressive. But not quite up to the old Calverly Quarry.)

The other reason nuts weren't being used was that by the dictates of popular wisdom they would be useless in sandstone. It sounds crazy now, of course, but if enough people say something often enough it becomes a case of the emperor's new clothes. I made up a set anyway, hexagonal building nuts with the threads drilled out, and soon enough we were all using them. Around this time I, along with quite a few other climbers, became interested in trying to keep the cliffs looking as natural as possible, without breaking our necks in the process. Another group tended to lean more toward bolts. And so began the sad soliloquy: to bolt or not to bolt. It was more than just a question—it was the opening salvo of the great bolt wars of the sixties.

I became a treacherous double agent. After having murdered the impossible on Echo Point and Vespians Wall, I received orders from high command to return to the scenes of the crimes and dispose of these embarrassing souvenirs of rusting monkey business. It was like a hardened eighteen-year-old hooker trying to atone for the innocent sins of the sixteen-year-old virgin!

My duplicitous maneuverings became positively tortuous in their complexity. I invented a new method for calculating the amount of available daylight and the position of the sun. It went something like this: if my companion was terrified and insisting on a bolt, I'd look into the sky and move the sun downward, and explain that we were almost out of daylight and there wasn't enough time to place one. If, on the other hand, it was me who was terrified, I'd move the sun way up into the heavens and create all the time that was needed put one in. Eat your heart out, Galileo! Isaac Newton took a pounding as well. The principle that "what goes up must come down" began to include the condition that "it must reach the top first." Alas, poor siege tactics! I knew them well! And, as far as protection went, it was paraphrased as "what goes in must come out."

It was during this period of rapid change that Bryden and I did our second route on Bluff Mountain. Unlike our climb of a year earlier, on which we'd placed quite a few bolts, I was hoping that our collection of crude nuts would allow us to climb this one without placing any. What actually happened is a good cautionary tale that says a lot about the tempo of the times. About halfway up I reached a sloping shelf and made a belay with two medium nuts. When Bryden arrived he looked at it and we started having one of those funny domestic quarrels that climbers come to love. I went into my Galileo routine and threw in the Joe Brown look for good measure, but Bryden wasn't buying. Hard words were exchanged. I finally won him over with those three famous words: "Mate! It's bombproof!"

He disappeared around a bulge but after a while the rope stopped moving. We couldn't hear each other over the wind, so I started leaning out on the slings to see what was happening. Just as Bryden clipped into his first runner, a sling over a spike, the bombproof nuts blew out. Bryden started screaming, "What's going on?" I kept shouting, "Nothing! Nothing!" as I tried to clamber back onto the shelf. It was the one time he got really angry. He even threatened divorce the moment we got to the top. He would have had sole custody of the crackajack and could have denied me visitation rights, so it's just as well that we somehow remained friends. And good friends at that. That little spike is one of my personal sacred sites.

By the time I got back from Europe in 1966 the Americans were discovering nuts and we were discovering hard steel American pitons. Glossy climbing magazines from England and America started to appear and—this is the most important thing—the time delay between the climbing literature and what was actually happening overseas shrank from about twenty years to about two weeks!

In all my rantings and writings I've never said much about grading, so perhaps another detour is in order. When I wrote my guidebooks to climbing in the Blue Mountains, I was so appalled by the uselessness of the English system and the confusions of the European systems that it seemed best to just dump the lot in Sydney Harbor and start again. For example, the top English grade at the time—"extremely severe"—could include anything from riding an escalator to finding yourself on an overhanging greasy nightmare with no visible holds and nothing for protection except a tied-off twig.

Other examples? For a start, the grading systems being used in other countries all had an inbuilt and totally unrealistic glass ceiling, which tradition made difficult to change. Furthermore, they were all using subdivisions, which created false psychological barriers. And, finally, they were not working well in their country of origin, so why the hell should they work half a world away? An important aspect as well was Australia's great isolation from what was then a Eurocentric focus in world climbing, and especially a British focus. Because a trip to England was out of the question for most Australian climbers, there was a constant state of confusion about grading climbs at all. So we had the strange situation of climbers in Australia putting up climbs and not being able to grade them because the frame of reference for doing so was 12,000 miles away! Of course, climbs *were* graded, using the same system as in England, but lurking beneath this was the constant question, "But what would this be graded in Wales or the Lake District?"

What we needed was something simple and, more importantly, something that was consistent and our own. So I started a new grading system, beginning at 1 and proceeding one number at a time, with no subdivisions and no preordained limit.

My reasons for starting the grades at the level of hiking came from a desire to demystify and redefine the point at which climbing starts. There exists to this day the fallacy that climbing has to be difficult and is in some way a specialized activity that needs truckloads of shiny things. I simply wanted to start with the basic activity of walking uphill as being grade 1, and to let the hill get steeper at its own pace. To pretend that there is a magical and definable point at which walking ends and scrambling begins, or scrambling ends and "real" climbing begins, is just plain foolish.

I never liked the old adjectival way of grading climbs because it implies that there exists a universal criterion of ability. In other words, the guidebook writer, or whoever, is to some degree predicting the experience the climber can have, or should have, on a particular climb. When I was nineteen I worked as a climbing instructor for the Manchester Education Department. Most of the kids were in their mid- to late teens, but sometimes we'd get groups of little ones. Instead of taking them to the cliffs, we'd just take them out hill-walking the moors. But I often thought that if we had been allowed to take them climbing it would have been a pity to tell them that what they'd struggled up was graded "easy." Similarly, when I tried to make a living instructing climbing a year later in the Blue Mountains (a doomed and futuristic endeavor, that, if ever there was one—talk about optimistic), I was never too thrilled to be telling someone that what we had just climbed had been "mild severe," when to them it was maybe the most intense thing they had ever done.

One thing I was vocal about at the time was to emphasize that the system should be thought of as open-ended from the word go, and not be thought of as in any way having a ceiling. I wanted to ensure that what was being done should not be interpreted as any indication of what was possible.

One criticism of the Australian system is that there are too many numbers. But take away 1–7, which are there for small children and total beginners, and what remains is comparable, more or less, to the total number of subdivisions currently used in England and the U.S. Not that this is in itself any justification—to follow these countries simply because they have thicker, glossier, and more expensive magazines, and a bigger population of climbers, is no guarantee of anything at all.

A more pertinent criticism is that the grade doesn't take factors such as loose rock, length of climb, quality of protection, and seriousness into account. My response to this was and still is: "That's what words are for." It is interesting that the British climbers, historically a literate subculture in a traditionally literate country, should be leading the gang worldwide in the mumbo-jumbo-mystification steeplechase. No combination of numbers, letters, and symbols will ever convey information as accurately as words when it comes to describing these factors of a route. If on the fourth pitch there is no protection for sixty feet, what is the problem with saying, "On the fourth pitch there is no protection for sixty feet"? If the climb is very sustained, why not try communicating this piece of information by using words such as, "The climb is very sustained." Does anyone need to be told by a complex series of symbols that a ten-pitch climb ten miles from the closest road is going to be a different outing than a one-pitch climb on a roadside crag? Have these Poms been using too much vinegar on their fish and chips? What is the problem here?

And a final comment on this subject: what's wrong with leaving the guidebook in the bag? Give yourself a thrill! Bring back "the four Fs," as I and my old mate Alec Campbell used to recite to each other: "Fail on it, Fall on it, or Fly up the Fucker."

As increasing numbers arrive upon these shores in silver spacecraft, with bags full of shiny gizmos and badges bearing letters such as UIAA and BMC, the pressure to conform and be good little colonists may escalate. When they start trying to sell you the newest and best grading system, it might be worth looking 'em in the eye and in your best Australian accent telling them that you "do not want the uncooked crustacean."

This is no call for isolationism. It is a call for national individualism and for resistance to European and American cultural imperialism—be it in the form of mass culture or something as microscopic as climbing.

So the sixties moved along. Virtually all attention worldwide shifted temporarily to the granite cliffs of a valley in California, the name of which we didn't know how to pronounce. On the tongues of Australian and English climbers it was initially read to rhyme with "nose bite" (the most famous climber in Yosemite had a funny name, too—Royal Robbins). The climbs got harder, sure, but only within a parallel framework and to the same corresponding degree that equipment got better and ethics changed. So they got harder and they became incomparably easier. The great bolt war festered and flared: take no prisoners. A lot of new, improved equipment became available. In a word, things got complicated.

By the early seventies I became so disheartened by the bolting wars and associated ethical arguments that I decided to abandon ship. Various climbers would come round the house and try to re-inject some of the magic, but I was an obstinate patient. Joe Friend was one. Mike Law another. Mike actually managed to get me away on a few new routes. One day I went to watch him and Kim Carrigan bouldering and there was no question that I was seeing some hot stuff. They both started out very much as traditional climbers. It's funny to refer to what I used to do as traditional climbing, but it does have some truth to it. In my fantasies I was always Fred Botterill on that lovely slab on Sea Fell in 1903, and I guess I did try to approach the whole business with a keen awareness of the past.

Around 1975 the scene suddenly blossomed. Greg Child, Andrew Penney, and Giles Bradbury were all in there, and they in turn were joined by many others who I never met: Peisker, Baird, Smoothy, Moon, Wagland. So a whole new generation was out there and they took full advantage of that new grading system and just started adding numbers: 27, 28, 29! There was no need to form any subcommittees and blow a year's climbing on paperwork and arguing in the pub.

Later still, the "Preparing the Virgin for Sacrifice" wars started—that is, the "starting at the top and doing it all before you actually do it" routine that has now become common practice—but that was no longer my battle and I was glad.

And now to find an entire new generation of climbers arguing about what is basically the same old stuff with new twists makes me feel very optimistic. I hope I will be forgiven for still caring enough to have thrown in my two cent's worth. Bolting, chipping, gluing, starting from the top, hangdogging, pinkpointing, redpointing, having or not having beta—it's enough to drive a man into the grip of the grape. It may serve us well to remember, though, that just as aid climbing, as an end in itself, became more or less passé or at least not the ultimate skill to aspire to—the times will change again and today's hardest and most highly prized bolted sport routes may well come to be viewed as the quaint relics of a passing phase that climbing had to go through. Climbs have their own market value within the psyche of each generation. Personally, I believe that the most valued climbs of the future will be the ones where all that exists will be the illusion of the *absence* of previous human passage—as opposed to those climbs that bear the rusting evidence of it.

As the cliffs pass from the care and stewardship of one generation into the hands of the next, the attendant ceremony of the changing of the guard often becomes an antagonistic exercise rather than a liberating ritual. This is to be expected, given the fact that none of us can say just exactly what it is that we are trying to guard. Now, seeing as the worst possible scenario in any quest for the Holy Grail would be to actually find the bloody thing, this inability to define exactly what we are guarding might be its saving grace.

I remain especially spiritually connected to two areas: the gritstone outcrops of Yorkshire—just as big and wild as they seemed to me as a thirteen-year-old—and the sandstone cliffs right here in the Blue Mountains. Whenever I return to Australia to play music, I always make time to visit this neck of the woods. I end up skulking around my old haunts and some of the new areas and various cliffs I wanted to climb but never did; looking to see what sort of shape the cliffs are in; soloing the odd easy favorite; or trying to explain to my non-climbing companions the content within the silence of the stone. God knows what I expect find, but the good part is that I always find it. And the tricky part is that having found it, I still don't know what it is.

Many years ago I spent two solid months working on a book in which I tried to formulate some of these same ideas that I am speaking of today. Oh, it was ambitious, with chapters such as "Climbing As an Art Form," "Climbing As a Sport," "Climbing As This & That," and at the end of it all I threw the lot into the flames. Holes everywhere; everything contradicted and fell over itself. Nothing panned out. It still doesn't. It still remains a mystery, and I find myself a middle-aged man in the embarrassing position of having to admit that the thirteen-year-old boy might have been right all along. Climbing may be as good a way to serve one's time as any—it may even be better than most.

If I can do it without sounding maudlin or pretentious, I'd like to dedicate the spirit in which I've tried to speak to the memory of someone who was perhaps my closest climbing companion, at least in matters of the heart. He held me on the south side of Bungonia, in the Warrumbungles, and on Dogface. His name was Alec Campbell. My nickname for him was "Menluff," a lighthearted tip of the hat to both Alec and the great English climber John Menlove Edwards. Alec was conscripted to fight in Vietnam. When he came home he went straight into the nuthouse. I used to visit him there and sit on the bed and listen to his ravings, most of which had me in stitches. A few weeks after being discharged he took a gun and blew his brains out.

I've mentioned the names of many climbers tonight. However, two of the biggest influences on my approach to high-angle silliness were not directly connected with climbing at all. One was a slim volume, *The Diary of Vaslav Nijinsky*, the phenomenal pre-World War I Russian dancer. The other was the letters of Vincent van Gogh. I'd like to try to start winding down with one of my favorite quotations from Mr. van Golf Ball. I should explain that the "bulb trade" he mentions is a reference to the tulip-growing industry, which became a national obsession—an early form of a futures exchange, so speculative and widespread that it actually started to undermine the Netherlands's monetary system and was eventually banned by the government. So the very simple and beautiful act of growing a flower was transformed into something similar to groveling about on the floor of a stock exchange. Here's part of a letter from Vinny boy to his brother, in 1885:

> You must let me maintain my pessimism about the art trade as it is these days, for it does not at all include discouragement. This is my reasoning... Supposing I am right in considering that curious haggling about prices of pictures to be more and more like the bulb trade. I repeat, supposing that, like the bulb trade... so the art trade... will disappear as it came, namely rather quickly. The bulb trade may disappear, but the flower growing remains. And I for myself am contented, for better or for worse, to be a small gardener, who loves his plants.

My climbing heroes were Fred Botterill, Menlove Edwards, Bryden Allen, Joe Brown, Royal Robbins—it's a long list and there are many names on it. I probably shouldn't be using the word heroes, as it implies a certain naiveté. I should be more modern and use the expression "role models." But there is something so fundamentally different in the two concepts that I have no choice other than to appear out of step and stick to the word "heroes."

Young climbers today have their own lists of new names, and a lot of the indefinable attraction of the whole racket is somehow woven into the connecting thread that unites the eras and places these various names represent. Even now, as a broken-down old fart, I feel a tremendous kinship with some of these young climbers, though they are doing stuff technically far harder than anything we were doing in the Jurassic Period. At the same time I feel an unbreakable bond with climbers of my own and previous generations. The central focus of the fetish of most young contemporary climbers may have moved closer and closer to the pure beauty and sheer technical difficulty of a single move, whereas the central focus of my fetish was how far back the last runner was. But it's all relative, or at least it can be. From Tricounis to modern slippers, if you're truly interested in taking a walk on the wild side you still can; and it doesn't really matter what you're wearing on your feet when you're shitting in your pants.

THE ADVENTURE OF THE SPECKLED HAND

Robert Walton

"And there you have a complete account of the sexual rites of passage of the maids of Bakwhuristan."

"Watson, you astonish me!"

"Not at all."

"I assure you, Watson, you have just rendered a unique narrative. Of particular interest was the dance of the silver needles prior to the maids' encounter with the naked young men. The maids' abandoned movements and their gleeful flourishing of the needles lends piquancy to the tale, especially in light of what they ultimately do."

"Just so, Holmes."

"Now, Watson, are you ready for the next pitch?"

"You're on belay."

"Quite." Holmes turned to face the rock. He rubbed his hands together, took a deep breath, slowly exhaled. Then he began to climb. Swiftly and with lithe competence, he liebacked up a groove. The dihedral steepened. He shifted into a bridge and proceeded more slowly. At last he stopped. Keeping his hands well away from the crack at the back of the corner, he inspected it minutely. He shifted his weight, unclipped a number 2 Camalot and inserted it as high as he could reach. He backed this up with a number 2 Friend somewhat lower. He clipped the rope to both bits of gear and called down, "Tension, Watson."

Watson squinted up into the Yosemite granite-glare. "Is this hangdogging entirely necessary, Holmes?"

"Absolutely, dear fellow."

Watson sighed and took in slack.

Holmes removed an implement from his rucksack, inserted it into the crack, and manipulated it for several moments. He made one deep, vigorous, final thrust and exclaimed, "That's it!" Something writhed. Holmes placed the implement and whatever he'd plucked from the crack into his rucksack.

"Holmes, what is it? Bad rock?"

"No, Watson, it's murder, cold-blooded murder. You may lower me now."

"What *are* you talking about, my dear man? Aren't you going to finish the pitch?"

"It's not necessary."

"What about the gear?"

Holmes shook his head impatiently. "Leave it." He continued studying the inside of his rucksack through the pursed opening at the top. "A windfall for the next impoverished climber who comes this way."

At the base Watson finished coiling the rope and swung it over his sturdy shoulder. He glanced up and saw Holmes peering intently at the ground. "What are you looking at?"

"Footprints."

Watson's eyes widened with alarm. "A bear's?"

"No, Watson, they are the footprints of a gigantic climber. I suspect LeStrade has been here. Size 49 Firés, at the very least. You are aware of my monograph on climbing shoes?"

Watson nodded wearily.

"Come, we must make haste back to Camp 4. LeStrade has been called in to consult with the FBI. We must make certain of several facts before he and his Scotland Yard oafs muddy the waters. And we need but little more to complete our case."

Shade and sunlight, like the pelt of a great leopard, lay in a mottled pattern across the tents of Camp 4. Holmes, seated in a folding chair, head bent forward, fingers pressed to temples in intense concentration, spoke at last. "When we viewed the body yesterday, Watson, did you notice anything of interest?"

Watson, seated on a boulder next to their yellow tent, stopped massaging his toes. "Nothing out of the ordinary. The usual trauma associated with a lengthy fall."

Holmes looked up. "You're sure?"

Watson shrugged. "What else would there be? It was devilish bad luck that Mr. Monarch fell just as he reached the end of the difficult section, but such things happen to solo climbers."

Holmes peered intently at Watson. "Was it bad luck?"

Watson nodded. "Or a loss of concentration."

"No, Watson. Rob Monarch was murdered."

Watson sighed. "There you go again, Holmes. Monarch's death was an obvious, though unfortunate, accident."

Holmes continued. "You saw no spots on his left hand?"

"Spots?"

"Four red spots just above the left ring finger."

"I did not note them."

Holmes looked over his shoulder. "Ah, our first guest has arrived." He rose.

A man of medium height with enormously wide shoulders stepped into the campsite. His head was leonine, and thick locks of yellow hair cascaded over the bunched muscles of his shoulders. His tapered torso was encased in an electric-purple lycra tank-top.

"Watson, may I introduce you to Monsieur Napoleon Pectoral, the foremost French climber of this generation."

Pectoral inclined his head in acknowledgment. "You are too kind."

"Not at all. Monsieur Pectoral, please be seated." Holmes indicated a folding chair directly opposite his. "Perhaps some refreshment? Oh, Mrs. Hudson!"

"Coming, Mr. Holmes." The tent made caterpillar-like motions, and a silver-haired head poked through its narrow entrance. "Coming, Mr. Holmes." A small, plump woman, dressed in a full-length purple frock, emerged from the tent with some difficulty. At last she stood before them.

"Mrs. Hudson, would you be so kind as to get some tea for Monsieur Pectoral?"

Pectoral shook his head. "No, *merci,* no tea. Mineral water only. I train."

Mrs. Hudson curtsied and turned toward the table.

"Now, Monsieur Pectoral, I asked to speak with you in order to clear up some details

Illustrations: *Steve Wood*

about Rob Monarch's accident."

Pectoral shrugged. "He fell."

"Quite, but why did he fall?"

Pectoral glanced heavenward and spread his hands in a gesture of perplexity. "Who can tell?"

"You were rivals, were you not?"

Pectoral leaned forward, muscles rippling across his broad chest. "Monsieur Holmes, Monarch had bad feelings for me. He was old, almost thirty-five. And I am the best. Many feel the—what is it?—the envy for me. It cannot be helped. I ignore it."

Holmes nodded. "Indeed. You have, I understand, quite extensive climbing experience, don't you, Monsieur Pectoral?"

"Yes."

"You have climbed worldwide?"

"Yes."

"Even Africa?"

"*Certainement.* Five years ago I climb in Mali, ze great red cliffs of Mali."

Holmes nodded. "Have you been there recently?"

Pectoral shuddered. "No! Once was enough! I hate ze—how do you call zem?—ze bugs. Too many stinging bugs! *Merde!* I will never go back there. Yosemite ees much better. Only ze bears here. Bear ees better than bug!" He shuddered again.

Mrs. Hudson returned, carrying a silver tray on which rested a crystal goblet filled with mineral water. She discreetly offered it to Pectoral.

Pectoral took the goblet with his left hand. With his right he gently reached out and chucked Mrs. Hudson under the chin. "You are so sweet, *ma cherie.*"

Mrs. Hudson blushed scarlet to the roots of her silver hair. She murmured, "Oh, Monsieur Pectoral, anything for you."

Pectoral smiled dazzlingly up at her. "You mean zat, *cherie?*"

Mrs. Hudson's blush deepened. She made a cooing sound and looked down at her boots.

Holmes, ignoring the byplay, said, "Watson, please hand me the Audubon Field Guide to insects and spiders."

Watson rose, plucked the book from an improvised shelf behind a boulder, and handed it to Holmes, who immediately became absorbed in its index.

Pectoral said, "*Cherie,* what is your name?"

Mrs. Hudson, her substantial bosom heaving noticeably, whispered, "Penelope."

Pectoral set the goblet down beside his chair. "Penelope, such a musical name. Penelope, will you come 'ave a glass of wine with me?"

Mrs. Hudson dropped the silver tray. It clanged off a rock and came to rest against Watson's shin. Watson gaped at their continuing exchange.

Pectoral took Mrs. Hudson's hand. "Then, *cherie,* perhaps we dine at ze Ahwahnee? You have money, of course?"

Mrs. Hudson giggled, a highpitched and strident sound. "Money, oh, I have loads of money. Working night and day for the great Mr. Holmes." She tilted her head toward the oblivious detective. "I never get a chance to spend what little he pays me. We shall fling money to the winds, Napoleon!" She simpered shyly. "May I call you Napoleon?"

He smiled magnanimously. "You call me Nappy! All ze beautiful girls do."

"Oh, Nappy!" she gushed, "let's find that wine! I so like a glass of Chateau Rayne-Vigneau at this time in the afternoon."

Pectoral rose from his chair, knocking it over with his muscle-roped thigh. "Your weesh ees my desire, *cherie,* and your desire ees my duty."

Mrs. Hudson seized his arm. Gazing raptly at each other, they left the camp.

Holmes closed the field guide with an emphatic thump. "That verifies it, Watson."

Watson, rubbing his shin, closed his mouth and turned to the detective. "Holmes, Pectoral just left."

"It does not matter."

"But, Holmes, he's made off with Mrs. Hudson!"

"Do not be overly concerned, Watson. Pectoral is fit and should survive the experience. Mrs. Hudson's appetites have moderated since she turned seventy. Now, our next guest should be coming soon."

"Our next guest?"

"Yes, and unless I mistake myself, here she is."

A young woman, so slender that she appeared much taller than she actually was, stepped close to the chair overturned by Pectoral.

"Watson, allow me to present Katrin Montana, a rising star among competition climbers."

Katrin, her sherry-colored eyes sparkling and her lustrous auburn hair catching every ray of sunlight, smiled at Watson. "Charmed!" she said. "I am so pleased to meet the indefatigable Doctor Watson!"

Watson rose, cleared his throat, surreptitiously brushed a spot of salsa from his tweed knickers, tugged at his tie, and said, "It is my pleasure, I'm sure."

Holmes picked up the overturned chair. "Please be seated."

Katrin sat and smiled sweetly up at Watson.

Holmes called out, "Oh, Mrs. Hudson? Mrs. Hudson!"

Watson leaned close to Holmes. "She's gone. She left with Pectoral."

Holmes threw up his hands and exclaimed, "Oh, my word, you're right! Watson, be a good fellow and get Ms. Montana some refreshment." He turned to her. "You would like?"

"Iced tea."

"Iced tea, Watson."

Watson inclined his head in a slight bow, turned and left.

Holmes seated himself and leaned toward Katrin. "Now, Ms. Montana, I wish to clear up some details about the tragic death of Rob Monarch. You knew him?"

Katrin lowered her eyes. "I did."

"You were in fact his lover, were you not?"

"I was, Mr. Holmes, years ago. We have not been close, or even friendly, for ever so long."

"I see. The parting, then, was not amicable?"

Katrin folded her hands in her lap. "He was very angry, very disturbed. I was merely sad."

"You initiated the separation?"

"Yes. It was time, though he didn't realize this. I meant him no harm. You see, I very much needed to concentrate on my climbing. He just couldn't understand or accept that."

Holmes nodded. "I see. Ah, Ms. Montana, have you traveled widely?"

Surprised, Katrin looked up. "Why, no, not really."

"You've never visited Africa?"

Katrin shook her head. "Africa? Never. I'd love to visit Africa someday, but I can't imagine when that day will come."

"Very good." Holmes leaned back and stared up at the distant ceiling of pine boughs. Deep in thought, he sat in silence for several moments.

Watson returned, but Holmes paid him no heed. Smiling, Watson held a pitcher beaded with drops of condensation. "Ms. Montana," he asked, "would you like a cool glass of tea?"

"Please call me Katrin."

Watson's smile widened. "Of course, Katrin."

"And, no, Doctor, I no longer wish to drink tea."

Watson's smile crumpled.

She leaned forward, eyes wide, lucent, and humid. "I would much prefer a drink of something stronger at the Mountain Room Bar."

Watson carefully set the pitcher down next to Holmes, offered Katrin his arm, and said, "My dearest Katrin, anything to oblige."

She rose, took his arm in both hands, tucked it close beside her bosom, and said, "You are so gallant, Doctor."

"Please call me John."

"John, perhaps we can have a light supper, too. You have money, of course?"

Watson grimaced and his eyebrows rose. "Well, little enough of my own."

Katrin stiffened and hastily released his arm. Watson, nodding at Holmes, continued hurriedly. "But I can get lots and lots of his money!"

Katrin smiled and again clamped down on Watson's arm. "Good." She glanced at the meditating detective. "And what about him?"

"Oh, don't bother about him. He could remain like that for hours. Most likely, he will. He won't even notice we're gone."

"Then let us depart. I'm frightfully thirsty. A glass of Berncasteler Doctor seems eminently appropriate, don't you think?"

"Ah, you enjoy the Moselles?"

"Very much so. Now, John—dear John—tell me something about yourself. I do so want to know you better." Arm in arm, they strolled away into the late afternoon sunshine.

Holmes at last straightened in his chair. "Watson? I say, Watson!"

"Excuse me, Mr. Holmes?"

Holmes turned and saw a tall, heavily built man with graying hair. His arms and shoulders were powerfully muscled, but his stomach was running to fat. "I believe I saw Doctor Watson walking toward the hotel with an attractive young woman. I caught only a glimpse, but I think it was Ms. Montana."

Holmes smiled and rose. "You are quite correct. And you, sir, I presume, are Mr. Amen."

The man inclined his head. "Talbot Amen. Glad to meet you."

"Mr. Amen, please sit down."

Amen smiled slightly. "I must decline. I have another appointment, most urgent, and I came by only to see if we could arrange a later meeting."

Holmes made a dismissive gesture. "I am at your convenience."

"I understand you are a climber, Mr. Holmes."

Holmes studied Amen's face intently. His carefully composed features gave nothing away, but his blue-gray eyes were curiously flat and lifeless. Holmes finally said, "I do climb, Mr. Amen, but I am only a dabbler, a weekender if you will."

Amen smiled faintly. "Still, I should be honored if you would share a rope with me tomorrow morning."

"Gladly. Where shall we meet?"

"Glacier Point Apron, east of Monday Morning Slab. I thought we'd try the right side of Goodrich Pinnacle."

Holmes smiled. "The route on which Mr. Monarch met his unfortunate end."

Amen's smile broadened. "If this causes you discomfort, Mr. Holmes—"

"Not at all. Shall we say nine o'clock?"

"This next 5.11 variation is quite stimulating, Mr. Holmes. I shall lead."

"Mr. Amen, you have spent time in North Africa?"

Amen turned. "What makes you think that?"

"I am a connoisseur of modern poetry. I have read many of your works."

"You have?"

"I have."

"Then you are a discriminating and intelligent man. My poems, you see, appeal only to those possessed of superior intellect."

Holmes smiled. "Perhaps this explains why they are so rarely to be found in print."

Amen frowned. "Unfortunately, you are right. You are also right about my having spent time in Africa. I visited Casablanca and spent a considerable period in Marrakech. I, with several companions, did some exploratory climbing in the Atlas Mountains. Pray, how did you know?"

"I detected certain African rhythms, certain nuances of image in your poetry."

"Most perceptive of you, Mr. Holmes!"

"I also perceive that you are carrying a rather bulky stuff sack on the left side of your harness. Wouldn't you prefer to leave it with me before you embark upon this lead?"

Amen smiled. "No, it's no trouble. It contains only a few oddments that I occasionally find useful."

Homes nodded. "I thought I detected a movement from within the bag?"

Amen turned to the rock. "You have an overactive imagination, Mr. Holmes. Climbing."

Holmes grasped the rope leading through his belay device and replied, "Climb." He watched Amen rapidly gain height.

Higher, Amen called down. "Ah, look at this! Some fool has kindly left a Camalot and a Friend just above the crux moves!" Amen clipped the two pieces and looked at Holmes. "I shall pause for just a moment and rest!"

Amen bridged his legs wide. His body blocked Holmes's view of the crack. His left hand manipulated the pouch at his side, darted into it, removed something, moved the object out of view toward the crack.

Holmes called out, "Are you all right?"

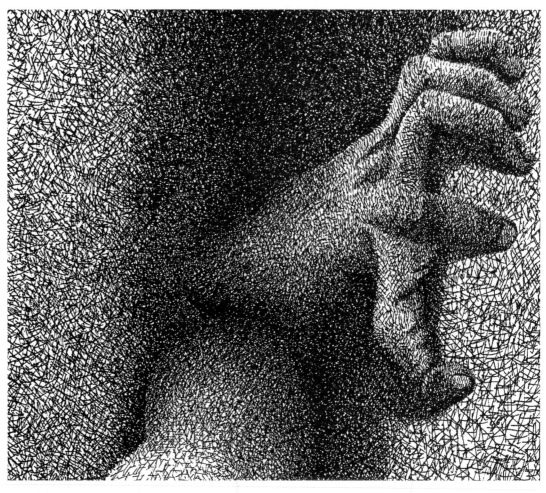

"Fine. I'm continuing now."

Amen moved out of sight above a bulge. Holmes continued to feed rope until Amen finally called down, "Off belay."

Holmes shouted up, "Belay off." He then looped a double-length runner and clipped it to his harness with two locking carabiners.

Amen called down, "Belay's good."

Holmes unclipped from the bolt anchors and answered, "Climbing."

"Climb."

Holmes moved up the pitch, quickly reaching the small stance just below the crux moves. Peering into the crack, scrupulously avoiding it with his hands, he reached high and clipped his double-length runner to both the Camalot and the Friend. Deep within the crack, something moved.

Amen queried, "Are you at the crux yet?"

Smiling slightly, Holmes yelled up, "Just below it. I'm moving up now. Up rope." As the rope came taut, Holmes took a deep breath, uttered a screeching cry, and launched himself away from the rock. The rope stopped him short.

"What is it, Holmes?"

Holmes screamed, "I'm bitten! My hand... it's on fire!"

Amen chuckled. "Is it? That will quickly pass. I daresay you will be dead long before your body hits the ground."

A series of shudders passed down the rope. In a weak voice, Holmes called out, "What, what are you doing?"

"I am cutting the rope, Holmes, with a shard of granite I laid by for that express purpose."
Still more weakly, Holmes called, "Why?"

"Your infernal curiosity, Holmes. You were too close to discovering my lifelong enmity for Monarch. He was seeking, yet again, to ruin me. I am about to close a multi-million dollar screenplay deal with agents representing Sylvester Stallone. It's a climbing epic and has a role for which Stallone is eminently suited. The role is loosely based on Monarch's past activities and he was threatening legal intervention. I had no choice but to eliminate him."

"How did you do it? And what bit me?"

Amen laughed. "That you must deduce, dear fellow... on your way to the ground!" Two white flowers of perlon blossomed. The rope parted.

Holmes swung safely onto his double runner as the rope hissed past him. Avoiding the ominous crack, he pulled himself up to the Camalot. He then reached high and placed a small Alien. He clipped a sling into it and stepped upward. Four more aid placements took him past the bulge. He stepped out of the last aid sling and climbed quickly and quietly up a friction slab. As he reached the end of the belay ledge, he saw Amen bent over at the far end, arranging a rappel with the trail rope.

Holmes stepped onto the ledge and spoke. "Mr. Amen?"

Amen whirled. "Good God! It's you, Holmes!"

Holmes smiled. "Your deprecation of both my deductive abilities and my climbing skills is disappointing. You have forgotten my experiences near Rosenlaui at the Falls of Reichenbach, Mr. Amen. I am intimately acquainted with 'surprise' solo climbing situations. Condescension, underestimation of one's foe, can be fatal flaws." Holmes reached down and plucked up the stuff sack Amen had removed from his harness. It moved voluptuously as he lifted it. "And this?"

Amen smiled sardonically. "You tell me, Holmes."

"I shall. As you said, the source of your enmity for Monarch was not hard to discover. I did so after your visit to our camp. This, coupled with the red spots on Monarch's hand and your familiarity with North Africa, led to an obvious conclusion."

Amen's smile broadened. "I see I shall have to deal with you in a more mundane fashion. Forgive me if I emulate my future business partner." Amen's hand plunged into his chalk bag.

Holmes shook the stuff sack vigorously, slid open the drawstring, and hurled it at Amen. Amen's hand, as it emerged from the chalk bag in a cloud of powder, held a ghost-white Baretta automatic. The stuff sack struck his chest. Four fat, black, crablike creatures with high-arched tails swarmed onto his chest and shoulders. He screamed. Rage-driven stingers plunged deep again and again. Amen screamed hoarsely one last time and fell backwards off the ledge.

Holmes watched his fall and mused. "*Scorpionida africanus,* the most deadly scorpion known to man."

"Oh, Mrs. Hudson?"

"She's at the medical center, Holmes," said Watson.

"Whatever is she doing there?"

"Visiting Pectoral." Watson puffed at a thin cheroot and then continued. "He should recover, by the way."

Holmes straightened and peered at Watson. "Recover from what? Surely Mrs. Hudson didn't... injure him in any fashion?"

Watson grinned. "No, no, no, Holmes. It was your incorrigible sloppiness that laid him low. He and Mrs. Hudson had an amorous tryst in the tent last night. At an intimate moment, Pectoral sat on that scorpion you collected the other day. Mrs. Hudson mistook his agony for ecstasy, and it was some little time before she summoned assistance. Still, he's a massive brute and the scorpion was a smallish one. And it stung him only once before it expired beneath his buttocks."

Holmes exclaimed, "The unfortunate man! I am culpable, Watson, most definitely culpable!"

"All's well that ends well, so to speak. Don't let it bother you, Holmes." Watson again puffed at his cheroot. "Tell me, old fellow, what made you discard Pectoral as a suspect?"

Holmes sniffed. "His obvious and unfeigned disdain for insects. I knew he'd never have the stomach for handling and transporting scorpions."

Watson looked critically at the cheroot and then tossed it into the fire ring. "And he's stupid."

Holmes raised and pointed a cautionary forefinger at Watson. "Do not be fooled, my friend. Stupidity is no impediment to malice. Stupidity often lends the power of single-mindedness to an evil deed."

"What about Katrin? What made you discount her?"

Holmes shrugged. "She'd never been to Africa. That was key to any knowledge of the creature I found lurking in the crack."

Watson nodded. "So it had to be Amen."

Holmes sighed. "And violence does in truth recoil upon the violent, Watson. He who dug a pit for another has fallen to his own doom."

Watson looked up. "But you shook the bag of scorpions, arousing their arachnid tempers."

Holmes smiled slightly. "I meant only to distract him, but, yes, I am no doubt directly responsible for Talbot Amen's death. However, I cannot say it is likely to weigh heavily upon my conscience."

Watson turned. "Ah, Holmes, about another matter."

Holmes arched his eyebrows. "I trust that your concupiscent infatuation with Ms. Montana is in full force?"

Watson grinned sheepishly. "Matters were proceeding exceedingly well last night when I suddenly ran short of funds. But we are to meet again this afternoon." Watson looked earnestly at his friend. "Could you do the decent, Holmes?"

Holmes gestured languidly toward the tent. "Of course, dear fellow. The red slipper is stuffed with money. Take what you need."

Watson turned and scrambled into the tent with indecorous haste. Holmes leaned forward in his camp chair, opened the clasps on a battered violin case, and removed a well-worn, well-cared-for instrument. He plucked up the bow, tightened it, and drew it across the strings. He adjusted the strings slightly and began to play. The opening notes of Sarasate's *Zigeunerweisen* mingled with golden evening light radiating from Sentinel.

Contributors

KENNETH BALDWIN resides in Canberra, a prime location near some of Australia's best rock climbing. As an inhabitant of the world's flattest continent, he sometimes flees his homeland for real mountains in New Zealand, Europe, and North America. A member of the first successful Australian expedition to the Himalaya (India's Dunagiri in 1978), he also took part in the Australian Baruntse Expedition to Nepal in 1988, which succeeded in everything except reaching the final summit. Baldwin has also enjoyed the delights of trekking in Tibet, Borneo, and Vietnam. The inspiration for "Mimi Dreaming" came from a journey through the red center of the Australian outback, where the balance between climbing access and cultural sensitivity to Aboriginal ties with the land reflects issues similar to those experienced by native peoples around the world. Baldwin is a laser physicist at Australian National University.

JEFF APPLE BENOWITZ resides in Fairbanks, Alaska, a city he says is famous for having "more armchair climbers per capita than anywhere else, and more days of darkness also—correlation factor unknown." Comments such as "four days of food will last two weeks if you don't eat" have led locals to question Benowitz's sanity, yet his route on the southeast spur of Hunter and his daring solo route on Foraker attest to his perseverance and perhaps his purported diet of "a raman a day." "A degree in geology never helped my rock climbing," he says, "but my secret black book of possible Alaskan firsts would make Beckey drool." Benowitz puts "writer" on every form that requires an entry for occupation, and we at *Ascent* applaud his iconoclastic approach to the art. His acquired "middle name," by the way, sports a lower case "a."

ALEX BERTULIS has practiced architecture for the past thirty years, encountering many distractions along the way: climbing the mountains of the Northwest, windsurfing, watercolor painting, and exploring the remote regions of our shrinking planet. One of his early exploits was the 1964 lead of the infamous "Lithuanian Roof" on Liberty Bell Mountain, in the North Cascades. "Since I'm too old to keep up with Fred Beckey," Bertulis says facetiously, "I'm going to shut down my office and take a year off and dedicate it to creative writing. My sources of inspiration will include my past: surviving World War II in Germany, the Soviet occupation of Lithuania, and my teenaged years in Watts (Los Angeles)." Bertulis might, or might not, return to Seattle and the Cascades once his sabbatical is finished.

CAMERON M. BURNS was born in Melbourne in 1965 and grew up roaming the peaks of Tasmania. In 1978 he immigrated to the United States and began rock climbing on the basalt crags of New Mexico. After completing a degree in architecture at the University of Colorado, he spent several years working in the film industry in Hollywood. Burns abandoned this to spend four months climbing in the Sierra Nevada with Steve Porcella and this led to a joint book, California's Fourteeners, and a full-time writing career. He has written for dozens of newspapers and magazines around the world and has won six awards for his reporting for the *Aspen Times*. He's also written several climbing guides, including one to Kilimanjaro and Mt. Kenya. He lives in Basalt, Colorado with his wife, Ann, an untamable dog named Lefty, and two cats.

GREGORY CROUCH's first climbing experience was an ignorant foray up an unclimbed (and since unrepeated) section of choss in the Hudson Highlands of New York while he was a West Point cadet. That first climb included an unplanned bivy in a poison-ivy patch and later disciplinary action, but Crouch was nevertheless hooked. Without climbing, and the tenuous grasp on sanity it provided him, he would not have graduated from West Point—nor survived his tenure as an infantry officer. Since leaving the army, he has climbed and traveled extensively in North and South America, bouncing between Patagonia, Alaska, Yosemite, and Boulder. Crouch is a writer and photographer who contributes regularly to climbing publications. Currently, he lives in Santa Barbara, California, with his wife, DeAnne, and dreams of climbing in Asia and writing the Great American Novel.

STEPH DAVIS skipped a calculus class at the University of Maryland in 1991 to go rock climbing and rarely looked back, although she stuck around in school long enough to get her master's degree at Colorado State University with a thesis entitled "The Reality of Experience in Mountaineering Literature." After two weeks in law school, Davis embarked on a career of waiting tables, guiding, and rock climbing throughout the world. Never one to go halfway, she made her alpine debut in Patagonia, did her first big wall in wintertime in the Black Canyon of the Gunnison, and chose a 160-foot Indian Creek crack for her first 5.13 redpoint. In 1997 she received the American Alpine Club's Youth Award for Alpine Achievement. Her writing has appeared in *Rock & Ice, Climbing,* and *The Mountain Yodel.* Davis lives in Moab, Utah, with a small dog called Fletcher.

JOHN EWBANK, described in the 1971 *Ascent* as being "a unique blend of athlete, artist, and evangelist," began climbing at twelve on the gritstone quarries and edges of the Yorkshire moors. At fifteen, after his family immigrated to Australia, he ran away from home, determined to make a living as a climber. In the mid-1960s, while still a teenager, Ewbank founded *Thrutch,* Australia's first climbing magazine; later, he invented the country's now-famous openended grading system. In the mid-1970s, disgusted by the Great Bolt Wars, he stopped serious climbing for many years but is now back to his old love: unfashionable ground-up first ascents of loose and scary trad routes. Ewbank lives in New York City, where he is a writer and musician, and where his six-year-old daughter, Jane, loves to empty chalk bags into a powdery pile on the gym floor and draw pictures.

BRUCE FAIRLEY is a small-town lawyer practicing in Golden, British Columbia, deep in the heart of some of the beautiful mountain country on earth. He has long found climbing and its literature to be a fruitful springboard into avenues of philosophic inquiry. Fairley, editor of the *Canadian Mountaineering Anthology,* is currently working on a new collection called *Climbing and Ideas.* As an environmental advocate, he recently helped protect the pristine Cummins Valley, in the Rocky Mountain Trench, from development; it is now a park. From time to time Fairley heads for the hills, where he's made new routes on the east face of Mt. Sir Donald, the west ridge of Mt. Gilbert, and the north buttress of the "completely unknown" Wahoo Tower, in the remote Coast Mountains. Some of these routes, he says, "are probably worth repeating."

PATRICIA FAREWELL is a poet who enjoys hiking, cross-country skiing, and swimming, and much of her writing is inspired by the mountains and the sea. She makes her living as a writing teacher, working with children in schools throughout Westchester and Rockland counties in New York. Her poetry has been published in *New York Quarterly, Paris Review, American Poetry Review,* and other magazines and anthologies. Farewell's first book, *Raising the Devil,* has been a finalist for a number of prizes, and her award-winning poem "From the Lighthouse" is part of a ninety-foot sculpture that marks the entrance to the Atlantic City Gateway. Farewell has long been promising her husband that she'll climb *Too Steep for My Lichen* at the Gunks with him. To get in shape for this, she hangs from the edge of a bookshelf and reads poetry and mountaineering books.

TERRY GIFFORD, climber, poet, and raconteur, escaped from the flat Fens of Cambridge to be a student at Sheffield. He has lived there ever since, climbing whenever he can on the famed gritstone crags west of the city. Gifford, who teaches literature and environment at Bretton Hall College of Leeds University, is the founder and director of the annual International Festival of Mountaineering Literature, sponsored by the college and now in its thirteenth year. He is also poetry editor of *High* magazine. John Muir is another of Gifford's interests, and he is the editor of two omnibus collections of the naturalist's writings, published by the Mountaineers. His frequent climbing partner, the painter Julian Cooper, who is represented herein in black and white, has worked on huge canvases in Peru at 16,000 feet. Cooper's dealer is Michael Richardson, at the Art Space Gallery in London.

JOHN HARLIN was planning to enter the scientific life when he was offered a job guiding in Rocky Mountain National Park. Later, after completing his epic three volume *Climber's Guide to North America,* he threw himself fully into the publishing world. In 1987 he became an associate editor at *Backpacker,* which he left in 1989 to become editor of *Summit,* a thirty-five-year-old publication that he relaunched to provide a sophisticated literary perspective on all facets of the global mountain world. When *Summit* was sold in 1995, Harlin returned to *Backpacker* as its Northwest field editor while maintaining his home in Oregon with his artist wife, Adele Hammond, and their sweetheart, Siena. Besides rock climbing, Harlin loves to carve intricate routes from snowy summits. He was the first to ski, both alpine and Nordic, from the summit of Longs Peak; he also Nordic skied Peru's highest peak, 22,205-foot Huascaran.

JOHN HART has been beating around the hills of the western U.S. for some forty years but remarks that lately the hills have taken to beating back. "I'm a jack of several outdoor trades and master of none," he says modestly. "I'm a semicompetent climber, mountaineer, backpacker, and desert rat." The situation described in "No Other Annapurnas" has taken a turn for the better; thanks to an artificial knee, he's on the hoof again, swarming up plastic walls and local cliffs with *Ascent* editors and friends. Hart's numerous books include *Walking Softly in the Wilderness: The Sierra Club Guide to Backpacking; Storm Over Mono: The Mono Lake Battle and the California Water Future; Hiking the Great Basin;* and *The Climbers,* a poetry volume in the University of Pittsburgh series. Hart lives in Marin County, California, but "not among the elite."

DENNIS HIGGINS teaches computer science at the State University of New York at Oneonta. Besides climbing, writing, and teaching, he revels in crosscountry skiing and takes part in occasional ski races, even winning some now and then. A bad knee finally won out over triathlons, bike racing, downhill skiing, and humping big loads in the big mountains. Higgins has climbed in Washington State and New England, but usually gravitates toward New York's Shawangunks, which he's been visiting for more than two decades. He says that "unlike most of the contributors to this volume, I have no first ascents and have never been to Patagonia or the Sola Khumbu or Waddington." Higgins has written for *Rock & Ice* and *The Climbing Art,* and his fictional piece "On Shoulders of Giants" appeared in the 1989 *Ascent.*

DAVE INSLEY and Moammar Bonswali (better known as Jason Keith) are long-time friends who have scaled dozens of routes together throughout the Colorado Plateau, including first ascents of Tower Butte and the north face of Toothrock. Insley moved from Kansas to Arizona when he was fourteen and began a compelling love affair with the mountainous regions of the western United States. His twenty years of climbing have included first ascents in the Teton and Superstition ranges, as well as in numerous desert locales. Insley, a songwriter and musician, lives in Scottsdale, where he is additionally occupied as a partner in a river-rafting business. When not busy with all this, he and his wife, Brenda, tend to a garden and three cats. In his spare time he works as a rodeo clown and a daredevil stunt driver.

AMY IRVINE, indoctrinated into climbing during her freshman year at U. C. Berkeley, fourteen years ago, has climbed throughout North America and Europe. Although a traditionalist at heart, she excelled at sport climbing and found herself spending less time in the mountains and more time competing in climbing competitions. Irvine has long had an enduring commitment to both environmental and women's issues; after completing a degree in feminist studies she went on to conduct women's climbing seminars and now writes frequently about the natural world and women's issues. She says she has a love-hate relationship with the world of climbing and related ventures, because they are "landscapes scarred by masculine values." At press time, Amy Wroe Bechtel is still missing; Irvine finds that the tragedy has reinforced her feelings, paranoid or otherwise, about the precarious positioning of women in the outdoors.

JOE KELSEY advised the editors to use the same biographical information that appeared in the last volume. "Tell them I'm six years older and a little grayer," he told us. We can add a few details to this. Kelsey has been writing for *Ascent* since 1968—six articles all told—and his eloquence and wry humor have delighted several generations of climbers. He still spends summers in Wyoming, exploring his great love, the Wind River Range. An expert on this fabulous place, he was a natural to write a guidebook to it, and his revised hiking and climbing guide, published by Chockstone Press, appeared a few summers ago. Kelsey still winters in the San Francisco Bay Area, still works with computers, still has a couple of golden retrievers (if not the same ones), and still climbs with verve and finesse.

DOUGALD MACDONALD began climbing at Dartmouth College in the late 1970s and has since climbed throughout the U. S., Europe, and South America. He has lived in Colorado since 1987 and makes frequent trips to the desert crags and towers around Moab, Utah, where he has accomplished numerous first ascents. After a long stint as editor of the *Denver Business Journal,* Macdonald quit in 1994 to pursue writing projects and climbing. Since then his articles have appeared in many magazines, but mostly in *Rock & Ice,* where he served as news editor and editor before forming a publishing company that purchased the magazine at the end of 1997. He has climbed six Zion walls and has done one more route with Chris McNamara: the probable first hammerless ascent of the *North America Wall* on El Capitan.

JOHN MIDDENDORF began climbing in 1974 at the Telluride Mountaineering School, where he was able to sample Dave Farny's ample collection of mountaineering books. Inspired by the literature (including early issues of *Ascent*), he made the pilgrimage to Yosemite in 1977 and thrived on the challenge of his first big route, the northwest face of Half Dome. Realizing the need for improved tools, Middendorf combined his engineering expertise (gained at Stanford) and climbing knowledge to design and manufacture portaledges and other gear—and A5 Adventures was created in 1987. In 1992 he climbed the Great Trango Tower with Xaver

Bongard. This alpine-style ascent, using the most modern lightweight tools, brought new standards of elegance, length, boldness, and difficulty to one of the world's biggest vertical rock faces. Middendorf has also done stunning new routes in Yosemite, Zion, and Baffin Island.

DAVID PAGEL, born and raised in Minnesota, has burned a lot of gas during his twenty-four-year climbing career. His appetite for the classics has carried him from El Capitan to the Lotus Flower Tower, in the Northwest Territories, and to the north face of the Eiger, where in 1989 he consummated a lifelong obsession with that fearsome wall. Greatly impressed by this climb, he vowed someday to buy Anderl Heckmair dinner—and the result is the article herein. Pagel is the author of *Superior Climbs,* the definitive guide to the cliffs of the north shore of Lake Superior, and has written extensively for *Climbing,* where he's a contributing editor. His self-deprecating humor, he assures us, "is neither a reflection of false modesty nor a cry for help—just a reflection of my paunchy self in a mirror." Pagel, who lives in Duluth, works in film and video production as a writer, camera operator, and editor.

AMELIA RUDOLPH is a artist/athlete who has been a student of movement since she started ballet lessons at six. She founded her own dance company, Project Bandaloop, in 1991. Bandaloop was born out of a growing love for climbing and the Sierra. "I was fascinated to watch the action at the intersection of climbing and dance," she says. Some of her favorite climbs have been the *Harding Route* on Mt. Conness, *The Shield* on El Capitan, and bringing her housemate up Cathedral Peak as her very first climb. Rudolph briefly competed at the sport, regionally placing in the top three for several years. Last season's aerial highlights included rappel-dancing from the Vasco da Gama Tower in Portugal at the World's Fair and from skyscrapers in Houston—and performing at the UN Conference on Climate Change in Buenos Aires.

ANDY SELTERS began climbing in the Trinity Alps/Mt. Shasta area of northern California, where he had many adventures struggling up first ascents with only modest experience. At twenty-three he let his degree in biology wither and embraced fulltime climbing and guiding, eventually leading trips to the Himalaya and Alaska. Selters often took advantage of such guided trips to tag on a personal expedition, such as the Thalay Sagar epic described within. He's also climbed new routes on Cholatse and Great Trango Tower. Fascinated by the peoples of the Himalayan regions, he took a bike ride across Tibet in 1987 and a few years later started-ed co-leading charitable and cultural treks in Ladakh. Selters, who lives below the eastern Sierra, has written Glacier Travel and Crevasse Rescue and several hiking guides.

DAVID STEVENSON began climbing in 1971 and cites his days on the north ridge of Mt. Kennedy, in the St. Elias Range, as the formative experience of his mountain life. In his twenties he claimed to subscribe to the start-slowly-then-taper-off school of mountaineering. Some time later that dictum would slip from self-deprecating joke to self-fulfilling prophecy. He now aspires to a single Grade IV per year. Stevenson's fiction has appeared in *Ascent* and has been featured more recently in the *Mountain Yodel.* "Climber As Writer" was written shortly before he became book-review editor of the *American Alpine Journal.* He lives with his wife and two children in the rural Midwest, where he teaches writing and literature at Western Illinois University. The family spends summers on the east side of the Sierra, where Stevenson works as a naturalist for the U.S. Forest Service.

JOHN THACKRAY, surely one of the few Scots ever raised in Brazil, is a confessed counter-phobe who has climbed new routes in the Cordillera Real in Bolivia and elsewhere. One of the highlights of his climbing career was the first ascent of Thalay Sagar, in India's Garhwal district, in 1979. He's climbed and ski-toured extensively on this continent, and the *Ascent* editors agree that he looks much "craggier" each year, yet climbs with increasing finesse, as Joe Kelsey describes in this volume. For ten years Thackray was the book-review editor of the *American Alpine Journal*, and he has written for the *Himalayan Journal, Climbing,* and *Mountain.* He makes a living as a business and financial journalist in New York and London. This erudite world traveler lives in posh quarters in Manhattan, with wife Pat and various dogs and guests.

STEPHEN VENABLES grew up in the English county of Surrey, far from rocks or mountains. He skied in the Alps at age nine and at sixteen did his first rock climbs at Fontainebleau. He started alpine climbing with the Oxford University Mountaineering Club in 1972 and five years later went on his first expedition, climbing new routes in the Afghan Hindu Kush. That was the first of many Himalayan trips, the most enjoyable of which was the 1988 Anglo-American ascent of a new route up the Kangshung (East) Face of Everest in Tibet, when he reached the summit alone, without oxygen. Venables has also done many new routes in South America. He has written five books, one of which, *Painted Mountains,* won the coveted Boardman-Tasker Prize. Now earning his living as a writer and lecturer, he lives in Bath, England with his wife and two sons.

BOB VIOLA has been climbing walls, both big and little, since moving west from Illinois in the mid-70s; his checkered employment history includes stints as an oil-field worker, ski instructor, and particle-accelerator designer. Several years ago he was introduced to the climbers' news group on the Internet and loved the freeflowing anarchy of this forum. This, he says, was "wonderfully unencumbered by the moderating influence of copyeditors and libel attorneys. Amid this sea of spew and creative syntax, I noticed a compelling new genre emerging: the Big-Wall Tale of Woe. As rigidly structured as a sonnet, the classic BWTW is an account of an heroic (though emotionally vulnerable) protagonist's attempt to gain spiritual redemption by climbing El Cap. The narrative must be short on humor and long on hellish introspection. It was a literary form that begged for parody."

ROBERT WALTON has been a climber for twenty-three years and counting. He's also been a teacher at San Lorenzo Middle School in King City, California, for thirty years. These two facts, he says, "tells much about my impaired mental competence." Although his wife, Phyllis, doesn't climb, their two sons—Jeremy at Reed College and Jon presently in high school—play on the cliffs with Walton when they have the time, which isn't often enough. Walton has written three books for children ("I can retire on royalties in the year 2058"), and his fiction, garnering prestigious prizes over the years, has been published in *Ascent, The Climbing Art,* and elsewhere. Inspired by oldtimers such as Dave Gregory and Allen Steck, he intends to climb as much as possible before retiring—and then get serious about the sport.